GATHERING

FIRST PRINTING   JUNE 1987   5,000 COPIES
SECOND PRINTING   NOVEMBER 1987   10,000 COPIES

Additional copies may be obtained by addressing
THE GATHERING
c/o The Blue Bird Circle
615 W. Alabama
HOUSTON, TEXAS 77006

Order forms are included in the back of the book
$12.95 per copy plus $2.00 for postage & handling

PRINTED BY HART GRAPHICS, INC.
8000 SHOAL CREEK BLVD.
AUSTIN, TEXAS 78758

About the Artist

Frank T. Gee was born in 1948 in Canton, China. His family fled during the Communist Revolution, and Frank lived for six years in Hong Kong with his mother and sister while his father worked in the United States and saved to bring the family here. They settled in Nashville, Tennessee. Frank went to the Memphis Academy of Arts after his high school graduation, majoring in advertising, painting, and print making. After graduating in 1972, he worked as a layout artist, designer and illustrator for the Methodist Publishing House in Memphis, Tennessee. In 1975, Frank established his own business to reproduce and distribute his limited edition prints. He has had over 40 shows throughout the United States and won numerous awards and honors. He is a member of the Tennessee Watercolor Society and the American Society of Animal Artists. The Blue Birds greatly appreciate the generosity of this fine artist in donating the use of his painting "Gathering Place" for their cookbook cover.

Acknowledgements

We appreciate those who offered their recipes to be used in our cookbook. We are so very grateful to those who tested and tasted, typed and proofed. Without their generous help in every phase, we would never have been able to complete this project.

We also acknowledge with grateful appreciation the following whose knowledge and use of the computer made our cookbook a reality:

Nancy Bryan, who supervised the work on the Clinic's computer,

Pat Boone, who was in charge of the Shop's computer, and

Craig and Katherine Rench, who worked many long hours on their personal computer, typing, editing and re-editing.

The Blue Birds thank each and every one involved in the creation of *The Gathering*.

Cookbook Committee

Chairmen:

Speight Anderson
Shari Carroll
Willie Mae McGinty
Carolyn Purifoy

Advisor:

Virginia Kennedy

Co-Chairmen:

Jo Anne Cassin
Jessie Lee Cain
Emoline Cron
Julia Jordan
Nancy Kerr
Pat McMahen
Mary Peterson
Sharon Rathjen
Sarah Shaw
Sherra Wax
Margaret Weaver

History:

Betty Broyles

Artist:

Frank T. Gee

Contributors

Albritton, Ann Moulton
Allbritton, Carol
 Covington
Allen, Mary Bradley
Anderson, Bronwyn
 Williams
Anderson, Speight
 Williamson
Andrus, Mary Jean
 Wright
Atmar, Eugenia Hare
Bahm, Elvine Schiurring
Baker, Barbara Ann
 Smith
Baker, Dorothy Stuckey
Baldwin, Marguerite
 Emmert
Barnett, Betty Pizer
Beeson, Mary Jo
 McAngus
Bergstrom, Janet
 Rendleman
Beyer, Mary Tom Luton
Bintliff, Alice James
Bishop, Lynette Caldwell
Bludworth, Rita Allyson
 Smith
Bonham, Lucia
 McKinney
Boone, Pat Holliday
Bowman, Ola Morgan
Bracht, Kitty Anderson
Breeding, Frances
 Conlon
Brown, Cynthia L.
Broyles, Betty Bills
Bruce, Valerie Olsen
Bruce, Julie Townsend
Bryan, Rachel Boynton
Bryan, Nancy Nichols
Bullock, Peggy
 Richmond
Burkholder, Tommye
 Carter
Burrow, Vassa Woodley
Bute, Judy James
Cain, Mary Margaret
 Holmes
Cain, Jessie Lee Roark
Caldwell, Beverly
 Frambach
Cameron, Frances
 Goughs.
Campbell, Sallie Sanford
Cannon, Claudia Sparks
Capps, Emily Tyson

Carroll, Shari Collins
Carter, Helen Reeves
Caughlin, Jo Ann Boyle
Chapman, Mary Lou
 Whitney
Chiles, Marie E.
Christy, Gloria Parker
Coale, Mary Wade
 Winkler
Cockrell, Yvonne
 Bownds
Cody, Muriel Fursteneau
Cole, Frances
 Brandenberger
Collie, Gladys Stanley
Colpitts, Gwen Gates
Cooke, Dorothy Evans
Coolidge, Sue "Dot"
 Roemer
Copeland, Patricia
 Sammons
Couch, Vicky Daniels
Couch, Patsy Sue Lyles
Craft, Ann Logan
Crites, Carolyn
Cron, Emoline Dehnert
Dawson, Charlotte
 Drennan
Day, Patricia Rourke
Degnan, Barbara Ryman
Delhomme, Roberta
 Matthews
Dickson, Nancy Nelson
Dissen, Kathleen
 Delaney
Doehring, Sally Walston
Duffie, Maryanne
 "Jackie" Jackson
Dundas, Barbara Bering
Eidman, Vesta Veatch
Evans, Billie Aderman
Fariss, Elsie Rain
Farley, Stella
Farren, June Dunlop
Faught, Fay Beringer
Ford, Ann Suggs
Ford, Jane Stroud
Foy, Martha Overall
Frazar, Ellen Brooks
Freeman, Marion
 Merseburger
Fruth, Mary K.
 Nicholson
Gayle, Jane Colley
Gentle, Marjorie Keeland
Giles, Nell Montgomery

Goldthwaite, Mildred
 Cabiness
Gorman, Marilynne
 Capps
Graves, Barbara Pitman
Graves, Betty Ann
 Johnson
Greenwood, Frances
 Samuell
Greer, Margaret Griffith
Greer, Ann Painter
Hagans, Patricia "Patty"
 Coyle
Hare, Bertha McIntosh
Harrington, Mary Alice
 Wade
Hayes, Elsie Cottrell
Haynie, Bette Flossel
Heacker, Bettie Holik
Henry, Rue Evans
Hervey, Doris
 Delhomme
Holmes, Kathryn Voelkel
Hooper, Susanne Catlett
Hopkins, Natalie
 Hopkins
Houck, Pat West
Hueter, Winkie
 Winkelmann
Hughes, Myrial Reed
Hulett, Lucille Conyers
Hurst, Lorraine Mallory
Jamison, Margaret
 Bundy
Japhet, Mildred
 Richards
Johnson, Sally
 Schneider
Joiner, Virginia White
Jones, Vivian Kuntz
Jordan, Julia von
 Blucher
Kanaly, Virginia
 "Ginger" Johnson
Keenan, Virginia Meek
Keitt, Imogene Wright
Kennedy, Virginia Scott
Kenyon, Martha Pyle
Kerr, Nancy Taube
Kleas, Lelah Broussard
Kolber, Jeriann
 Whitcomb
Kucera, Jean Whitbread
LeBlanc, Peggy
 Carpenter
Ledbetter, Elise Fonville

Lefferty, Mildred Carraher
Lewis, Ruth Chambers
Livingston, Florence David
Logue, Fanelle Dornak
Lucke, Nancy Johnson
Manning, Debbie Lyn Mathis
McCanse, Victoria Harris
McCardell, Essie Hill
McClure, Loyce Townsend
McKenzie, Sidney Taylor
McKinney, Lucile Knight
McMahen, Pat Dixon
Miele, Gymme Odom
Mills, Jane McInnis
Mills, Virginia Jackson
Montague, Judy Baldwin
Moore, Martha Scott
Moore, Karen McKinney
Morse, Anna Sloane Gose
Morse, Ervie Mueller
Murphy, Deanna Cook
Murphy, Evelyn Smith
Newnam, Mary Ann McLeod
Nixon, Helen Phillips
Olsen, Mary Love Parks
Parker, "Bebe" Fischer
Parsons, Dorothy Smith
Peterson, Mary Weismann
Peterson, Doris Sather
Pimlott, Mary Kathryn DuRoss
Plumhoff, Franchelle Williams
Poe, Gayle Ramey

Price, Lillian Hutton
Prokop, Jane Brown
Purifoy, Carolyn Bauernschmidt
Rain, Sara Ann Williams
Ramey, Norma Carter
Rathjen, Sharon Thompson
Redford, Martha Kay Frazier
Reed, Ann Brittain
Reynolds, Mary Dean Grimes
Riedel, Bobbie Graham
Rolle, Zat Zatarain
Sayers, Paige Hoffman
Settegast, Carlita Wollbrett
Shaw, Sarah Boyd
Sherbert, Charlene McAlpine
Smeck, Jane Leach
Smith, Jule Collins
Smith, Walta Jean Sturgis
Smith, Sherren Bess
Smith, Jeanne Black
Snyder, Mary Helen Wilson
Sparks, Sissy Rouse
Stanley, "E" Lockhart
Sterling, Dakota Ehman
Streit, Yvonne Tuttle
Taber, Ruth Rietz
Talbott, Edna Sallee
Taylor, Shirley Thornton
Thweatt, Mary Jo Russell
Tomlinson, Velma Crafton
Townsend, Kay Daniel

True, Naomi Robertson
Tunks, Annelle Gardner
Tuttle, Vita Daniels
Tyson, Judy Gilbert
Udden, "Teeta" Marks
Untermeyer, Marguerite Graves
Urban, Lois Ball
Vater, Dorris Knolle
Verheyden, Ruby Wilson
Vittrup, Nan Barnhill
Watson, Audrey Martin
Wax, Sherra Sharman
Weaver, Irene Jurries
Weaver, Margaret Pierce
Wehner, Jo Alice McDonald
Wells, Mildred Porter
Werlin, Faleska Mossner
White, Marguerette Hughes
White, Margaret Lunsford
Wilkinson, Roslyn Adcock
Williams, Sonny Paul
Williams, Ann Catlett
Williams, Jean Hilliard
Winters, Nell Sterquell
Winters, Betty Hamm
Withrow, Raedelle Evans
Wood, Diane Evans
Wooddy, Mary Belle Manning
Woodfin, Johnie Slaughter
Wright, Jean Corley
Zama, Nancy Connor
Zion, Dr. Thomas E.

History

In 1923 a small group of women from the First Methodist Church in Houston, Texas, met to dedicate their time and talents to community service. The Blue Bird Circle, named for the "blue bird of happiness" and a circle of love, became a nondenominational organization which today has more than 500 members.

Providing health and happiness for children soon became the primary goal of The Blue Bird Circle. In 1934 a hospital for crippled children was built, and Circle members volunteered their services there. By 1951 this "little hospital" had evolved into a seizure clinic — a much-needed treatment center for children with epilepsy and other neurological disorders.

As this clinic rapidly expanded, so did the Blue Birds' fund-raising activities. Since 1924 Blue Birds have made Easter baskets and hemmed tea towels for sale. In 1955 the first Blue Bird Gala was presented — an exciting annual event that continues today.

A resale shop was opened in an old house in 1959. Today, used clothing, household goods and furniture are sold to thousands of Houstonians in a new block-long building that also houses meeting rooms and project facilities. Blue Birds are proud of their reputation as the "Neiman-Marcus of resale shops." The recently expanded shop provides community residents an opportunity to purchase previously-owned merchandise at affordable prices. More than 200 Blue Birds devote their time to this endeavor.

Along with the 4,000 or more Easter baskets that are made and sold each year, the Circle members boil, dye, decorate and sell 30,000 Easter eggs.

Just as Easter is a symbol of hope, The Blue Bird Circle Clinic for Pediatric Neurology is also a symbol of hope for the 2,500 young patients who are treated there each year, regardless of ability to pay. This unique clinic, located since 1977 in the Neurosensory Center of The Methodist Hospital in The Texas Medical Center, is nationally regarded as one of the finest in its field. It serves as the teaching arm of the Baylor College of

Medicine in the field of pediatric neurology. The Blue Bird Circle, with the cooperation of The Methodist Hospital System, funds this clinic, and more than 100 Blue Bird volunteers assist the medical staff in its operation.

Today, the dream of unlocking the mysteries of epilepsy and other neurological problems that plague the young patients is becoming a reality. In 1985 The Blue Bird Neurogenetic Research Center was established. This center, with the dedicated services of its excellent medical staff, provides the tools to alleviate and eradicate some of these ravaging diseases of childhood.

Working countless hours each year with hearts, minds and hands, the Blue Birds share their talents to bring the "blue bird of happiness" into the lives of the clinic patients and the community.

Sharing has been a tradition in The Blue Bird Circle since its beginning. In this book we share our favorite recipes with you.

Table of Contents

Appetizers & Beverages

Baked Cheese

1 round loaf of bread	1 round ball of soft cheese, such as Brie

Hollow out bread to 1" thickness, reserving bread pieces. Place unwrapped cheese into hole and cover with foil. Bake at 400° for 30 minutes. Use bread pieces to dip into hot cheese.
Yield: 6-8 servings

Chutney Cheese Ball

2 3-ounce packages cream cheese	½ teaspoon curry powder
1 cup grated sharp Cheddar cheese	¼ teaspoon salt
	2 tablespoons chutney
4 teaspoons sherry	2 tablespoons chopped chives

Soften cheeses. Place cheeses, sherry, curry and salt in food processor and blend well. Roll into a ball. Top with chutney and sprinkle with chives. Serve with crackers.
Yield: 20 Servings

 This can be doubled or tripled and put into a springform pan. It's pretty on a large crystal or silver tray. Use extra hot chutney if you like it hot.

Pineapple Cheese Ball

2 8-ounce packages cream cheese, softened	½ green pepper, finely chopped
1 teaspoon seasoned salt	1 cup chopped pecans
1 tablespoon chopped onion	1 cup chopped fresh parsley
1 15-ounce can crushed pineapple, drained	

Mix cream cheese, salt and onion. Blend in pineapple, green pepper and pecans. Chill and shape into one large or two small balls. Roll in chopped fresh parsley. Serve with crackers.
Yield: 3½ cups

Cheesy Cheese Ball

¾ pound blue cheese, crumbled
2 4-ounce jars Kraft's olive pimiento cheese spread
2 4-ounce jars Kraft's Old English cheese spread
8 ounces Woody's smoke-flavor cheese
2 4-ounce packages Kraft's garlic cheese
2 4-ounce packages Kraft's jalapeño cheese
1 4-ounce can chopped ripe olives
⅛ teaspoon white pepper
⅛ teaspoon garlic powder

Let the cheeses come to room temperature. Put all ingredients into a mixing bowl and blend well. Keep in refrigerator until serving time. Serve with assorted crackers.
Yield: 90-100 appetizers

Variation: Add ¼-½ cup chopped and seeded jalapeños to give the cheese a bite.

Toni's Texas Pecan Spread

1 8-ounce package cream cheese
2 tablespoons milk
2 ounces dried beef, washed and chopped
¼ cup minced green pepper
2 tablespoons minced onion
½ cup sour cream
1½ teaspoons garlic salt
½ teaspoon pepper

Preheat oven to 350°. Blend cheese and milk. Stir in beef, green pepper, onion, sour cream and seasonings. Mix very well and pour into a 1 quart baking casserole.

Topping:
2 tablespoons butter
½ teaspoon salt
½ cup chopped Texas pecans

Melt butter; add salt and pecans. Sauté until lightly brown. Spread over cream cheese mixture and bake at 350° for 20 minutes. Serve hot with wheat crackers.
Yield: 8 servings

Variation: May add ½ cup chopped water chestnuts.

Curried Mushroom Pâté

1 pound fresh mushrooms
4 tablespoons butter
½ cup chopped onion
1 tablespoon curry powder
1 teaspoon salt
⅛ teaspoon ground pepper
1 8-ounce package cream cheese

Clean and chop fresh mushrooms. In a large skillet melt butter and sauté mushrooms and onions for 5 minutes. Stir in curry, salt and pepper. Cook and stir for 5 minutes. Cool. Beat cream cheese until fluffy and fold into the cooled mushroom mixture. Cover and refrigerate. Serve with crackers.
Yield: 6-8 servings

Pâté

1 medium onion	¾ teaspoon cognac
1 pound chicken livers	¾ teaspoon white pepper
1 cup chicken stock	½ cup whipped heavy cream
2 teaspoons salt, divided	1 package unflavored gelatin,
1½ cups butter	optional

Boil onion, chicken livers, chicken stock and ½ teaspoon salt for 10 minutes. Strain and discard liquid. Place in processor and add butter, cognac, 1½ teaspoons salt and the pepper. Process until smooth. Cool. Fold in whipped cream. Place in pâté bowl. May be decorated with flowers made of carrots, green peppers, etc., then covered with gelatin, dissolved and ladled over pâté. Keep refrigerated until served.
Yield: 2 cups

Smoked Turkey Pâté

1 cup smoked turkey, finely ground	½ cup chopped pecans
	2 tablespoons chopped parsley
1 8-ounce package cream cheese, softened	Tabasco sauce, to taste, optional
3 tablespoons mayonnaise	

Combine turkey, cream cheese and mayonnaise. Serve in pâté bowl or shape into a ball and roll in chopped pecans and parsley. Will freeze. A beautiful way to use left-over smoked turkey.
Yield: 2 cups

Variation: May use 1 cup plain, roasted turkey and ¼ teaspoon liquid smoke

Crab Dip

1 8-ounce package cream cheese, softened	Tabasco sauce , to taste
	2 garlic cloves, pressed
1 tablespoon milk	20 pitted black olives, sliced,
3 tablespoons chopped green onion	optional
	1 pint fresh crab meat
1 teaspoon prepared horseradish	1 cup grated Swiss cheese
½ teaspoon salt	1 cup sliced almonds
pepper, to taste	

Preheat oven to 375°. Blend cream cheese and milk until smooth. Add onion, horseradish, salt, pepper, Tabasco and garlic. In a 2 quart buttered glass casserole, layer cream cheese mixture, olives, crab meat, Swiss cheese and almonds. Bake at 375° for 15 minutes or until hot and cheese is melted. Serve with crackers or toast rounds.
Yield: 8-10 servings

Piquant Vegetable Dip

1 cup mayonnaise	2 tablespoons onion, finely chopped
4 teaspoons soy sauce	
1 teaspoon ginger, optional	2 tablespoons milk
	1 teaspoon vinegar

Mix all ingredients with a spoon. Serve in a pretty bowl. The easiest and best vegetable dip ever.
Yield: 1½ Cups

Rockport Shrimp Dip

1 8-ounce package cream cheese, softened	¼ cup minced chutney
	1-1½ cups cooked, diced shrimp
1 tablespoon curry powder	½ cup sour cream
¼ teaspoon garlic powder or fresh crushed garlic	2 tablespoons milk

Blend cream cheese, curry, garlic and chutney. Mix sour cream and milk; add shrimp. Combine with cream cheese mixture. Gently mix well and refrigerate to mingle tastes. Serve with crackers. Bland crackers are the best, so as not to overwhelm the mixture's flavors.
Yield: 12 servings

Shrimp-Artichoke Dip

2 16-ounce cans artichoke hearts, not marinated	2 4½-ounce cans shrimp, drained and chopped
1 0.7-ounce package Good Seasons Italian dressing mix	2 cups mayonnaise

Mix all ingredients together the day before and refrigerate overnight. Serve with chips or crackers.
Yield: 8-10 servings

Shrimp Mold

1   can tomato soup
1   8-ounce package cream cheese
1   envelope unflavored gelatin
¼   cup cold water
1   pound cooked shrimp, chopped
1   cup mayonnaise
1   small grated onion
½   cup chopped celery

¼   cup chopped green pepper
1   tablespoon lemon juice
1   tablespoon Worcestershire
    sauce
¼   teaspoon salt
    pepper, to taste
    garlic powder, to taste

Heat soup and dissolve cheese in soup. Dissolve gelatin in cold water and add to soup mixture. Cool about 30 minutes and add remaining ingredients. Pour into a slightly greased 2 quart mold. This may be used as a spread served with crackers.
Yield: 20-25 appetizers or 8 slices

Variation: This may also be used as a luncheon salad made in a 2 quart glass dish and sliced into squares. Serve on lettuce ruffles.

Gouda Shrimp Puffs

½   cup vegetable oil
¼   cup butter or margarine
½   cup water
¾   cup plus 2 tablespoons flour
3   eggs
    dash of Tabasco sauce

¼   teaspoon salt
⅛   teaspoon pepper
1   cup shredded Gouda cheese
1   tablespoon chopped chives
1   4½-ounce can of shrimp, drained
    and chopped

Heat the vegetable oil to 350° in skillet. Melt butter in a medium saucepan; add water and bring to a boil. Add flour, stirring until mixture leaves sides of pan; remove from heat. Add eggs, one at a time, beating well at medium speed of electric mixer after each addition. Stir in the remaining ingredients. Drop the mixture by teaspoonfuls into a hot skillet. Fry about 5 minutes or until golden brown, turning once. Drain on paper towels. May be kept warm in 200° oven for 1 hour before serving.
Yield: 3 dozen

Glazed Ham Balls

2   pounds ground ham
1   pound ground pork
2   cups bread crumbs

2   eggs
1   cup milk

Preheat oven to 325°. Mix ingredients into small balls. Put into a large glass baking dish.

Glaze:

1   cup brown sugar
1   teaspoon dry mustard

½   cup vinegar
½   cup water

Mix ingredients for glaze in saucepan and heat until sugar is dissolved. Pour over ham balls. Bake at 325° for 1 hour, uncovered, spooning glaze over ham balls several times to keep them moist.
Yield: 90-100 small balls

Patsy's Delight
(Hot Cocktail Wieners)

1	18-ounce jar red currant jelly	1	tablespoon cornstarch
4	tablespoons mustard	1	tablespoon water
¼	teaspoon salt	2	5-ounce packages cocktail
2	tablespoons brown sugar		wieners

Melt jelly and add mustard, salt and brown sugar. Thin cornstarch with water and add to mixture. Cook and stir until it thickens. Add cocktail wieners (may be cut in halves) and slowly heat. Serve in a chafing dish.
Yield: 20-25 servings

Sweet and Sour Meatballs

2	pounds extra lean ground beef, room temperature	2	8-ounce cans water chestnuts, finely chopped
3	teaspoons salt	¾	cup milk
½	teaspoon pepper		

Preheat oven to 350°. Mix all ingredients and chill. Shape into balls about the size of a walnut. Bake on a cookie sheet until cooked through and lightly browned — 15-20 minutes. It is not necessary to turn during baking. Serve in a chafing dish with Sweet and Sour Sauce.

Sauce:

4	tablespoons cornstarch	2	green peppers, chopped
1	cup sugar	2	20-ounce cans pineapple chunks
1	cup vinegar		with juice
2	tablespoons soy sauce		

In a large saucepan heat all ingredients, stirring until thickened. Pour over meatballs in chafing dish and serve with toothpicks or small forks.
Yield: 30-40 meatballs

 One sauce recipe will be enough for several recipes of the meatballs. Meatballs may be cooked ahead of time and frozen for several weeks. Thaw before reheating and adding to sauce.

Artichoke and Parmesan Phyllo Pastries

3   6-ounce jars marinated artichoke hearts
1   small garlic clove

¾   cup freshly grated Parmesan cheese, divided
12   16 × 12″ sheets of phyllo

Stack the phyllo between sheets of waxed paper and cover with a damp towel. Preheat oven to 375°. Drain artichokes, reserving the marinade. In food processor blend artichokes, garlic and ½ cup Parmesan. Lightly brush 1 sheet of phyllo with marinade and sprinkle with 2 teaspoons remaining Parmesan. Cover with another sheet of phyllo and lightly brush with marinade. Using a sharp knife, halve the sheets lengthwise; then cut crosswise into thirds — about 6 × 5″. Working with one section at a time, place a rounded teaspoon of the artichoke filling in the center. Gather the corners of the phyllo and twist to close over the filling. Repeat steps with all remaining phyllo and filling. Bake on a greased cookie sheet at 375° for 15 minutes or until golden brown.
Yield: 36 pastries

Antipasto Salad

1   bunch broccoli
1   head cauliflower
1½   pounds mushrooms
1   medium zucchini, peeled
1   green pepper
1   medium onion, diced

1   5¾-ounce can pitted ripe olives
1   16-ounce can green beans
1   8-ounce bottle herb and spice salad dressing
½   teaspoon garlic powder

Cut broccoli, cauliflower, mushrooms, zucchini and pepper into bite-sized pieces. Mix with onions and cans of olives and green beans, juices included. Add dressing and garlic powder. Stir thoroughly; cover and refrigerate. Drain before serving. Place on serving tray with toothpicks.
Yield: 15-16 servings

Ceviche

1   pound fresh fish fillets (never frozen)
3-4   limes
1   teaspoon salt
½   cup coarsely chopped fresh tomato
¼   cup coarsely chopped green pepper

½   cup coarsely chopped onion
½   teaspoon finely minced and seeded serrano chili, optional
4-6   tablespoons cilantro leaves, finely minced

Remove any remaining bones from fillets and cut into ½-¾″ cubes. Place in a 2-quart glass bowl. Cover with lime juice and sprinkle with salt. Turn gently. Cover tightly and refrigerate for 30 minutes. Turn again and refrigerate overnight. The next day drain and discard the lime juice. Carefully mix and add remaining ingredients. Refrigerate at least another 2 hours or preferably overnight. Drain before serving with toothpicks.
Yield: 6-8 servings (approximately 1 quart)

 Scallops or shrimp may be substituted for fish. Avoid any oily fish, such as cod.

Ham (or Tuna) Stuffed Tomatoes

2   2¼-ounce cans deviled ham or 1   2   tablespoons prepared
    3¼-ounce can of tuna   horseradish
2   tablespoons sour cream   1   pint cherry tomatoes

Mix ham or tuna with sour cream and horseradish. Slice tops off tomatoes. Remove pulp and drain shells on paper towels. Fill shells with ham or tuna mixture. Cover and refrigerate.
Yield: 15-16 tomatoes

Pancho Villa's Pie

1   16-ounce can refried beans   1   avocado, chopped
2   cups shredded lettuce   1   cup shredded Cheddar cheese
1   small onion, chopped   1   cup picante sauce
1   tomato, chopped   tostados

On a tray, spread beans ¼" thick. Then layer in order: lettuce, onion, tomato, avocado and cheese. Serve with picante sauce and tostados.
Yield: 16 servings

Variation: Substitute guacamole for chopped avocados.

Hamburger Ro-Tel Dip

1½-2 pounds ground beef   1   can Ro-Tel tomatoes
1   green pepper, coarsely chopped   garlic salt, to taste
1   large onion, coarsely chopped   1   tablespoon jalapeño pepper
2   pounds Velveeta cheese   juice, optional

In skillet, cook meat, green pepper and onion. Drain very well. Put Ro-Tel tomatoes into blender container and blend to cut up the tomatoes. Melt Velveeta in a double boiler. When melted, blend in Ro-Tel tomatoes. Stir in meat mixture. Season with garlic salt and jalapeño juice. Serve in chafing dish with chips. This dip freezes very well.
Yield: 30 servings

Mushroom Croustades

24 slices thin Pepperidge Farm bread	2 tablespoons soft butter

Lightly butter bread. Cut a 3″ round with a cookie cutter from each slice of bread. Fit into small muffin tins, forming cups. Bake 10 minutes at 400°. Remove from pans and cool.

Filling:

1 cup finely chopped mushrooms	1 teaspoon salt
3 tablespoons chopped shallots or onions	⅛ teaspoon cayenne pepper
	1½ tablespoons chives
6 tablespoons butter or margarine, divided	1 tablespoon chopped parsley
	1 teaspoon lemon juice
2 tablespoons flour	2 tablespoons grated Parmesan cheese
1 cup whipping cream	

Preheat oven to 375°. Sauté mushrooms and shallots in 3 tablespoons butter. Cook until moisture evaporates. Sprinkle flour over mixture and stir in. Pour in cream, stirring constantly. Bring to boil. Reduce heat to simmer and cook I minute longer until thickened. Remove from heat and stir in seasonings, herbs and lemon juice. Fill croustades. Sprinkle with Parmesan and dot with remaining butter. Bake for about 10 minutes. Serve hot.

Yield: 24 appetizers

 Croustades can be frozen on a cookie sheet and then stored in a plastic container. Thaw in refrigerator 4 hours before baking.

Cheese Fondue Squares

¼ pound butter or margarine	3 cups milk, scalded
¾ pound New York sharp Cheddar cheese, grated	salt and pepper, to taste
	Tabasco sauce, to taste
3 eggs, slightly beaten	10 slices bread, crusts trimmed

Preheat oven to 350°. Mix butter and cheese in double boiler. Add eggs, milk and seasonings. Place trimmed bread slices in an ungreased 12 × 8″ casserole, using two rows of bread. Pour cheese mixture slowly over all. Let stand several hours or overnight. Bake in a pan of water for 35-45 minutes or until firm. Cut into 1″ squares.

Yield: 96 appetizers

Barbecued Party Oysters

2 quarts oysters, drained	¼ cup A-1 steak sauce
1 cup flour	¾ cup Chipotle pepper sauce
salt and pepper, to taste	2 tablespoons Worcestershire
¼ teaspoon cayenne pepper	sauce
½ pound butter	¼ cup sherry
¼ cup lemon juice	

Dredge oysters in a mixture of flour, salt, pepper and cayenne pepper. Melt butter in a large skillet and sauté oysters a few at a time. Keep oysters warm in a chafing dish until all have been cooked. Add remaining ingredients to skillet. Heat thoroughly but do not boil. Pour over oysters and serve immediately with toothpicks.
Yield: 8-10 servings

 Chipotle pepper sauce can be found at a specialty food store or at a Mexican market.

Hot Seafood Canapés

1 6-8 ounce package frozen king	2 tablespoons parsley
crab meat	¼ teaspoon dried crushed basil
8-9 ounces Camembert cheese	1 loaf unsliced French bread (14-
½ cup butter	16" long)

Thaw, drain and slice crab. Remove rind from cheese and cut into chunks. Melt butter; add cheese, parsley and basil. Cook over medium heat until blended, stirring constantly. Fold crab into cheese mixture. Cut bread in half, lengthwise. Spread each half with mixture. Place on baking sheet, mixture side up. Broil 6" from heat until top is hot and bubbly. Cut into wedges to serve. To make ahead of time, spread mixture on bread halves; wrap in foil and refrigerate up to 24 hours. Just before serving, broil according to directions.
Yield: 2½ dozen wedges

Hot and Spicy Seafood Dip

2 large tomatoes	3 or more minced peppers (torrido,
3-4 large garlic cloves, minced	banana or jalapeño for desired
1½ pounds cooked seafood (shrimp,	hotness)
crab, scallops, clams or lobster)	½ cup chopped onion
4 8-ounce packages cream cheese	2 tablespoons minced cilantro,
	optional
	tortilla chips

Peel, seed and chop tomatoes. In the top of a double boiler, fold together all ingredients; stir gently over hot water until well mixed. Serve in a heated chafing dish with sturdy tortilla chips.
Yield: 10-12 servings

Variation: Use half Muenster cheese.

Harvest Popcorn

2 quarts popped popcorn (about ⅓ cup unpopped)
2 1½-ounce cans shoe string potatoes
1 12-ounce can mixed nuts

⅓ cup butter
1 teaspoon dill weed
1 teaspoon Worcestershire sauce
½ teaspoon salt
1 teaspoon lemon pepper

Preheat oven to 350°. Combine popped corn, potatoes and nuts in a large mixing bowl. Melt butter and add dill weed, Worcestershire, salt and lemon pepper. Pour over the popped corn mixture and mix well. Pour into a 15×10×1″ pan and bake in a 350° oven for 8-10 minutes. Stir once while baking. Cool and store in tightly covered tins.
Yield: 6-8 servings

Sweet and Spicy Almonds

3 tablespoons peanut oil
2 cups whole blanched almonds
½ cup plus 1 tablespoon sugar, divided

1½ teaspoons salt
1½ teaspoons ground cumin
1 teaspoon cayenne pepper

Heat the oil in a heavy skillet over medium heat. Add the almonds and sprinkle the ½ cup sugar over them. Sauté until the almonds become golden brown and the sugar caramelizes. This happens the minute the sugar melts. Remove the almonds from the pan and toss in a bowl with the salt, cumin, pepper and the remaining sugar. Place on waxed paper to cool. Serve warm or at room temperature. Store in an airtight box or tin.
Yield: 2 cups

Wedding Punch

2 6-ounce cans frozen orange juice
2 6-ounce cans frozen lemon juice
6 cups water
1 46-ounce can pineapple juice

1 cup sugar
2 tablespoons almond extract
2 12-ounce bottles ginger ale, chilled

Mix all ingredients except the ginger ale in a large 4-5 quart container. Place in freezer for several hours, stirring occasionally to keep it mushy. Add the ginger ale just before serving.
Yield: 20 cups

 This has been used for country weddings in this area for years.

Almond Tea

6 cups water, divided	⅔ cup lemon juice
3 regular tea bags	½ teaspoon vanilla
¾ cup sugar	1 teaspoon almond extract

Boil 2 cups water, pour over tea bags in a tea pot; set aside. Boil 4 cups water with sugar for 5 minutes. Combine both mixtures. Add remaining ingredients. Refrigerate.
Yield: 6 cups

Christmas Eggnog

24 eggs, separated	1 quart heavy cream
2 cups sugar	2 quarts milk
1 quart bourbon	1 quart vanilla ice cream
2 cups brandy	ground nutmeg

Beat egg yolks and sugar until thick. Add bourbon and brandy, stirring constantly. The liquor cooks the eggs. Add cream and milk and continue stirring. Break up ice cream and add. Beat egg whites until stiff and fold into mixture. Refrigerate at least 30 minutes before serving. Sprinkle lightly with nutmeg.
Yield: 30 punch cups

David's Orange Blossom Tea

2 cups fresh orange juice	sugar to taste
2 cups tea	

Mix orange juice with tea and sweeten to taste. Serve over ice.
Yield: 1 quart

Milk Punch

1 gallon low fat milk	24.8 ounces white rum (or a fifth)
1 gallon vanilla mellorine	1 cup white crème de cacao
12 ounces bourbon (or ½ of a fifth)	

Mix above ingredients in large container and freeze. Take from freezer about 2 hours before serving. It will be icy.
Yield: 50 punch cups

Mocha Punch

3 cups sugar	½ gallon good vanilla ice cream
2 cups water	½ gallon whole milk
2 ounces Folger's coffee crystals	

Boil sugar and water until clear. Stir coffee crystals into hot sugar water. Refrigerate until needed. When ready to serve, chop up the ice cream and mix with coffee syrup and milk.
Yield: 25-30 punch cups

 Wonderful wedding or shower punch.

Orange-Strawberry Wake-Up

1	cup orange juice	½	cup non-fat powdered milk
1	10-ounce package frozen strawberries, partially thawed	½	cup cold water
1	egg	4	orange twists or 4 fresh strawberries

Mix orange juice and strawberries in blender. Add egg, powdered milk and water. Blend until smooth. Pour into glasses and garnish each with orange twist or fresh strawberry. Serve immediately.
Yield: 4 small glasses

Party Punch

3	quarts unsweetened pineapple juice	1½	cups lemon juice
3	cups orange juice	4	28-ounce bottles ginger ale, chilled
⅓	cup lime juice	2	28-ounce bottles soda, chilled

Combine juices and chill. Before serving, add chilled ginger ale and soda.
Yield: 60 punch cups

Strawberry Punch

2	cups crushed strawberries (preferably fresh)	1	cup sugar
3	lemons		fresh strawberries or cherries
2	cups unsweetened pineapple juice		mint leaves
		3	28-ounce bottles ginger ale, chilled

Mix strawberries with juice from lemons and let stand for 30 minutes. Add pineapple juice and sugar, stirring until sugar dissolves. Refrigerate overnight. Fill metal salad ring with water, strawberries or cherries, and mint. Freeze. To serve, unmold ice ring into large punch bowl and add chilled punch and ginger ale.
Yield: 30 punch cups

Texas Tea

3	quarts water	15-20	lemon drop candies
1	family size tea bag	1	cup fresh mint leaves

Bring water to a boil; add tea bag, lemon drops and mint leaves. Remove from heat and let cool before removing tea bag and mint leaves.
Yield: 3 quarts

Be sure to use fresh, pungent mint. Old mint (nearing seed-time) lacks flavor.

Wonderful coffees: Before perking coffee, add 3-4 drops of almond extract and a light sprinkle of ground cardamon to the grounds. Ground cinnamon may also be used. Both give a wonderful taste and a lovely smell.

Salads & Soups

Carrot and Caper Salad

4   cups carrots, julienned
½   cup black olives, halved

⅓   cup capers
¼   cup scallions, chopped
     red tip, bibb, or other lettuce

Combine the first four ingredients and toss with dressing.

Dressing:
¾   cup oil
¼   cup vinegar
2   tablespoons Dijon mustard

½   teaspoon salt
¼   teaspoon pepper

Combine all ingredients and toss with the salad. Serve on lettuce leaves.
Yield: 6 servings

Marinated Carrots

2   16-ounce jars fingerling carrots,
     drained

1   medium onion, thinly sliced

Marinade:
1   15-ounce can tomato sauce
1   cup sugar
¾   cup vinegar

⅓   cup oil
1   teaspoon Worcestershire sauce
1   teaspoon dry mustard

Combine carrots and onion slices. Mix marinade and pour over carrots and onions. Marinate overnight.
Yield: 8-10 servings

Fresh carrots may be used. Cook al dente and cool before use.

Cobb Salad

6   cups of 3 different kinds of
     salad greens in bite-sized pieces
1   ripe avocado, sliced crosswise
2   medium fresh tomatoes, cut into
     eighths
1   hard-cooked egg, quartered

3   cups slivered cooked breast of
     chicken
6   slices crisp bacon, cut into ½-
     inch pieces
2   tablespoons snipped chives

Russian dressing:
1   cup prepared mayonnaise
2   tablespoons chili sauce
4   tablespoons milk
4   tablespoons finely chopped
     stuffed green olives
2   tablespoons finely chopped
     onion

2   tablespoons finely chopped
     green pepper
4   tablespoons lemon juice
½   teaspoon salt
2   tablespoons prepared
     horseradish

Place lettuce in salad bowl. Arrange avocado and tomato and quartered egg around edge of bowl. Mound slivered chicken in center. Pour dressing on top of chicken and sprinkle bacon and snipped chives on top. Pass extra dressing in bowl.
Yield: 6 servings

Crab Salad

1 pound Alaskan King Crab or 3 cans, drained	½ cup chopped green pepper
2 tablespoons minced onion	2 teaspoons Worcestershire sauce
2 cups chopped celery	½ teaspoon salt
½ cup chopped stuffed olives	¼ teaspoon pepper
½ cup fresh parsley, chopped	¼ cup vinegar
	½ cup salad oil

Mix all together and serve chilled on lettuce leaves.
Yield: 4-6 servings

English Pea Salad

1 17-ounce can LeSueur English peas, drained	½ cup cubed American cheese
¾ cup chopped dill pickles	½ cup mayonnaise
½ cup chopped onion	½ tablespoon dill pickle juice

Combine all ingredients. Chill several hours before serving.
Yield: 4-6 servings

 Great picnic salad!

Congealed Broccoli Salad

2 10-ounce packages frozen chopped broccoli	Tabasco sauce, to taste
2 envelopes unflavored gelatin	2 teaspoons Worcestershire sauce
⅔ cup cold water	dash garlic powder
2 cups chicken broth	green food coloring, as desired, optional
2 cups mayonnaise	4 hard-cooked eggs, grated
3-4 tablespoons lemon juice	paprika

Cook broccoli in salted water; drain and set aside. Soften gelatin in water. Bring broth to boil in medium sauce pan. Remove from heat. Stir in gelatin mixture and all remaining ingredients except the eggs and paprika. Place broccoli and grated eggs in lightly oiled 3 quart oblong baking dish. Top with gelatin mixture. Sprinkle with paprika. Chill until firm. Cut into squares. Serve on a lettuce leaf.
Yield: 12-15 servings

Gazpacho Salad

6   small zucchini, diced finely
4-5 tomatoes, diced finely
2   green peppers, diced finely
3   cucumbers, diced finely

1   large onion, diced finely
3   avocados, diced finely
10 pitted ripe olives

Dressing:
¼ cup vinegar
½ cup olive oil
    pinch of cumin

1   tablespoon chopped parsley
2   teaspoons finely chopped
    shallots
    cracked black pepper

Layer in order, interspersing olives, in a glass bowl. Sprinkle with cracked pepper. Pour dressing over vegetables and chill.
Yield: 8-10 servings

 This is easily tripled and looks lovely on a buffet table.

Green Goddess Salad

Dressing:
3   tablespoons vinegar with
    tarragon
1   garlic clove, minced
½ teaspoon salt
½ teaspoon dry mustard
1   teaspoon Worcestershire sauce
2   tablespoons anchovy paste

3   tablespoons snipped scallions
½ cup snipped parsley
1   cup mayonnaise
½ cup sour cream
⅛ teaspoon black pepper

Combine all ingredients in a blender and mix well. After serving, store remainder in a tightly covered jar in the refrigerator.
Yield: 2½ cups

Salad:
1   quart mixed greens, in fork-size
    pieces
2   tomatoes, quartered

1   cup cleaned, cooked shrimp,
    optional

Add ⅓ cup of dressing to salad greens and shrimp. Toss lightly. Garnish with tomato wedges.
Yield: 6-8 servings

Quick Cucumber, Tomato and Onion Salad

2   medium cucumbers, peeled and
    sliced
3   large tomatoes, diced
1   medium purple onion, thinly
    sliced

½ cup red wine vinegar
1   cup Kraft red wine vinegar and
    oil salad dressing
    salt and pepper, to taste

Mix all ingredients. Chill several hours before serving.
Yield: 4-6 servings

Corn Slaw

1   12-ounce can Niblets corn with
     pimientos and green peppers
½   medium onion, finely chopped
1   large tomato, finely chopped
½   green pepper, finely chopped

1½ cups grated cabbage
1   tablespoon sweet pickle relish
¼   cup vinegar
¼   cup mayonnaise
     salt and pepper, to taste

Mix drained corn with all other ingredients. Chill and serve.
Yield: 6 servings

 This is pretty in a glass bowl and goes well with ham, brisket, or chicken.

Zesty Coleslaw

4   cups shredded cabbage
1   green pepper, chopped
1   small onion, chopped
1   cup raisins

1   cup mayonnaise
½   cup Durkee's sauce
2   tablespoons white vinegar
    salt and pepper, to taste

Combine cabbage, green pepper, onion and raisins. Mix mayonnaise, Durkee's sauce and vinegar; pour over cabbage. Salt and pepper to taste.
Yield: 6-8 servings

 This is better if it is made early in the day.

Stuffed Lettuce

1   head iceberg lettuce
2   ounces Roquefort or bleu cheese
1   8-ounce package cream cheese,
    softened

2-3 tablespoons milk
1   tablespoon onion, grated

Hollow out center of lettuce, leaving a 1" shell. Beat cheese and milk until smooth. Add onions and mix thoroughly. Stuff lettuce with mixture. Chill until firm. Cut into crosswise slices and serve with homemade French dressing.

French dressing:
¾   teaspoon dry mustard
½   teaspoon black pepper
½   teaspoon paprika

½   teaspoon sugar
2   ounces cider vinegar
6   ounces salad oil

Mix all ingredients.
Yield: 4-6 servings

Frosty Cranberry Salad

1   16-ounce can whole cranberries
1   cup sour cream

1   16-ounce can crushed pineapple, drained
¼   cup sifted powdered sugar

Stir ingredients together. Line 2 refrigerator trays with aluminum foil. Pour mixture into trays and freeze.
Yield: 8 servings

Fruit Salad Merveilleux

1   8-ounce package cream cheese, softened
1   6-ounce jar maraschino cherries, drained and finely chopped
1   20-ounce can crushed pineapple, drained

3   cups small marshmallows
1   cup chopped pecans
½   pint whipping cream, whipped and sugared to taste
1   3½-ounce can angel flake coconut

Whip cream cheese. Mix all ingredients and chill overnight. Serve on lettuce leaves.
Yield: 10-12 servings

Green Grape Salad

2   pounds seedless green grapes

Wash and remove stems.

Dressing:
2   teaspoons grated orange peel
¼   cup brown sugar

¾   teaspoon nutmeg, or to taste
1   cup sour cream

Mix orange peel, brown sugar and nutmeg into sour cream. Stir the dressing well and mix with the grapes using a spatula or wooden spoon so the grapes will remain whole. Dressing should be made several hours before serving.
Yield: 8 servings

Mozel's Fruit Salad

4 eggs, well beaten	8 navel oranges, peeled and
½ cup pineapple juice	sectioned
juice from 2 lemons	5 bananas, sliced
½ cup sugar	1 20-ounce can chunk pineapple,
½ pint whipping cream	drained
	18 large marshmallows, diced

Cook the eggs, pineapple juice, lemon juice and sugar until thickened. Refrigerate overnight if possible. Whip the cream. Add the fruit and fold into egg mixture. Refrigerate until ready to serve.
Yield: 16 servings

Peanut Brittle Salad

1 12-ounce box peanut brittle	2 cups small marshmallows
1 20-ounce can pineapple chunks,	4 large bananas, sliced
drained well	3 packages Dream Whip, whipped
1 20-ounce can Royal Ann	
cherries, drained well	

Crush brittle. Add fruit. Fold in whipped Dream Whip. Allow to stand 3-4 hours before serving.
Yield: 12-18 servings

Pretzel Surprise Salad

2⅔ cups pretzels, lightly crushed	2 10-ounce packages frozen
1½ sticks margarine, melted	strawberries, thawed
1 8-ounce package cream cheese	1 20-ounce can crushed pineapple
1 cup sugar	1 3-ounce box strawberry Jello
1 8-ounce container Cool Whip	

Combine pretzels and margarine and put in a 9×13″ pan. Bake 10 minutes at 350°. Cool. Cream the cheese and sugar. Add Cool Whip and mix. Spread over the pretzels when they are cool. Drain the defrosted strawberries and pineapple; measure enough juice or add water to make 2 cups. Heat and dissolve the Jello in the juice. Cool until nearly set and add the fruit. Pour over the other two layers. Refrigerate.
Yield: 12 servings

Asparagus Ring

2	cans green asparagus	1	cup heavy cream, whipped
2	envelopes unflavored gelatin	1½	teaspoon salt
½	cup cold water	2-3	dashes Tabasco sauce
2	cups asparagus liquid and water	2	tablespoons parsley flakes
¾	cup mayonnaise	3	tablespoons lemon juice
2	tablespoons minced onion	1½	cups slivered almonds

Drain asparagus, reserving juice. Soften gelatin in cold water. Heat asparagus juice with water added to make 2 cups. Dissolve gelatin in the hot liquid, then refrigerate. When mixture is partly set, add mayonnaise, onion, salt, Tabasco, parsley and lemon juice. Fold in whipped cream. Cut asparagus into small pieces and add to gelatin. Add almonds. Mix well and spoon into individual molds or a 2 quart ring mold. Chill until firm.
Yield: 12 servings

Beet Salad

1	16-ounce can beets, shoestring cut	½	cup cold water
1	8-ounce can crushed pineapple	1	tablespoon unflavored gelatin
1	3-ounce package lemon gelatin	1	tablespoon vinegar
1	3-ounce package black cherry gelatin		

Drain beets and pineapple well, reserving liquid. Add water, if necessary, to make 3½ cups. Heat; add and dissolve the fruit gelatin. Soften the plain gelatin in cold water and dissolve in the hot mixture. Add vinegar, pineapple and beets, mixing well. Put in a large greased mold or in individual greased molds.
Yield: 10-12 servings

 Serve with horseradish-mayonnaise dressing.

Variation: Use 2 cans of beets and omit pineapple. Add 1 cup chopped celery, 1 tablespoon chopped onion, and 1½ tablespoons horseradish.

Blueberry Salad

1	l5-ounce can blueberries and 1 cup juice	1	banana, mashed
2	3-ounce packages lemon Jello	½	pint whipping cream, whipped, or Dream Whip, prepared
2	cups pineapple juice		

Heat blueberry juice to boiling and add to Jello. Add pineapple juice. When slightly set, add banana and fold in cream or Dream Whip.
Yield: 2 quarts or 10 molds

 A tart dressing may be used, or lemon yogurt.

Cranberry Orange Salad

1 3-ounce package cherry gelatin	½ navel orange with rind
1 cup boiling water	1 cup chopped pecans
1 cup sugar	½ cup chopped celery
1 pint fresh cranberries (2 cups)	

Dissolve gelatin in boiling water. In food processor or blender, chop cranberries and orange with rind. When gelatin is cool, combine with all ingredients and mix by hand. Pour into mold.
Yield: 8 servings

Creamy Tuna Salad Mold

1 envelope unflavored gelatin	1 7-ounce can tuna, drained and
½ cup cold water	flaked
1 10¾-ounce can cream of celery	½ cup shredded carrot
soup	⅓ cup chopped celery
1 3-ounce package cream cheese	1 tablespoon lemon juice

Sprinkle 1 envelope unflavored gelatin on ½ cup cold water to soften. Place over boiling water. Stir until gelatin is dissolved. Blend cream of celery soup with cream cheese. Add dissolved gelatin, tuna, shredded carrot, chopped celery and lemon juice. Pour into 1 quart mold. Chill until firm. Unmold and serve on crisp salad greens.
Yield: 4 servings

Variation: 2 tablespoons grated onion, 2 tablespoons minced pimiento, 1/2 cup tiny canned peas, 1 hard-boiled egg, chopped, and dash of Tabasco sauce may be added.

Mango Salad

1 3-ounce package lemon gelatin	8 ounces cream cheese, softened
1 3-ounce package orange gelatin	1 12-ounce can mango nectar
2 cups boiling water	

Dissolve gelatins in the water. Mix the cream cheese with mango nectar in the blender. Add to gelatin. Pour into a mold and chill several hours.
Yield: 6-8 servings

Spiced Orange Mold

1	11-ounce can mandarin oranges	1	3-ounce package orange gelatin
1/8	teaspoon salt	1	cup cold water
1	3" stick cinnamon	1	tablespoon lime juice
1/2	teaspoon whole cloves	1	tablespoon lemon juice
1/4	teaspoon whole allspice	1/2	cup coconut or chopped pecans

Drain oranges and reserve syrup. Add enough water to syrup to make one cup. In small saucepan combine syrup, salt, cinnamon, cloves and allspice. Cook over low heat for 10 minutes. Remove from heat and let stand covered for 10 more minutes. Return to heat and bring to a boil. Strain hot syrup and add gelatin, stirring until dissolved. Add cold water, lime juice and lemon juice. Chill until mixture is partially set. Stir in coconut or pecans and oranges. Pour into 3 cup mold. Refrigerate.
Yield: 4 servings

Avocado Anchovy Dressing

1	egg	2	large avocados
1/2	teaspoon dry mustard	3	shallots
4	ounces salad oil		garlic powder, to taste
1	teaspoon Worcestershire sauce	1	ounce anchovy fillets, drained
	juice of 2 lemons	4	ounces mayonnaise
1/4	teaspoon Tabasco sauce	1/2	teaspoon saffron
1/2	teaspoon salt		

Blend egg and mustard. Add oil and mix. Add Worcestershire, lemon juice, Tabasco, salt and pepper. Peel avocados and cut into chunks. Chop shallots and add garlic powder. Blend all together with anchovies. Add mayonnaise and saffron. Chill for 2 hours.
Yield: 1½ pints

Variation: For a dip, substitute cream cheese for mayonnaise

Banana Dressing

1	medium banana	1	tablespoon lemon juice
1/2	cup pineapple juice	1/4	teaspoon salt
1/2	cup vegetable oil	1	tablespoon sugar

Blend all ingredients in blender. Serve over fresh fruit.
Yield: approximately 1 cup

Fresh Fruit Dressing

1 egg, beaten	juice of 1 orange
1 cup sugar	juice of 1 lemon

Combine ingredients in sauce pan and bring to a boil. Cook 1 minute. Pour into a pint container and store in refrigerator. Use as much on salad as desired.
Yield: 1 pint

 Fresh fruit salad with dressing added may be made well in advance. The fruits, even bananas, will not darken.

Fruit Salad Topping from Rome

1 cup sugar	½ cup pineapple juice
2 tablespoons flour	¼ cup orange juice
½ teaspoon salt	¼ cup lemon juice
4 egg yolks or 2 whole eggs	1 16-ounce carton Cool Whip

Combine dry ingredients with eggs. Gradually stir in juices. Place over medium heat and cook until thickened. Chill and fold into Cool Whip. Serve over a fruit salad or mix with the fruit.
Yield: 1 quart

Lemon-Dill Vinaigrette Dressing

juice of 2 lemons	1 green onion, finely chopped
2 tablespoons fresh dill or 2 teaspoons dried dill	dash of cayenne pepper
1 teaspoon salt	½ cup light olive oil
¼ teaspoon black pepper	½ cup mayonnaise

Mix all ingredients. Chill.
Yield: 1½ cups

 Delicious dip for raw vegetables

Roquefort Dressing

1 tablespoon milk	½ cup mayonnaise
½ pound Roquefort cheese or blue cheese	juice of ½ lemon
¼ cup salad oil	dash garlic powder
	salt, to taste

Soften cheese with milk. Add oil, a few drops at a time, and mash into cheese with a fork until all the oil is used and the cheese is creamy. Add remaining ingredients and stir until well blended. If a thinner dressing is desired, add a little more milk.
Yield: approximately 1 cup

Vinaigrette Dressing

6   tablespoons salad oil
3   tablespoons wine vinegar
1   teaspoon dry mustard
⅛   teaspoon black pepper
1   teaspoon parsley flakes or
    chopped fresh parsley

½   teaspoon tarragon leaves
1   teaspoon chopped chives
1   teaspoon garlic salt
1   teaspoon chopped capers
1   hard-cooked egg white, finely
    chopped

Combine all ingredients and chill at least one hour.
Yield: approximately ½ cup

Especially good for fresh asparagus or sliced tomatoes.

White French Dressing

1   egg
1½ cups vegetable oil, chilled
1   scant teaspoon salt
⅓   teaspoon white pepper

⅓   teaspoon English mustard
4   teaspoons white vinegar
4   teaspoons fresh onion juice

Beat egg until thick. Add oil a few drops at a time. Add salt, pepper, mustard, vinegar and onion juice. Chill well to season before serving.
Yield: approximately 2 cups

Artichoke Soup

1   10¾-ounce can cream of celery
     soup
1   soup can of cream
1   8-ounce can artichokes, drained
     and finely chopped

¼   cup sherry
     dash of Tabasco sauce
1   teaspoon chicken bouillon
     granules
2   teaspoons dried onion flakes

Mix all ingredients and heat until well blended. Put into food processor and blend until smooth. Serve either hot or cold.
Yield: 4 servings

Black Bean Soup

1	16-ounce package black beans	2	quarts water
12	slices bacon, fried and drained	1	quart chicken stock
1	medium onion, chopped	2	teaspoons salt
4	carrots, sliced	1	teaspoon pepper
4	ribs celery, sliced	1	cup sherry
2	garlic cloves	1/2	teaspoon cayenne pepper
2	bay leaves	6	sliced scallions
1/2	teaspoon thyme		

Soak beans overnight. Drain beans and mix with all other ingredients except sherry, cayenne and scallions. Cook uncovered 1 1/2 hours. Add sherry and cayenne and simmer for 30 minutes more. Add the scallions when served.
Yield: 6-8 servings

Carolyn's Tamale Soup

2	pounds lean ground beef	1	teaspoon chili powder
1	package onion soup mix	1	2 1/4-ounce can sliced, ripe olives
1	23-ounce can Ranch Style beans		salt and cayenne pepper, to
1	16-ounce can whole kernel corn		taste
1	16-ounce can tomato sauce	1	10 1/2-ounce can beef broth, as
1	20-ounce can whole tomatoes		needed
		1	16-ounce can tamales

Brown ground beef. Add soup mix, beans, corn, tomato sauce, tomatoes, chili powder, olives and all juices. Add salt and pepper. Simmer these ingredients for at least 30 minutes; the longer it cooks, the better the flavors mix. Add beef broth if additional liquid is needed. Cut the tamales into bite-sized pieces and add during the last 15 minutes of cooking time.
Yield: 6-8 servings

Cheese Beer Soup

1/4	cup butter, melted	1	pound Velveeta cheese, cubed
1/4	cup flour	1 1/2	cups milk
1/4	cup cornstarch	1	12-ounce can beer
32	ounces chicken stock	1/2	teaspoon salt
1/2	cup minced onion		dash white pepper
1/2	cup minced celery	1/2	cup chopped parsley
1/2	cup minced carrots		

Add flour and cornstarch to melted butter and brown. Slowly add stock, stirring constantly. Cook until slightly thickened. Add vegetables and simmer 20 minutes. Stir in cheese until melted. Add milk and beer. Reduce heat immediately. Cook another 5 minutes. Season to taste with salt and pepper. Garnish with parsley. Serve hot.
Yield: 8 servings

Chicken Oyster Gumbo

2½-3 pound chicken, cut up
    salt and red and black pepper,
    to taste
½   cup salad oil
½   cup flour
1   large onion, chopped
2   quarts hot water
1-2 pints oysters, undrained

2   ribs celery, chopped
½   green pepper, chopped
½   cup chopped parsley
½   cup chopped green onion tops
6-8 slices crisp bacon, crumbled
    gumbo filé, optional
    hot cooked rice

Season chicken with salt and peppers. Heat oil in heavy iron pot. Add chicken and cook until browned. Remove chicken from pot and stir in flour. Cook over medium heat until a dark-brown roux is formed, stirring constantly. Add onion, cooking until tender; then add chicken. Gradually stir in the water, blending well. Bring to a boil and simmer for about 1 hour or until chicken is tender. Remove chicken bones from gumbo, if desired. Season to taste. Add oysters, celery, green pepper, parsley and green onions. Simmer for 20 minutes. Just before serving, add bacon. Thicken with gumbo filé if desired. Serve over rice.
Yield: 8-10 servings

Chicken Mushroom Soup

1   stick butter, melted
½   pound fresh mushrooms,
    chopped
¼   cup onions, chopped
2   10¾-ounce cans cream of
    mushroom soup

2   cups milk
4   chicken breasts, cooked and
    chopped
1½ cups very thin noodles, cooked,
    drained and rinsed

Sauté the mushrooms and onions in melted butter until soft. Add the soup and milk, mixing well. Add the chicken and noodles and cook 45 minutes over low heat.
Yield: 3-4 servings

Cold Carrot Soup

3   cups chicken stock
2   tablespoons butter, melted
1   medium yellow onion, finely
    chopped
6   medium carrots, peeled and
    chopped

1   small white potato, peeled and
    chopped
    salt and white pepper, to taste
1   cup cream
¼   cup chopped parsley

Bring chicken stock to a boil. Sauté onions and carrots in butter, stirring constantly, about 15 minutes. Transfer to a 2 quart soup pot. Stir in potato, salt, pepper and chicken stock. Return to a boil, lower heat and simmer partially covered for 20 minutes. Skim off excess butter. Pureé the mixture in a food processor. Transfer to a bowl and chill thoroughly. Stir in cream just before serving. Garnish with parsley.
Yield: 6 servings

Colonel Red's Chili

4	tablespoons oil, lard or bacon drippings	3	garlic cloves, finely minced
1	large onion, chopped coarsely	2	15-ounce cans tomato sauce
3½	pounds lean beef, venison, moose, elk or antelope meat, coarse chili grind	1	cup water
		6	tablespoons chili powder
		4	cubes beef bouillon
		1	teaspoon oregano

Remove any fat or gristle from meat. Heat the oil in a large skillet and sauté onion until transparent. Place onion in a large stockpot. In the skillet, cook the meat until well browned; transfer to the pot. Add remaining ingredients and bring to a boil. Lower heat to a simmer and cook 1½-3 hours, stirring occasionally.
Yield: 6-8 servings

Variation: Add canned red kidney beans 20 minutes before serving.

Crab Chowder

½	cup chopped onion	1	8-ounce can cream-style corn
½	cup chopped celery	3	tablespoons chopped pimiento
3	tablespoons butter, melted	¼	teaspoon salt
3	cups milk	¼	teaspoon thyme
1	10¾-ounce can cream of potato soup	1	bay leaf
8	ounces crab meat	¼	cup sherry
		¼	cup snipped parsley

Cook onion and celery in butter until tender. Add remaining ingredients except sherry and parsley. Cook until heated thoroughly, stirring often, about 15 minutes. Stir in sherry. Heat 2 minutes more. Remove bay leaf. Garnish with parsley.
Yield: 4 servings

Crab Soup

1	10¾-ounce can cream of asparagus soup	1	cup crab meat
1	10¾-ounce can cream of celery soup	3	soup cans of milk
1	10¾-ounce can cream of mushroom soup	¼	cup sherry parsley for garnish

Mix all ingredients. Heat. Add parsley.
Yield: 6 servings

Easy Tortilla Soup

¼	cup butter or margarine, melted	2	cups chicken broth
1	onion, chopped	1	10-ounce can Ro-Tel tomatoes
½	green pepper, chopped	¾	cup grated American cheese,
1	10¾-ounce can cream of		divided
	mushroom soup	24	tortilla chips
1	10¾-ounce can cream of		
	chicken soup		

Sauté onion and green pepper in butter. Add soups and broth. Simmer 5 minutes. Add Ro-Tel tomatoes and simmer 10 minutes more. Add ½ cup cheese and tortilla chips. Serve hot, garnished with additional cheese.
Yield: 8-12 servings

 This soup improves as it "sits". Cook ahead, if possible — at least the day before.

French Market Soup

1	1½-pound package French Market bean soup mix	2	garlic cloves, minced
3	quarts water		salt and pepper, to taste
	ham hock	1	pound link sausage, sliced
	bouquet garni, optional	2	boneless chicken breasts, cut into bite-sized pieces
1	22-ounce can tomatoes, including juice	½	cup red wine
2	onions, chopped	½	cup chopped parsley
4	ribs celery, chopped		

Wash and drain beans. Add 3 quarts water, ham hock and bouquet garni if desired. Simmer covered 2½-3 hours. Add tomatoes with juice, onions, celery, garlic, salt and pepper. Simmer covered 1½ hours. Add sausage and chicken breasts. Simmer 30-40 minutes. Before serving, add ½ cup red wine and chopped parsley.
Yield: 10-12 servings

Variation: Bay leaves and thyme may be substituted for bouquet garni, and a large green pepper may be added.

 French Market bean soup mix includes ¹/₄ cup of each: black beans, navy beans, red beans, garbanzos, pinto beans, split peas, black-eyed peas, lentils and baby lima beans.

Gazpacho

6	tomatoes, chopped	2	6-ounce cans V-8 juice or Snap-E-Tom if you like it hot
2	cucumbers, chopped		
½	cup chopped green pepper	1	10½-ounce can beef broth
½	cup chopped onion	⅓	cup olive oil
½	cup chopped celery	3	tablespoons lemon juice
			salt and pepper, to taste

Combine tomatoes, cucumbers, green pepper, onion and celery. Add V-8 juice, beef broth, olive oil and lemon juice. Salt and pepper to taste. Let mixture stand overnight.
Yield: 6-8 servings

Monterey Jack Soup

½	cup finely chopped onion	1	10¾-ounce can cream of chicken soup
½	cup peeled, seeded and chopped tomatoes		
1	4-ounce can chopped green chilies, drained	1½	cups warm milk
			dash of pepper
½	clove of garlic, minced	1½	cups grated Monterey Jack cheese
1	cup chicken broth		

Combine onions, tomatoes, chilies, garlic and broth. Cook until vegetables are tender. Remove from heat and slowly stir in soup and milk. Return to heat, stirring constantly while adding the remaining ingredients.
Yield: 4 servings

Variation: For a spicier soup, use Monterey Jack cheese with jalapeños.

Mushroom Soup with Ham

1	ham bone	¾	cup uncooked rice
2	quarts water	¼	teaspoon black pepper
2	ribs of celery, chopped	1	teaspoon salt
1	large onion, chopped	2	tablespoons butter, melted
1	bay leaf	½	pound mushrooms, chopped
1	10¾-ounce can cream of mushroom soup	1	teaspoon minced parsley
		2	teaspoons dry mustard

Simmer first 5 ingredients for 2 hours. Strain and skim broth. Cut lean ham bits from bone and return to broth. Stir in soup, rice and seasonings. Cook long enough for rice to be done. Sauté mushrooms in butter; add with parsley and mustard to the soup.
Yield: 6-8 servings

Mushroom and Chive Bisque

½ cup butter	2 cups chicken broth
2 cups finely chopped mushrooms	¼ cup sherry, optional
4 tablespoons flour	¼ cup finely chopped chives
¼ teaspoon dry mustard	2 cups half and half
1 teaspoon salt, or less	

Melt butter and sauté mushrooms until soft. Add flour, mustard and salt; cook 1 minute. Pour in chicken broth and cook until thickened. Add sherry and chives. Process in Cuisinart or blender; then add half and half. Serve hot.
Yield: 8 servings

Oyster Spinach Soup

5 tablespoons butter	2½ cups minced fresh oysters
5 tablespoons flour	1½ cups chicken stock, very hot
½ teaspoon nutmeg	3 cups half and half, heated
1-2 teaspoons salt	2 10-ounce packages frozen
red pepper, to taste	chopped spinach, cooked and
1 teaspoon Tabasco sauce	drained well
¼ cup minced green onion	thin lemon slices
1 garlic clove, minced	

Melt butter; add flour, seasonings, green onions and garlic. Cook until onion are limp and mixture has thickened. Add oysters and continue cooking until oysters begin to curl. Stir frequently. Add stock and cream. Mix well. Add cooked spinach. Bring mixture to a boil. Remove from heat at once. Pour into soup bowls. Garnish with a pat of butter or a very thin slice of lemon; sprinkle with red pepper.
Yield: 4-6 bowls or 6-8 cups

Portuguese Bean Soup

2 ham hocks, or cut up ham	1 bunch parsley, chopped
12 ounces Portuguese sausage or other kind	2 15-ounce cans kidney beans, drained and rinsed
1 pound diced potatoes	1 15-ounce can tomato sauce
2 onions, chopped	1 teaspoon freshly ground pepper
3 celery ribs with tops, chopped	½ teaspoon hot pepper sauce
2 medium carrots, diced	1 bay leaf
1 green pepper, chopped	

Sauté meat. Add all other ingredients and water to cover. Bring to a boil, skimming off foam. Reduce heat and simmer 2 hours.
Yield: 8 servings

Chirp: For a hot soup in a hurry, mix 1 10¾-ounce can green pea soup with 1 10½-ounce can beef bouillon, 1½ cups milk, and 1 teaspoon celery powder. Heat in a double boiler.

Puchero de Sonora (Pork Soup)

1½	pounds pork tenderloin			salt and pepper to taste
6	cups beef broth			cayenne
2	tablespoons chili powder		4	tortillas, cut in bite sizes
1	6-ounce can tomato pureé		2	15-ounce cans garbanzo beans
1	teaspoon oregano		1	15-ounce can hominy
1	tablespoon fresh cilantro			
4	green chilies, chopped			

Place pork tenderloin in deep freeze until it hardens but is not frozen. At that point it is easy to cut into bite-sized squares. Cook pork slowly in beef broth with chili powder for 1 hour. Add remaining ingredients and cook for ½ hour. Serve in soup bowls.
Yield: 8 servings

 Garnish on the side: 1 bowl picante sauce, 1 bowl sliced radishes, 1 bowl finely shredded lettuce. Place desired amount on top of soup.

Queen's Chicken Soup

1	cup diced carrots		1	cup diced cooked chicken
1	cup diced celery		1	cup diced cooked ham
1	small onion, diced		⅓	cup flour, divided
¼	cup diced green pepper		1	quart hot milk
½	cup butter, divided		3	hard-cooked eggs, diced
1	quart chicken stock			

Sauté vegetables in half the butter for 10 minutes. Add remaining butter. Thicken with the flour. Add chicken stock and boil gently 10 minutes. Add chicken and ham. Stir in the milk and eggs.
Yield: 10-12 servings

Quick Shrimp Bisque

1	stick butter, divided		1	bunch green onions, chopped
3	heaping tablespoons flour		1	6½-ounce can minced clams
3	cups hot water		1	cup chopped boiled shrimp
3	teaspoons instant bouillon			juice of 1 lemon
1	8-ounce can tomato sauce			pinch each of red and black
1	garlic clove, minced			pepper
				pinch of thyme
			¼	cup sherry or to taste
				chopped parsley

Melt 6 tablespoons butter in heavy pan. Blend in flour and slowly add water and bouillon. Stir in tomato sauce and set aside. In another pan, sauté garlic and onions in remaining butter. Add to sauce. Stir in clams with juice, shrimp, lemon juice, peppers and thyme. Heat and add sherry. Garnish with parsley.
Yield: 4 servings

Seafood Gumbo

3-4 cups water
1 10-ounce package frozen cut okra
1 15-ounce can tomatoes
2 bay leaves

salt and pepper, to taste
cayenne pepper, to taste
4 small garlic cloves, minced
½ green pepper, finely chopped

Bring to a boil. Reduce heat and simmer while making roux.

Roux:
4-5 tablespoons bacon drippings or any fat

4-5 tablespoons flour

Put in a heavy iron skillet. Use a little more flour than fat. Stir constantly over low heat until the roux turns dark brown. Do not use high heat and be careful not to burn. When roux is done, add to base mixture. Check spices and adjust if needed.

Seafood:
1 pound picked crab

1 pound peeled shrimp.

Add seafood during last 10-15 minutes. Serve with rice.
Yield: 4-6 servings

 Use raw cleaned crab bodies when available.

Sherry Crab Soup

1 10¾-ounce can tomato soup
1 10¾-ounce can green pea soup
1 10½-ounce can consommé
1 6½-ounce can crab meat or 8 ounces fresh crab meat

½ pound cooked shrimp
½ cup whipping cream
sherry, to taste

Combine ingredients and heat in double boiler. Thin with water if needed.
Yield: 4-6 servings

Summer Squash Soup

2 medium onions, chopped
¼ cup plus 2 tablespoons butter or margarine, melted
4 cups diced yellow squash
2 cups chicken broth

½ teaspoon white pepper
1 teaspoon celery salt
½ teaspoon dried whole tarragon
2 cups milk

Sauté onions in butter until tender. Add next five ingredients. Cook over low heat 10 minutes or until squash is tender. Remove from heat and stir in milk. Place squash mixture in food processor and process until smooth. Serve hot or cold.
Yield: 6½ cups

Sopa de Lima (Lime Soup)

1 3-3½-pound broiler chicken, cut up	1 medium onion, quartered
10 cups water	2 teaspoons salt or less, to taste
6 peppercorns	¼ teaspoon thyme
3 cilantro or parsley sprigs	¼ teaspoon oregano
1 celery rib, cut up	

Place stock ingredients in a large Dutch oven and bring to a boil. Reduce heat and simmer uncovered for 1½ hours, skimming occasionally, until chicken is tender. Remove chicken and strain broth. Debone chicken and cut meat into pieces.

Soup:

2 tablespoons vegetable oil	½ medium green pepper, chopped
1 garlic clove, minced	2 large tomatoes, peeled, seeded and chopped
1 medium onion, chopped	1 lime
	3 tablespoons cilantro

Heat oil in Dutch oven over medium heat; sauté garlic, onion and green pepper until tender, about 3-4 minutes. Add tomatoes and cook 5 minutes. Add broth and heat thoroughly. Stir in cilantro. Squeeze in the juice from the lime and drop the lime into the hot broth for just about a minute. Remove the lime and discard. Add chicken and adjust the seasonings. Simmer another 10-20 minutes.

Garnish:

oil for frying	¾ cup finely chopped onion
6 corn tortillas, cut into 8 wedges	¼ cup Serrano chilies, minced
lime slices	

While soup simmers, heat oil in skillet to 350° and fry the tortilla wedges until golden brown. Drain. To serve, place 8 wedges in each bowl and add soup. Mix the onion and chilies. Pass the onion mixture and lime slices or sprinkle on top.
Yield: 6 servings

Split Pea Soup with Ham

1 pound dried split green peas	½ medium onion, finely diced
8 cups cold water	½ turnip, finely diced
2-3 cups diced ham	salt and pepper, to taste
1 carrot, finely diced	3-4 sprigs parsley, minced
1½ ribs celery, finely diced	
celery leaves, finely chopped	

Wash and pick through peas. Put peas in large pot with 8 cups cold water. Add ham and other ingredients. Bring to boil early in the day; reduce heat to simmer and cook slowly, stirring occasionally, nearly all day. Taste to see if ham has provided enough salt to soup before adding salt. Add seasonings to taste. Garnish with parsley.
Yield: 6-8 servings

Sweet Potato Vichyssoise

2   cups chopped leeks (can use
    onions, but will be stronger
    flavor)
½   cup chopped green onions, white
    part
1   tablespoon margarine
1   medium garlic clove, minced
2½ cups (about ¾ pound) peeled
    diced sweet potatoes

3   cups chicken broth
½   teaspoon salt
¼   teaspoon white pepper
⅛   teaspoon cayenne
1½ cups milk
1   tablespoon chopped chives

In a large saucepan, cook both kinds of onion and the garlic in margarine. Cover and cook over low heat for 15 minutes until soft but not browned. Stir in sweet potatoes and broth. Bring to a boil; then reduce heat and simmer about 25 minutes until vegetables are tender. Cool. Pureé in blender or food processor until smooth. Return to saucepan. Add salt, pepper, cayenne and milk. Simmer just until heated through. Do not boil. Ladle into bowls, sprinkling chives over each serving or put in refrigerator and chill for at least three hours. Serve cold.
Yield: 6 servings

 This is a delicious and nutritious dish. It has few calories (160 per serving) and contains fiber, protein and beta carotene.

 Rye cheese toast is a good accompaniment for soups. Toast rye bread and butter on one side; sprinkle with grated Swiss cheese and fresh Parmesan. Broil until bubbly.

Breads & Sandwiches

Bread is mainly flour, water, yeast and salt, possibly enriched with milk and oil, flavored with dazzling products of the countryside — grains, herbs, vegetables, fruits and nuts. Breads can be simple, earthy, elegant or refined — rough country loaves with herbs, sweet holiday breads dense with raisins and nuts, imaginative multi-grain breads with a variety of tastes and shapes. All give delicious pleasure.

Bread Hints for Planning Time

1. Yeast breads are amazingly durable. Don't be afraid to adjust the bread to your schedule.
2. The addition of butter coats the gluten strands of sweet dough and slows the rising, as do fruits, nut fillings and some cheeses.
3. The slower the rise — the greater the flavor.
4. The less kneading — the longer the rise.
5. Cooling slows down the rise.
6. The more yeast — the quicker the rise.
7. Active dry yeast is about twice as potent in relation to its weight as fresh yeast. A 7 gram envelope of active dry yeast is the equivalent of an 18 gram cube of fresh yeast.

Delicious Ice Box Rolls

1 package dry yeast	½ cup butter
½ cup warm water	1 cup milk, warmed
3 eggs	5 cups flour
1 teaspoon salt	melted butter
½ cup sugar	

Dissolve yeast in warm water for 1 hour. Beat eggs with salt, sugar, butter and warm milk. Add to yeast mixture. Add flour and mix well. Place in refrigerator overnight. Roll out approximately ½″ thick and cut into rounds. Dip in butter and place in a pan. Let rise in a warm place 3½ hours. Bake at 375° for 12-15 minutes.
Yield: 3 dozen

Cloverleaf Ice Box Rolls

2 cups buttermilk	1 teaspoon salt
1 package dry yeast	1 teaspoon baking soda
4½ cups flour	½ cup Crisco
¼ cup sugar	

Warm buttermilk to lukewarm; dissolve yeast in buttermilk. Sift flour, then measure. Sift together flour, sugar, salt and soda. Cut Crisco into flour mixture. Add milk and beat until smooth. Put into greased bowl, cover with damp cloth and set in refrigerator until ready to use. To form the cloverleaf, pinch off small pieces of dough and roll into ½" balls, placing 3 in each muffin cup. Brush with melted butter and let rise 1½-2 hours in warm place. Bake at 375° for 15-20 minutes.
Yield: 3 dozen

Garden's Icebox Rolls

1 cup shortening	½ cup warm water
¾ cup sugar	3 eggs, slightly beaten
1½ teaspoons salt	7½ cups sifted flour
1 cup boiling water	1 cup water
2 packages active dry yeast	melted butter

Combine shortening, sugar and salt. With wooden spoon, beat until smooth and creamy. Add boiling water; stir until smooth. Set aside to cool. In large bowl, sprinkle yeast over ½ cup warm water; stir until dissolved. Add shortening mixture to yeast, along with eggs; mix well. Add flour alternately with 1 cup water. Beat until smooth. Grease top of dough; cover bowl tightly with foil. Refrigerate overnight.

To shape, remove a fourth of the dough at one time from the refrigerator. On a lightly-floured surface, roll into a rectangle 12×10". Brush with 2 tablespoons melted butter. Roll up jellyroll fashion. With sharp knife, cut crosswise into 12 pieces. Place cut side down in greased muffin cups. Cover with cloth and let rise in warm place until doubled in bulk, about 1 hour. Bake at 400° for 15-20 minutes.
Yield: 4 dozen

 For bread sticks, dip split hot dog buns into melted butter seasoned with garlic powder and Worcestershire sauce. Cut into thirds; sprinkle with Parmesan cheese and bake at 200° for 1½ hours.

Finnish Easter Bread

5¼-6¼ cups flour, divided
¾ cup sugar
½ teaspoon salt
1 teaspoon ground cardamom
1 tablespoon grated orange peel
1 teaspoon grated lemon peel
2 packages active dry yeast
¾ cup milk
½ cup water
½ cup margarine
2 eggs
½ cup chopped blanched almonds
½ cup golden raisins

In a large bowl, thoroughly mix 1½ cups flour and next six ingredients. Combine milk, water and margarine in a saucepan. Heat over low heat until liquids are very warm (120°-130°). Margarine does not need to melt. Gradually add to dry ingredients and beat 2 minutes at medium speed of electric mixer, scraping bowl occasionally. Add eggs and 1 cup flour. Beat at high speed 2 minutes, scraping bowl occasionally. Stir in enough additional flour to make a stiff dough. Turn out onto lightly-floured board. Knead until smooth and elastic, about 8-10 minutes. Place in greased bowl, turning to grease top. Cover, let rise in warm place, free from draft, until doubled in bulk, about 1½ hours. Punch dough down; turn out onto lightly-floured board. Knead in almonds and raisins. Roll out to a 16×10″ rectangle. Lightly roll up from long side as for jellyroll. Place seam side down in a greased 10″ tube pan. Pinch ends together to form a ring. Cover; let rise in warm place, free from draft, until doubled in bulk, about 1½ hours. Bake at 375° for 40-50 minutes. Remove from pan and cool on rack.
Yield: 1 10″ ring

 Good served with Camembert, Brie, Edam or Gouda cheese.

Horns

3 cups flour
½ pound butter
1 cake yeast
½ pint sour cream
3 egg yolks, beaten

Put flour in bowl with butter; cut in with knife or pastry blender until crumbly. Dissolve yeast in sour cream and add to flour and butter. Add egg yolks. Mix well and form into loaf. Wrap in waxed paper. Place in refrigerator overnight.

Filling:
2 cups nuts, chopped
1 cup sugar
1 teaspoon vanilla
dash of cinnamon
milk enough for spreading consistency

Roll out dough half at a time on floured board to ¼″ thick. Cut into squares; spread with filling. Roll, starting from corner, and shape into a crescent. Place on greased cookie sheet. Bake at 350° for 15 minutes.
Yield: 2 dozen

Margie's Angel Biscuits

5 cups flour	1 cup plus 3 teaspoons shortening
1/4 cup sugar	1 package dry yeast
3 teaspoons baking powder	1/4 cup warm water
1 teaspoon soda	1 cup buttermilk
1 teaspoon salt	1 cup sour cream

Sift dry ingredients together and cut in shortening. Dissolve yeast in warm water, add buttermilk and sour cream. Mix well. Roll out 1/2" thick and cut with cutter. Brush tops with melted butter. Bake at 400° for 15 minutes.
Yield: 3 dozen

Gingerbread

1 cup shortening	1¾ teaspoons soda
1 cup sugar	1 cup buttermilk
3 eggs	1 cup unsulphured syrup (Brer Rabbit or Cane Syrup)
3 cups flour	
1½ teaspoons salt	1 cup raisins, optional
2 teaspoons ginger	1 cup nuts, optional
1 teaspoon nutmeg	

Cream sugar and shortening; add eggs and beat well. Sift dry ingredients. Add alternately with buttermilk and soda. Add syrup and beat well. Add raisins and nuts. Fill greased muffin cups about half full or a 9 × 13" pan. Bake at 350° for 20 minutes for muffins and 30 minutes for pan.
Yield: 36 muffins

Pumpkin Bread

4 eggs	2 teaspoons nutmeg
3 cups sugar	2 teaspoons cloves
1 cup oil	2 teaspoons cinnamon
1 cup water	2 teaspoons allspice
1 16-ounce can pumpkin	1 teaspoon vanilla
3½ cups flour	1 cup pecans, chopped, optional
2 teaspoons soda	1 cup raisins, optional
1/2 teaspoon salt	

Beat eggs and sugar. Add oil, water and pumpkin; mix well. Sift together dry ingredients and add to pumpkin mixture. Beat in vanilla. Add nuts and raisins and stir in by hand. Grease 4 1-pound coffee cans thoroughly. Pour batter into cans and bake at 325° for 60 minutes.
Yield: 4 loaves

Poteca Christmas Bread

Filling:

2 cups chopped walnuts or pecans	⅓ cup sugar
¾ cup milk	1 cup raisins
¾ cup honey	

Mix all ingredients in a large heavy saucepan. Bring to a boil and cook about 5 minutes, stirring constantly. Remove from heat and cool completely before spreading over dough.

Bread:

2 packages yeast	½ cup sugar
⅓ cup water	2 teaspoons salt
1 cup milk	3 cups flour, divided
½ cup margarine, divided	2 eggs

Soften yeast in water. Heat milk and ¼ cup margarine until blended. Do not boil. Measure sugar and salt into a large bowl; add hot milk mixture and stir until dissolved. Cool to lukewarm. Add about 1½ cups flour and beat well. Add enough more flour to make a soft dough. Turn out on a lightly-floured board and knead until smooth and satiny, about 5-8 minutes. Shape into a ball and place in a greased bowl. Grease surface of dough lightly. Cover with a cloth and let rise in a warm place until doubled in bulk, about 1 hour. Then remove cover and punch down. Let rest for 10 minutes. Meanwhile, melt the remaining margarine. Divide dough into thirds. Roll out each portion to a rectangle about 10×20″. The dough will be very thin. Spread with the filling. Roll up like a jellyroll, starting with the narrow edge and seal the edges underside. Repeat with the remaining dough. Place on a greased baking sheet and brush tops lightly with melted margarine. Let rise until doubled, about 30 minutes. Bake at 375° for 30-35 minutes or until golden. Remove from oven and brush again with margarine.
Yield: 3 loaves

Zucchini Pineapple Bread

3 eggs	½ teaspoon baking soda
1 cup oil	1 teaspoon salt
2 cups sugar	2 teaspoons baking powder
2 teaspoons vanilla	1-2 teaspoons cinnamon
2 cups peeled, coarsely shredded zucchini	1 cup walnuts, chopped
1 8¼-ounce can crushed pineapple, well drained	1 cup raisins
3 cups flour	

Beat together eggs, oil, sugar and vanilla until light and foamy. Stir in zucchini and drained pineapple. Sift together dry ingredients. Stir gently into zucchini mixture. Fold in walnuts and raisins. Pour into two floured and greased 9×5″ loaf pans. Bake at 350° for 1 hour.
Yield: 2 loaves

Walnut Bread

Glaze:

1   egg   ½   teaspoon salt

Insert steel knife in food processor and blend egg and salt for 2 seconds.

Bread:

1   cup warm water   3   tablespoons walnut oil
¼   cup firmly packed brown sugar   1   teaspoon salt
1   envelope dry yeast   1½ cups small walnut pieces
3   cups bread flour, divided
½   cup whole wheat flour

Combine water, brown sugar and yeast; stir to blend. Let stand until foamy, about 10 minutes. Combine 2½ cups bread flour with whole wheat flour, walnut oil and salt in work bowl of food processor. With machine running, pour yeast mixture through feed tube and blend until dough cleans inside of bowl and is uniformly moist and elastic, about 40 seconds. If dough is too wet, add reserved ½ cup bread flour through feed tube, 1 tablespoon at a time. Push dough down into blade. Transfer to work surface and work in walnuts. Place in greased bowl turning to coat all surfaces. Cover bowl with damp towel. Let stand in warm draft-free area until doubled in volume, one hour. Punch dough down and turn onto well floured surface. Shape into smooth ball. Transfer to greased pie pan. Drape loosely with greased plastic wrap. Let stand in warm area until doubled, 35-40 minutes. Preheat oven to 400°. Brush with glaze. Bake for 30-40 minutes until well browned and sounds hollow when tapped.
Yield: 1 round loaf

All-Bran Muffins

2   cups buttermilk   2   eggs
2   cups Kellogg's All-Bran Cereal   1   teaspoon salt
2   teaspoons soda   1½ cups flour
½   cup butter or margarine   1   cup raisins, optional
¾   cup sugar

Put buttermilk, All-Bran and soda in mixing bowl and let stand 5 minutes. In another bowl, cream butter and sugar. Beat in eggs. Add salt and flour and blend. Add buttermilk mixture, mixing all together. If using raisins, dust them first with flour before adding to the batter. Fill greased medium sized muffin tins ⅔ full and bake 350° for about 12 minutes. Do not overbake.
Yield: 24 muffins

Banana Muffins

½ cup margarine	½ teaspoon salt
1 cup sugar	¾ teaspoon baking soda
2 eggs	½ teaspoon cinnamon
¾ cup ripe bananas, mashed	¼ teaspoon nutmeg
1¼ cups flour	1½ cups pecans, chopped

Cream margarine, add sugar and eggs. Beat. Stir in bananas. Add sifted dry ingredients. Add nuts. Fill greased muffin pan ¾ full. Bake at 350° for 20 minutes.
Yield: 12-14 muffins

Variation: Substitutions may be made as follows: coconut for pecans; ¹/₂ cup raisins or ¹/₂ cup mini chocolate chips with ¹/₂ cup pecans. If baked and frozen, defrost 1 hour and place in warm oven for 20 minutes.

Blueberry Muffins

3 cups flour, sifted	1 cup blueberries
4 teaspoons baking powder	2 eggs, beaten
½ cup sugar	¼ cup butter, melted
½ teaspoon salt	1 cup milk

Sift the dry ingredients together and mix in the blueberries. Mix eggs, shortening and milk together. Combine the two mixtures. Stir gently just to dampen the flour and allow the mixture to stand for 15-30 minutes. Fill greased muffin pans ⅔ full. Bake at 350° for 20 minutes.
Yield: 15 muffins

Fresh, canned or frozen blueberries can be used.

This is wonderful with Orange Butter (page 61).

Carrot Muffins

1½ cups flour	½ teaspoon salt
1 cup sugar	⅔ cup oil
1 teaspoon baking powder	2 eggs, beaten
1 teaspoon cinnamon	1 cup grated carrots
1 teaspoon vanilla	½ cup crushed pineapple with juice

Sift together dry ingredients. Add remaining ingredients and beat 2 minutes. Pour into greased medium-size muffin pans. Bake at 375° for 25 minutes.
Yield: 24 Muffins

Date Muffins

1 8-ounce package dates, coarsely chopped	½ cup whole wheat flour
¾ cup boiling water	½ cup sugar
¼ cup corn oil	⅓ cup walnuts, coarsely chopped
½ teaspoon vanilla	½ teaspoon baking soda
1 cup flour	

Grease muffin tins to make 12 large or 24 small. Stir together dates, boiling water, corn oil and vanilla. In another bowl stir together the flours, sugar, walnuts and soda. Add to the date mixture and stir until the flour mixture is moistened. Spoon into greased muffin tins. Bake at 375° for 20 minutes. Immediately remove from pan.
Yield: 2 dozen small, I dozen large.

 These freeze well.

French Puffies

⅓ cup margarine, softened	¼ teaspoon nutmeg
½ cup sugar	½ cup milk
1 egg	¾ cup sugar
1½ cups flour	1 teaspoon cinnamon
½ teaspoon baking powder	½ cup margarine, melted
½ teaspoon salt	

Cream margarine, sugar and egg. Sift flour, baking powder, salt and nutmeg and add to margarine mixture alternately with the milk. Fill greased muffin tins ⅔ full and bake at 350° for 20 minutes. During baking, mix sugar and cinnamon in small bowl. When muffins are done, remove immediately from the pans and dip each muffin top in the melted butter and then roll in the sugar and cinnamon.
Yield: 12 muffins

Texas Pecan Oatmeal Muffins

1 cup quick-cooking oatmeal	1 cup flour (half or all whole wheat)
1 cup buttermilk	1 teaspoon baking powder
½ cup margarine	½ teaspoon salt
¾ cup brown sugar	½ teaspoon soda
2 eggs	½ cup chopped pecans

Soak oatmeal and buttermilk one hour. Add margarine and sugar which has been beaten together. Add eggs. Sift dry ingredients together and add to buttermilk mixture. Add pecans. Fill greased muffin pans ⅔ full. Bake at 400° for 20 minutes.
Yield: 12-18 muffins

Broccoli Corn Bread

1   10-ounce box frozen chopped
broccoli, thawed and drained
2   tablespoons chopped onion
1   6-ounce carton small curd
cottage cheese

1   stick margarine, melted
4   eggs, beaten
1   8½-ounce box Jiffy corn bread
mix

Mix the first five ingredients. Add the corn bread mix last. Pour into a 9 × 13″ pan. Bake at 400° for 20-25 minutes.
Yield: 12 squares

Variation: For a corn bread that is not sweet, substitute two 6-ounce packages of Morrison's Corn-Kits.

Cheesy Beef Corn Bread

½   pound ground beef
1   cup yellow cornmeal
¾   teaspoon salt
½   teaspoon soda
1   cup milk
1   17-ounce can creamed corn

2   eggs, beaten
¼   cup vegetable oil
8   ounces shredded Cheddar
cheese
1   onion, chopped
2-4 jalapeño peppers, chopped

Cook beef; drain and set aside. Combine cornmeal, salt and soda. Mix well. Add milk, corn, eggs and oil; mix. Pour half of batter into a greased and heated baking dish or skillet. Sprinkle with cheese, onion, peppers and ground beef. Top with remaining batter. Bake at 350° for about 50 minutes.
Yield: 8-10 servings

Baked French Toast

1   pound loaf of unsliced egg rich
bread
6   eggs
¼   cup sugar
2   cups half and half

¼   teaspoon cinnamon
¼   teaspoon nutmeg
¼   cup powdered sugar
syrup

Prepare and refrigerate the night before serving. Slice bread into 1″ diagonal slices and place in a 2 quart greased casserole. Beat eggs; add sugar, cream, cinnamon and nutmeg. Pour over bread. If it does not moisten bread well, add a little milk. Bake at 375° for 40 minutes. Dust with powdered sugar and serve with syrup.
Yield: 6-8 Servings

Variation: Use 1″ slices of cinnamon bread

 Quickie: Mix your favorite corn bread recipe and bake in a waffle iron.

French Pancake

2 tablespoons butter	½ cup flour
½ cup milk	2 eggs lightly beaten

Preheat oven 475°. Melt butter in 9" baking dish in oven. Mix milk, flour and eggs. Add egg mixture to baking dish and bake for 12 minutes. Remove from oven, put on serving plate and top with butter, preserves, sautéed apples or powdered sugar. Cut into wedges.
Yield: 2-4 servings

Sunday School Coffee Cake

3 cups flour	½ teaspoon salt
2 cups sugar	1¾ cup pecans, chopped, divided
1 cup shortening	½ cup sugar
1 teaspoon cloves	1 cup raisins
1 teaspoon nutmeg	2 cups buttermilk
1 teaspoon cinnamon	2 teaspoons soda

Blend first 7 ingredients like a pie crust. Save ¾ cup and add to it ½ cup sugar and ⅓ cup pecans for topping. To remaining flour mixture add raisins, pecans, buttermilk and soda. Blend well. Pour into baking dish, sprinkling topping mixture over the pastry. Bake at 350° for 45 minutes.
Yield: 16-20 servings

 May be frozen.

Golden Butter Waffles

2 eggs	4 teaspoons baking powder
1¾ cups milk	½ teaspoon salt
½ cup butter, melted	1 tablespoon sugar
2 cups flour	

Beat eggs. Add remaining ingredients and beat until smooth. Cook in waffle iron according to directions.
Yield: 2-4 servings

Brown Bread

1½ cups buttermilk	1 teaspoon baking soda
⅓ cup molasses	1 teaspoon salt
⅔ cup sugar	1 cup raisins
3 cups whole wheat flour	butter

Put buttermilk in bowl; add molasses and sugar. Blend. Put dry ingredients on top of milk mixture and gently blend entire mixture. Add raisins. Pour into a 9×5″ greased and floured loaf pan. Bake at 350° for 1 hour. After baking, remove from pan and place on large sheet of waxed paper. Spread top and sides with butter. Fasten paper around loaf securely to steam; remove paper when cold.
Yield: 1 loaf

Pear Preserves

1 quart cooking pears	2½-3 cups sugar

Peel and cut up pears. Pour sugar over all and let sit overnight. Next day stir mixture well, then cook slowly until liquid is a clear amber color. Put into sterile jars.
Yield: 3½ pints

Peach Jam

3 pounds peaches (4 cups)	1 1¾-ounce box Sure-Jell
1 lemon	5½ cups sugar

Finely chop the fruit and put into large saucepan. Add Sure-Jell. Place on high heat and stir until mixture comes to hard boil. Add sugar all at once; bring to full rolling boil. Boil hard for 1 minute, stirring constantly. Remove from heat; skim off foam. Ladle into sterile jars and top with paraffin.
Yield: 7 cups

Plum Rum Jam

3½ cups unpeeled Santa Rosa red plums (about 16 plums)	1 3-ounce package Certo pectin
7½ cups sugar	4 ounces rum
½ cup fresh lemon juice	

Combine first 3 ingredients. Stir and cook slowly until mixture comes to a rolling boil. Skim off foam. Boil hard for 3 minutes. Remove from fire. Add pectin and rum. Stir well for 5 minutes. Pour into sterile jars and seal.
Yield: 8 8-ounce jars

Orange Butter:

1	pound butter	½	pound powdered sugar
4	oranges		

Grate rind from 2 oranges. Extract juice from oranges and strain. Add grated rind to juice. Add powdered sugar and mix with the juice as much as possible. Add this to the butter in an electric beater; mix until well blended. Mold or place in container and chill.
Yield: 2 cups

Strawberry Butter

½	cup softened butter	pinch of cinnamon
¼	cup strawberry preserves	

Combine all ingredients. Use as a spread on hot biscuits or toast.
Yield: 3/4 cup

Seasoned Butter

1	1-ounce package Hidden Valley Ranch dressing mix	1	8-ounce carton soft margarine garlic powder, to taste

Add dry mix to margarine. Mix and season with garlic powder. Use on toast rounds, cooked vegetables, fish or pasta. Store covered in the refrigerator.
Yield: 1 cup

Chicken Luncheon Sandwich

1	10¾-ounce can cream of mushroom soup or cream of chicken soup	¾	cup milk
1	tablespoon onion, minced	8	bread slices, crusts removed
1	2-ounce jar chopped pimiento, drained	2	eggs, slightly beaten
		3	tablespoons milk
1½	cups chicken, diced	½	tablespoon fresh tarragon
3	tablespoons flour	2	cups potato chips, crushed
		½	cup slivered almonds

Mix soup, onion, pimiento, and chicken in a saucepan. Blend flour with milk and add to soup. Cook, stirring constantly, until thick. Chill. Place four slices of bread in a 9″ square pan and spread the chicken mixture on top. Cover with remaining bread. Chill several hours or overnight. Mix eggs, milk and tarragon. Cut sandwiches into halves. Dip both sides of each half into the mixture and then into crushed potato chips. Arrange on buttered cookie sheets and top with almonds. Bake at 350° for 25 minutes.
Yield: 4-6 sandwiches

Frozen Bourbon Burgers

2	pounds ground meat	1	teaspoon salt
2	tablespoons butter	1	cup sharp Cheddar cheese,
½	cup chopped celery		grated
⅔	cup chopped onion	¼-⅓	cup bourbon, optional
½	cup chopped green pepper		butter, softened
1	cup catsup		mustard, to taste
1	tablespoon Worcestershire	16-20	hamburger buns
	sauce		

Cook meat; drain. Add butter, celery, onion and green pepper and cook until vegetables are limp. Stir in catsup, Worcestershire, salt and cheese. Let cool. Split buns and spread each cut side with butter and then mustard. Put about ¼ cup of meat mixture into each bun and wrap each separately in foil. Store in freezer. To serve, heat foil-wrapped frozen burgers in 375° oven for 35 minutes. Or remove foil and wrap frozen burger in paper towel and microwave on "low" 5 minutes until heated through.
Yield: 16-20 burgers

Grilled Gouda and Apple Sandwiches

½	cup golden delicious apple, cut in ¼" slices	4	slices homemade-type bread
2	tablespoons butter, divided	2	tablespoons mango chutney
4	teaspoons Dijon mustard	2	slices Gouda cheese

Sauté the apple slices in 1 tablespoon butter, approximately 4 minutes. Drain. Spread 1 teaspoon mustard on each slice of bread and 1 teaspoon chutney on 2 slices. Cover the chutney with Gouda, then apple slices. Top with the remaining bread, mustard side down. Melt the remaining 1 tablespoon butter on a grill or in a skillet and cook the sandwiches, turning once. To serve, cut diagonally into quarters.
Yield: 2 sandwiches

Hot Chicken Sandwich

12	slices Pepperidge Farm white sandwich bread, divided	1	10¾-ounce can cream of mushroom soup
3	cups cooked, diced chicken	1	10¾-ounce can cream of chicken soup
½	cup sliced pimiento-stuffed olives	1	cup sour cream
½	cup sliced mushrooms	1	cup grated Cheddar cheese
½	cup Hellmann's mayonnaise		

Place 6 slices of bread in baking dish. Mix chicken, olives, mushrooms and mayonnaise and spread over bread. Cover with remaining bread. Mix soups with sour cream and pour over bread. Cover and refrigerate overnight. Bake uncovered at 325° for 20 minutes. Sprinkle cheese over top and return to oven to melt cheese. Serve hot.
Yield: 6 sandwiches

Open-Faced Turkey Sandwich

6   slices pumpernickel bread
12 slices cooked breast of turkey
2   tomatoes, sliced
1/2 cup finely diced green pepper, divided

1   cup mayonnaise
1/4 cup grated Parmesan cheese
1/4 teaspoon onion salt
1   2-ounce can mushrooms, diced

Arrange on each slice of bread, 2 slices of turkey and 2 slices of tomato. Sprinkle on 1 tablespoon of green pepper. Combine other ingredients and spread over top of sandwiches. Broil until bubbly and serve at once.
Yield: 6 sandwiches

Variation: Can use chicken.

Mexican Grilled Sandwich

1/2 pound chicken breast, cooked and diced
4   8" flour tortillas
1/4 cup sour cream

4   ounces Monterey Jack cheese, grated
garlic salt

Spread 1 tablespoon sour cream on each tortilla. Put chicken on half of tortilla and grated cheese on chicken. Sprinkle with garlic salt. Fold in half in dry skillet on medium heat, turning until heated through and cheese is melted.
Yield: 4 sandwiches

Party Beef Pitas

1   pound ground beef
1   cup chopped onion
1/2 cup julienned green pepper
8   ounces sliced, fresh mushrooms
1/4 cup catsup
1   tablespoon snipped parsley
1   tablespoon Dijon mustard
1   tablespoon steak sauce

1   teaspoon oregano
1/4 teaspoon rosemary
1/4 teaspoon salt
1/4 teaspoon pepper
2   cups grated Swiss cheese
1/2 cup grated Parmesan cheese
6   lettuce leaves, halved
6   pita breads, halved

Cook beef, onion and peppers until meat is browned. Drain fat. Stir in all ingredients except cheeses, lettuce and bread. Cook for 5 minutes. Stir in cheeses. Line pita halves with lettuce and fill each with 1/3 cup of meat mixture.
Yield: 6 sandwiches

Rich Boy Sandwich

1	pint oysters
	melted butter
	chopped parsley
	salt and pepper

champagne, sherry, or dry white wine
French bread

Drain oysters but do not wash. Melt butter in skillet. Add chopped parsley. Salt and pepper the oysters and add to butter. Cook until oysters begin to get firm. Pour champagne, sherry or wine over. Cover and steam for a few minutes. Serve over French bread.
Yield: 2 generous sandwiches

 For a first course to serve 6, use 2 pints of oysters.

Toasted Cheese Sandwiches

2	large sandwich loaves
1	pound sharp cheese, grated
3	sticks margarine, softened
1	teaspoon onion powder

1¼ teaspoons dill weed
1½ teaspoons Worcestershire sauce
¾ teaspoon Tabasco sauce
dash cayenne pepper

Mix all ingredients together except bread. Place 3 slices of bread together and trim crusts. Spread cheese mixture on bottom slice, top with 2nd slice. Spread cheese on this one. Top with 3rd slice and spread cheese on it. Cut into fourths. Spread cheese on all sides but not on the bottom. Use the cheese mixture sparingly. Place on cookie sheet. Cover with foil. Freeze. When frozen, place in bags and keep frozen until ready to use. To bake, place on cookie sheet and bake at 350° for 20 minutes.
Yield: 96 squares

Chipped Beef Filling

1	2½-ounce jar dried beef, chopped
1	8-ounce package cream cheese, softened
1	teaspoon grated onion

2 teaspoons horseradish
2 drops Tabasco sauce
½ cup chopped pecans

Rinse beef, pat dry. Mix all ingredients thoroughly. Use any bread desired. Also good to stuff celery or cherry tomatoes.
Yield: Approximately 1 pint

Chili-Cheese Sandwich Spread

1   pound Cheddar cheese, grated
1   4-ounce can chopped green chilies, drained
1   2-ounce can chopped pimiento, drained
1   cup chopped pecans
½   cup chopped ripe olives
¼-⅓ cup mayonnaise, or as needed
2   tablespoons finely chopped onion

Mix all ingredients. Cover and refrigerate until ready to make sandwiches — open, covered, finger or shaped sandwiches.
Yield: Approximately 1 quart

 For a spicier spread, use 1 can of whole green chilies, chopped

Cucumber Sandwich Filling

1   8-ounce package cream cheese, softened
3   tablespoons mayonnaise
1   cucumber, seeds removed, coarsely grated and drained
½   teaspoon finely chopped chives
½   teaspoon paprika
dash cayenne
dash onion salt

Cream gently together. Refrigerate 1 hour before spreading. Suitable for open face or covered sandwiches.
Yield: Approximately 1 pint

Ham Filling for Sandwiches

3   cups minced cooked ham
1   tablespoon minced ginger root
⅓   cup minced green onions
1   5-ounce can water chestnuts, drained and chopped
2   tablespoons mayonnaise
2   tablespoons Dijon mustard
1   teaspoon lemon juice
dash white pepper

Combine all ingredients and mix well. Serve with rye or white bread or in pita halves.
Yield: Filling for 6-8 sandwiches

Polly's Filled Rolls

1   small green pepper
1   small garlic clove
6   small green onions
1½ pounds cheese, half sharp and half American
8   ounces ripe olives
1   2-ounce jar pimiento
6   hard-boiled eggs
4   tablespoons olive oil
4   tablespoons chili sauce
4   tablespoons catsup
18 small oval French rolls

Finely chop the first 3 ingredients. Grate cheese. Chop olives, pimiento and eggs. Combine all ingredients. Scoop out French rolls. Fill each with filling. Bake at 275° for 25 minutes.
Yield: 18 rolls

Olive Nut Sandwich Spread

1   4¼-ounce jar chopped ripe olives
1   5-ounce jar Spanish olives with pimentos, chopped

16   pecan halves, chopped
      mayonnaise to spread

Mix all ingredients. Spread on bread for sandwiches or use on crackers.
Yield: 1-1½ cups spread

Turkey Sandwich Filling

1   5-ounce can boned turkey
     juice of 1 lemon
2   cups mayonnaise

2   cups finely chopped celery
1   cup finely chopped pecans
     salt, to taste
     pinch of sugar

This must be prepared the day before. Break up turkey with fork and add all ingredients. Cover and refrigerate overnight. You cannot add more mayonnaise after it has set.
Yield: Approximately 1 quart

Vegetable Ricotta Filling for Pita Bread

1   tablespoon butter
1   cup fresh mushrooms, chopped
16   ounces ricotta cheese
½   cup olives, chopped

1   cup shredded carrots
2   tablespoons basil, minced
     dash pepper and salt
     pita bread

Melt butter and sauté mushrooms until tender. Cool. Combine other ingredients. Stir in mushrooms and serve in pita halves.
Yield: filling for 8 pita halves

Watercress Sandwiches

12   slices bread, crusts removed
1   bunch watercress, divided
2   slices bacon
2   3-ounce packages cream cheese

2½   tablespoons mayonnaise
2   tablespoons butter
1   teaspoon onion, minced
     salt and pepper, to taste

Wrap bread in dry towel. Wash watercress, save 12 sprigs for garnish and chop remaining. Fry bacon and chop fine. Cream the cheese with mayonnaise and butter; add bacon, onion, watercress and seasonings. Spread on bread and roll up, sticking sprig of watercress in each end. Put in damp towel and refrigerate.
Yield: 6 sandwiches

Eggs, Cheese & Pasta

Brunch Eggs

6	Canadian bacon slices	¼	cup milk
2	10¾-ounce cans cream of chicken soup	8	hard-cooked eggs, sliced
		3	English muffins, split
⅓	cup sauterne wine	¼	cup chopped parsley
1½	teaspoons tarragon		paprika

Brown bacon in skillet or oven. Combine soup, wine, tarragon and milk. Heat until warm. Add sliced eggs. Lightly toast muffins. Place slice of bacon on each half. Spoon on sauce and sprinkle with chopped parsley and paprika.
Yield: 3-6 servings

Cheese Burek

1	pound hoop or farmer's cheese, crumbled	4	eggs
		1	teaspoon sugar
8	ounces feta cheese, crumbled	1	pound phyllo leaves
2	cups cottage cheese, drained	1	cup butter, melted

In a large mixing bowl, mix all the cheeses together until well blended. Combine eggs and sugar and beat well with an electric mixer. Fold eggs into cheese mixture, stirring until creamy. Place two sheets of the phyllo, folded, in a 9 × 13″ buttered casserole. Brush phyllo with melted butter. Cover with ¼ of cheese mixture. Repeat layering of the phyllo and cheese mixture, ending with the phyllo. Bake at 350° for 30-40 minutes or until brown and crispy. Let stand for 10 minutes before cutting into squares.
Yield: 12 servings

Spanakopita

1	cup chopped onion	4	eggs, beaten, or 1½ cartons of Egg Beaters
2	tablespoons safflower oil		
	salt and pepper, to taste	1½	teaspoons basil
2	10-ounce packages frozen chopped spinach, thawed and drained well	½	teaspoon oregano
		1	16-ounce package phyllo leaves
2	cups crumbled feta cheese	½	pound tub corn oil margarine, melted and divided
2	tablespoons flour	1	tablespoon anise or fennel seeds
2	cups light-line cottage cheese		

Cook the onions in the oil until soft, salting lightly. Then combine with spinach, cheese, flour, cottage cheese, eggs, basil and oregano. Spread 1-2 tablespoons of the melted margarine in a 9 × 13″ pan. Begin layering 8 phyllo sheets with the edges climbing the sides, brushing each layer with margarine. Then spread ½ of the filling over the phyllo. Repeat, ending with the remaining filling. Fold the excess phyllo sheets down along the edges, making neat corners. Continue layering as many more phyllo sheets and margarine as the baking pan will accommodate. Brush the final sheet with the remaining margarine. Sprinkle anise or fennel seeds over the top. Bake uncovered at 375° for 45 minutes until golden.
Yield: 8 servings

 This is a light and healthy entreé.

Sausage Grits Casserole

1	pound bulk sausage	2	eggs, beaten
1	cup uncooked grits	3	4-ounce cans chopped green
4	cups water		chilies, drained
½	cup butter		paprika
8	ounces sharp cheese, grated		

Cook, drain and crumble sausage. Cook grits in water. Remove from heat and add butter and cheese. Blend well. Stir in eggs and chilies. Pour into a greased 9 × 13″ casserole. Sprinkle with paprika. Bake at 350° for 45 minutes until bubbly.
Yield: 8-10 servings

 This may be prepared ahead and refrigerated 1-2 days before baking. Or freeze, then thaw before baking.

Eggs, Spinach and Sausage Treat

1	10-ounce package frozen chopped spinach, thawed and drained well	1	10¾-ounce can cream of mushroom soup
1	pound sausage (mild or hot)	½	soup can of milk
1	dozen eggs	1	cup grated sharp Cheddar cheese
	salt and pepper, to taste		

Preheat oven to 350°. Line bottom of a 2 quart oblong dish with spinach. Brown and drain the sausage and add to the spinach. Scramble the eggs; add the salt and pepper and spread evenly over the sausage. Mix soup and milk and pour over all. Top with the cheese. Bake for 30 minutes or until hot.
Yield: 6 servings

 This may be prepared ahead and refrigerated one day before baking.

Creole Eggs

1	large onion, chopped	1	tablespoon chili powder
6	medium green peppers, chopped	½	teaspoon black pepper
1	tablespoon butter	1	15-ounce can tomatoes, drained
1	teaspoon salt	1	16-ounce can small peas, drained
1	tablespoon sugar		
1	tablespoon Worcestershire sauce	8	hard-cooked eggs
		¾	cup buttered bread crumbs

Brown onion and peppers slowly in butter. Add drained tomatoes and peas. Add seasonings. Simmer 15 minutes.

White Sauce:

2	tablespoons butter	2	cups milk
4	tablespoons flour		

Melt butter and add flour. Stir until smooth. Add milk gradually. Combine tomato mixture with the white sauce. Pour into buttered casserole alternately with layers of sliced eggs. Top with crumbs and bake at 350° for 15 minutes or until bubbly.
Yield: 8 servings

Eggs Cecile

12	hard-cooked eggs	½	cup mayonnaise
1½	tablespoons lemon juice (or vinegar)	1	pound crab meat
2	teaspoons prepared mustard	1	8-ounce can button mushrooms, drained
1	teaspoon Worcestershire sauce	2	cups cream sauce
1	teaspoon salt		curry powder, to taste
½	teaspoon pepper		

Cut eggs in half lengthwise. Press yolks through sieve. Combine with lemon juice, mustard, Worcestershire sauce, salt, pepper and mayonnaise. Beat until smooth. Adjust seasonings and refill egg whites. Place in flat baking dish. Spread crab and mushrooms over the eggs.

Cream sauce:

6	tablespoons butter	1	cup milk
6	tablespoons flour		

Melt butter; mix in flour until smooth. Add milk and stir until thickened. Add salt, pepper and curry powder. Pour over crab mixture. Bake at 350° for 30 minutes or until bubbly.

Yield: 6 servings

Welsh Rarebit with Beer

1	tablespoon butter	½	teaspoon salt
1	pound sharp Cheddar cheese, grated	1	tablespoon Worcestershire sauce
¾	cup beer, divided	1	egg, beaten
	dash of cayenne pepper or Tabasco sauce	1	teaspoon cornstarch
1	teaspoon dry mustard		

Melt butter in top of a double boiler. Add the cheese and all but 1 tablespoon of the beer. Cook over hot, not boiling, water until the cheese melts. Combine the seasonings with the remaining tablespoon of beer and stir into the cheese. Combine the beaten egg with the cornstarch; stir into the cheese mixture and let it thicken slightly. Serve immediately over saltine crackers, toast or broiled tomato halves.

Yield: 4 servings

 Any cheese mixture that is left over can be refrigerated and served as a spread with crackers.

Cheese Soufflé

2 tablespoons butter, divided	7 eggs, separated
2 tablespoons flour	1 pound Swiss or sharp Cheddar
2 cups milk	cheese, grated
salt and pepper, to taste	1 4-ounce can sliced mushrooms, drained

Combine 1 tablespoon melted butter with flour, milk and seasonings. Stir until thickened. Set aside. Beat the egg yolks and add half of the cream sauce and half of the cheese. Brown the mushrooms in 1 tablespoon butter. Beat the egg whites until stiff. Fold in the mushrooms and the remaining cream sauce and cheese. Mix well. Pour into buttered baking dish. Place dish in pan of cold water and put into a cold oven. Bake at 350° for 1 hour.

Yield: 8-10 servings

Petit Spinach and Cheese Soufflés with Lemon Sauce

1½ cups grated Parmesan cheese	8 egg yolks
8 tablespoons butter, melted	12 egg whites
4 green onions, finely chopped	½ teaspoon salt
8 tablespoons flour	2 cups fresh spinach, finely
2½ cups milk, scalded	chopped (about half of a 10-
1 teaspoon salt	ounce bag)
¼ teaspoon pepper	extra Parmesan cheese for
dash of cayenne pepper	coating

Butter inside of eight petit soufflé dishes and sprinkle with grated Parmesan cheese. Set aside. Sauté green onions in butter; add flour and stir together about 2 minutes. Add scalded milk to mixture and whisk together until blended. Add seasonings and cook, stirring until the mixture boils. Remove from heat. Beat in egg yolks, one at a time, and allow to cool slightly. Beat egg whites with ½ teaspoon salt until stiff but not dry. Stir half of the whites into the yolk mixture. Stir in spinach and cheese and then gently fold mixture into the rest of the whites. Pour into soufflé dishes and sprinkle tops with extra cheese. Bake at 400° for 5 minutes, then at 375° for 15-20 minutes until tops are a lovely golden brown. Serve with lemon sauce.

Lemon Sauce:

2 tablespoons butter	¼ teaspoon salt
2 tablespoons flour	2 egg yolks, beaten
1½ cups chicken broth	2 tablespoons lemon juice

Melt butter and blend in flour. Gradually stir in chicken broth. Add salt. Cook, stirring constantly, until thickened and smooth. Add small amount of sauce to the egg yolks; then add the rest of the yolks to the sauce. Cook over low heat until thickened. Blend in lemon juice. Serve over soufflé.

Yield: 8 servings

 Sauce may be prepared ahead and reheated.

Soufflé San Miguel

½	cup grated Monterey Jack cheese	2	teaspoons Lawry's dried onions dash of garlic powder
½	cup grated Cheddar cheese	½	cup Bisquick
⅓	of a 4-ounce can chopped green chilies	¼	cup margarine or butter, melted
2	eggs, beaten	1-2	tomatoes, chopped
1	cup sour cream		Crazy Mixed-Up Salt or salt and pepper, to taste
1	cup creamed cottage cheese		

Combine the first two cheeses. Spread half on the bottom of a greased 9″ pie plate. Sprinkle green chilies on top of cheeses. Beat eggs. Combine sour cream, cottage cheese, seasonings, Bisquick and margarine or butter. Mix until smooth. Pour over cheese and chilies. Top with rest of the cheese, chopped tomatoes and seasonings. Bake at 350° for 25-30 minutes or until a knife in the center comes out clean.
Yield: 4-6 servings

Variation: Those who like it really hot might use more chilies or use jalapeño peppers.

Spoonbread Soufflé

2	cups milk	4	eggs, separated
½	cup white cornmeal	1	teaspoon baking powder
¼	pound butter or margarine	1	teaspoon sugar
1	6-ounce roll garlic cheese	1	teaspoon salt

Combine cold milk and cornmeal. Stir and cook over medium heat until consistency of thick cream sauce. Be careful not to burn. Remove from heat. Add butter and cheese and stir until smooth. Cool. Add well-beaten egg yolks, baking powder, sugar and salt. Mix well. This can be prepared to this point and set aside or put in refrigerator until ready to bake. Remove from refrigerator 1 hour before cooking.

Preheat oven to 350°. Beat egg whites until stiff and fold into cornmeal mixture. Turn into a well-buttered 2 quart baking dish. Bake 45 minutes or until top is puffed and golden brown. Serve with butter or with creamed chicken, crab or shrimp.
Yield: 6 servings

Confetti Pizza Crust

4 cups grated zucchini	½ cup grated Parmesan cheese
4 eggs, or 1 carton egg beaters	1 tablespoon fresh basil or 1
⅓ cup flour	teaspoon dried
½ cup grated skim mozzarella cheese	salt and pepper, to taste

Salt zucchini lightly and let it stand 15 minutes. Squeeze out excess moisture. Combine all crust ingredients and spread into a 9×13" baking pan, greased or sprayed with Pam. Bake at 350° for 20-25 minutes until the surface is dry and firm. Brush the top with oil and broil for 5 minutes. Then pile on all of your favorite pizza toppings, such as tomato sauce, sautéed mushrooms, strips of red and green pepper, sliced ripe olives, etc. Sprinkle with low-fat mozzarella cheese and bake for about 25 minutes more.
Yield: 4-6 servings

 A healthy way to enjoy pizza!

Cheese-Deviled Ham Quiche

¾ cup cracker crumbs	½ teaspoon salt
¼ cup melted margarine, divided	¼ teaspoon pepper
2 cups chopped onion	1 4-ounce can deviled ham
1 cup milk	¾ cup grated Cheddar cheese
2 eggs, beaten	

Toss the cracker crumbs with 2 tablespoons margarine. Press into a 9" pie plate. Sauté onions in remaining 2 tablespoons of margarine and spread over the crumbs. Add 1 cup milk to the beaten eggs. Add seasonings. Combine deviled ham with the cheese and mix with other ingredients. Spread over onions. Bake at 300° for 40 minutes. Let stand for 10 minutes before serving.
Yield: 6 servings

Crustless Crab Quiche

8 ounces fresh mushrooms, thinly sliced	4 tablespoons flour
2 tablespoons butter	¼ teaspoon salt
1 tablespoon chopped onion	4 drops Tabasco sauce
4 eggs	6 ounces fresh or canned crab
1 cup sour cream	2 cups shredded Monterey Jack cheese
8 ounces small curd cottage cheese	½ cup Parmesan cheese

Preheat oven to 350°. Sauté mushrooms and onions in butter. Remove and drain on paper towels. In food processor, blend eggs, sour cream, cottage cheese, flour, salt and Tabasco sauce. Pour into bowl and add onions, mushrooms, crab and cheeses. Pour into a 9" or 10" quiche pan that has been sprayed with Pam. Bake for 45 minutes. Let stand 10 minutes before serving.
Yield: 8 servings

Variation: 8 ounces of ham or shrimp may be substituted for the crab meat.

Tex-Mex Quiche

1   can chopped green chilies
1   pound Monterey Jack cheese, grated
1   pound medium sharp Cheddar cheese, grated
4   eggs, separated

⅔   cup evaporated milk
1   tablespoon flour
½   teaspoon salt
⅛   teaspoon pepper
2   tomatoes, sliced

Preheat oven to 350°. Place chilies and cheese in a 2 quart buttered casserole. Beat egg whites until stiff. Set aside. Combine egg yolks, milk, flour, salt and pepper. Fold in egg whites. Pour over cheese mixture and pierce with a fork. Bake 30 minutes. Place tomato slices on top and bake 30 minutes more.
Yield: 6-8 servings

Spinach Ricotta Quiche with Buttermilk Crust

1   cup flour
⅓   cup corn oil margarine

3   tablespoons cold buttermilk

Make dough by cutting flour and margarine together into small pieces. When mixture is uniformly blended, add buttermilk. Chill the dough one hour; then spread into a 9″ pie pan.

Filling:
2   tablespoons margarine, melted
½   pound chopped fresh spinach
1   small onion, chopped
½   teaspoon salt
½   teaspoon basil
    pepper, to taste
3   tablespoons flour

½   cup Weight Watchers' cheese, shredded
1   pound slim ricotta cheese
4   beaten eggs or 1 carton egg beaters
    dash nutmeg
1   cup low-fat yogurt
    paprika

Sauté the spinach and onion in the butter. Add seasonings. Mix in cheeses, eggs and nutmeg, blending well. Spread into unbaked pie shell. Top with yogurt and spread to edges of the crust. Sprinkle generously with paprika. Bake at 375° for 40-45 minutes.
Yield: 6 servings

Spinach Quiche

1   8″ frozen Pet-Ritz pie shell, thawed
2   10-ounce packages Stouffer's spinach soufflé, thawed
2   cups grated Swiss cheese

2   tablespoons butter
1   medium onion, chopped
8-10 mushrooms, sliced, or 4-ounce can sliced mushrooms, drained

To thaw spinach soufflé, let stand 4 hours at room temperature or in the refrigerator overnight. Preheat oven to 350°. Sauté onions and mushrooms in butter. Place in bottom of thawed pie shell. Cover with grated cheese. Spoon the defrosted soufflé into pie shell. Bake for 1 hour. Allow to cool 10 minutes before serving.
Yield: 6 servings

Mike and Charlie's Quiche

12 slices bacon
2 onions, sliced
2 cups coarsely-chopped ham
2 cups grated Cheddar cheese
2 cups grated Swiss cheese
1 tablespoon flour
2 10" baked pie shells
6 eggs, beaten
2 cups light cream, heated

1 teaspoon salt
½ teaspoon coarsely ground black pepper
½ teaspoon dry mustard
½ teaspoon cayenne pepper
½ teaspoon nutmeg
  paprika
  dried parsley flakes

Preheat oven to 350°. Fry bacon until crisp. Crumble bacon and reserve drippings. Sauté onion in bacon drippings until soft; remove and set aside. Sauté ham in the drippings for approximately 5 minutes. Combine cheeses and toss with flour. Sprinkle bacon, then onion, over bottom of pie crusts. Layer half of the ham and half of the cheeses. Add the remaining ham and top with the cheeses. Beat the eggs with the warm cream, salt, pepper, dry mustard, cayenne and nutmeg. Pour egg mixture over the filled pie shells; let stand 10 minutes. Sprinkle lightly with nutmeg, paprika and dried parsley. Bake for 30-40 minutes or until custard is set.
Yield: 10-12 servings

 To freeze, bake at 350° for 20 minutes. Cool. Wrap with foil and freeze. To serve, place while still frozen into a 350° oven and bake for 20 minutes.

Barbara's Chicken Spaghetti

3 slices bacon
1½ onions, finely chopped and divided
1 green pepper, finely chopped
4 chicken breasts
3 ribs celery, chopped
1 12-ounce package spaghetti
1 pound Velveeta cheese, cubed
1 2-ounce jar diced pimientos, drained

1 4-ounce can sliced mushrooms, drained
1½-2 cups chicken broth, or as needed
1 heaping teaspoon Beau Monde
  salt and pepper, to taste
  paprika
  Parmesan cheese

Fry bacon; drain and reserve drippings. Sauté 1 chopped onion and pepper in drippings. Boil chicken in water to cover with remaining ½ onion and celery. Strain and reserve broth. Debone and cut up chicken. Cook spaghetti as directed on package. Mix with hot chicken, cheese, bacon, sautéed vegetables, pimientos and mushrooms. Stir in broth, using enough to make it very moist. Add Beau Monde, salt and pepper. Pour into greased 2 quart casserole. Sprinkle with paprika. Bake at 350° for 30 minutes. Serve with Parmesan cheese.
Yield: 6-8 servings

 Spaghetti may be cooked in chicken broth.

Carbonera

2-3	slices bacon		salt and pepper, to taste
1/3	pound fettucini	3	tablespoons butter
1	garlic clove, minced	1/3	cup grated Romano cheese
1	tablespoon finely chopped parsley	1	egg yolk

Fry bacon until crisp. Drain and crumble. Cook fettucini. Meanwhile, put the bacon, garlic, parsley, salt, pepper and butter into the frying pan and keep warm. Mix the cheese and egg yolk. When the pasta is done, drain and add to other ingredients in the frying pan. Add the cheese/egg mixture and toss to coat. Turn onto a warmed platter and serve immediately with more Romano cheese if desired.
Yield: 2 servings

Easy Microwave Manicotti

1   10-ounce package frozen chopped spinach

Microwave the spinach on high until thawed. Drain well and set aside.

Sauce:

1	14½-ounce can whole tomatoes, undrained	½	cup water
1	8-ounce can tomato sauce	½	teaspoon salt
1	6-ounce can tomato paste	¾	teaspoon sugar

Quarter the tomatoes and combine with tomato sauce, tomato paste, ½ cup water and seasonings in a 1½ quart microwave-safe casserole. Cover and microwave until mixture is hot.

Manicotti:

1	teaspoon dried oregano	½	cup Parmesan cheese
½	teaspoon pepper	1	egg or egg substitute
½	teaspoon garlic powder	1	8-ounce package manicotti shells
1	15½-ounce carton slim ricotta cheese	½	cup warm water
2	cups shredded slim mozzarella cheese, divided		

Combine ricotta, 1 cup mozzarella cheese, Parmesan cheese, egg and spinach. Blend well. Stuff mixture into uncooked manicotti shells; arrange in a 12×8″ microwave-safe baking dish. Pour sauce over shells. Cover with plastic wrap. Microwave (high) 14-15 minutes. Rotate dish; add water. Microwave (medium) 18-20 minutes or until noodles are tender. Sprinkle with 1 cup mozzarella cheese. Microwave (high) uncovered for 2-3 minutes until cheese melts. Let stand for 5 minutes before serving.
Yield: 6 servings

Fideo

5	tablespoons bacon drippings or safflower oil	1	10½-ounce can consommé
1	5½-ounce package fideo vermicelli	1	4-ounce can whole green chilies, chopped and seeded
1	14½-ounce can tomatoes	½	teaspoon salt

Heat drippings or oil. Crumble fideo and brown, stirring constantly. Add other ingredients; cover and cook over low heat for 20 minutes.
Yield: 6-8 servings

Fettucini Florentine

2	10½-ounce packages frozen chopped spinach	2	shallots (not green onions)
1	tablespoon diet margarine	2	teaspoons dried tarragon
		2	tablespoons lemon juice

Cook and drain spinach according to package directions. Sauté shallots in margarine. Add to spinach along with tarragon and lemon juice. Place spinach mixture in lightly greased baking dish.

Fettucini:

1	pound fettucini		freshly ground pepper, to taste
3	tablespoons cooking oil	½	cup buttered, toasted bread crumbs
2	garlic cloves, finely chopped		
½	cup farmer's, Swiss or Gruyère cheese	1	cup Parmesan cheese

Cook noodles and drain. Mix oil, garlic and cheese together and add to noodles. Add pepper to taste. Place on top of spinach. Sprinkle liberally with Parmesan cheese and crumbs. Heat for l5 minutes at 350°. Place under broiler for 2-3 minutes or until golden brown.
Yield: 6 servings

 This is a satisfying low-cholesterol dish.

Jane's St. Louis Mostacholli

2	8-ounce package Mostacholli	2	4½-ounce cans mushrooms, stems and pieces, drained
3	pounds lean ground beef		
1	cup chopped onions	2	teaspoons oregano
1	15-ounce block chili (Owen's preferred)	1	teaspoon garlic salt
2	16-ounce cans tomatoes	1	tablespoon salt
2	8-ounce cans tomato sauce	1	teaspoon pepper
2	6-ounce cans tomato paste	1	drop anise oil
2	tablespoons sugar	2	cups water

Cook pasta according to package directions. Drain. Sauté ground beef and onions until well done. Cut chili into pieces and add to meat mixture. Add all other ingredients except pasta. Stir and simmer until mixture bubbles. Add sauce to pasta. Pour into a deep-dish baking casserole. Bake at 300°-325° for 25-45 minutes.
Yield: 12-16 servings

Jarlsburg Pasta Primavera

2	tablespoons butter	1	cup half and half
1	medium zucchini, sliced	¼	teaspoon basil
½	cup carrots, julienned	¼	teaspoon salt
⅓	cup green onions, cut in 1" pieces	⅛	teaspoon pepper
⅓	cup quartered mushrooms	1	cup shredded Jarlsburg cheese
1	small garlic clove, minced	1	cup broccoli flowerets, cooked
1	tablespoon flour	1	8-ounce package thin spaghetti, cooked and drained

In a large saucepan, melt butter and sauté zucchini, carrots, onions, mushrooms and garlic until just tender, stirring occasionally. Add flour and blend well. Gradually stir in half and half. Cook, stirring until thickened. Season with basil, salt and pepper. Add cheese and heat, stirring until cheese is melted. Add broccoli flowerets. Toss in pasta and serve immediately.
Yield: 4 servings

Frittata di Spaghetti Farcita (Stuffed Spaghetti Frittata)

½	pound spaghetti		pinch of salt
4	tablespoons butter, divided	½	cup mozzarella cheese, grated
⅓	cup grated Parmesan cheese, divided	4	ounces mild Italian salami, diced
2	tablespoons olive oil	3	eggs, slightly beaten
3-5	tablespoons chopped onion	⅛	teaspoon freshly ground pepper
1	cup canned Italian plum tomatoes, drained and chopped		

Cook spaghetti al dente. Drain and toss with half the butter and half the Parmesan cheese. Sauté onion in heated olive oil. Add tomatoes and salt. Cook for 15 minutes, stirring occasionally. Mix in mozzarella and salami. Mix eggs with pepper and combine with pasta. Mix well. Put remaining 2 tablespoons of butter into skillet and heat. Spread half the pasta evenly over the bottom of the skillet. Spread tomato filling over pasta. Then sprinkle on remaining Parmesan; cover with rest of pasta. Cook for 4 minutes over medium heat without stirring. Cook until just golden. Run under broiler 1 minute. Cut into wedges to serve.
Yield: 4 servings

Russian Noodle Casserole

5	ounces noodles	1	teaspoon salt
1	garlic clove, minced		few drops Tabasco sauce
½	cup chopped green onions	1	tablespoon Worcestershire sauce
2	tablespoons butter or margarine		
1	cup cottage cheese	1	cup grated Cheddar cheese
⅓	cup pine nuts		paprika
1	cup sour cream		

Cook noodles according to package directions. Sauté garlic and onions in butter. Mix all ingredients except Cheddar cheese and paprika. Place in well-greased casserole. Top with cheese and paprika. Bake at 350°, covered, for 20 minutes and then uncovered for 20 minutes more.
Yield: 4-6 servings

Lasagna

2 tablespoons olive oil	½ teaspoon sugar
2 garlic cloves, minced	1 teaspoon oregano
1 pound ground beef	½ pound lasagna noodles
1 envelope onion soup mix	¾ pound mozzarella cheese, shredded
1½ cups water	
1 8-ounce can tomato sauce	1 16-ounce carton small curd cottage cheese
1 6-ounce can tomato paste	
½ teaspoon salt	4 tablespoons grated Parmesan cheese
¼ teaspoon pepper	

Heat the oil and brown the garlic and meat. Stir in the dry soup mix, water, tomato sauce, tomato paste and seasonings. Cover and simmer for 30 minutes. Cook noodles according to package directions. Drain and rinse well with cold water. Put 3 tablespoons of meat sauce in a 9×13" casserole. Alternate layers of noodles, mozzarella, cottage cheese and meat sauce, ending with sauce. Sprinkle with Parmesan cheese. Bake at 350° for 30 minutes or until bubbly.
Yield: 8-10 servings

 Freezes well.

Pasta and Chicken Salad

6 ounces pasta twists	¼ teaspoon pepper
¼ cup sesame seeds	3 cups shredded cooked chicken
½ cup salad oil, divided	½ cup chopped parsley
½ cup soy sauce	½ cup thinly-sliced green onions with tops
½ cup white wine vinegar	
3 tablespoons sugar	8 cups torn spinach leaves, lightly packed
½ teaspoon salt	

Cook pasta according to package directions. Drain, rinse and cool. In a small skillet cook sesame seeds in ¼ cup oil over medium-low heat for 2 minutes, stirring. Cool. Stir in remaining oil, soy sauce, vinegar, sugar, salt and pepper. Pour over cooked pasta, add chicken and toss gently. Cover and chill for at least 2 hours. To serve, toss lightly with parsley, onion and spinach.
Yield: 8 servings

Shrimp Vermicelli Salad

2 pounds cooked small or medium shrimp	1 cup fresh lemon juice

Marinate shrimp overnight in lemon juice. Drain and add to vermicelli, below.

Vermicelli:

1 14-ounce package vermicelli (fresh is best)	½ teaspoon dried oregano
	½ teaspoon chopped chives
1 medium red onion, chopped	½ cup Italian dressing
1 medium green pepper, chopped	1 cup mayonnaise
1 tablespoon chopped parsley	salt and pepper, to taste
1½ teaspoons celery seed	

Cook vermicelli al dente. Drain and rinse in cold water. Add Italian dressing, mayonnaise and all other ingredients except shrimp. Add more mayonnaise if necessary.
Yield: 10-12 servings

Sauce for Spaghetti or Lasagna

1	large onion, minced	½	teaspoon marjoram
3	tablespoons salad oil	½	teaspoon basil
2	pounds lean ground beef		garlic powder, to taste
4	8-ounce cans tomato sauce		black and red pepper, to taste
1	cup Burgundy wine	1	teaspoon salt
½	teaspoon oregano	1	tablespoon sugar
½	teaspoon rosemary	12	ounces vermicelli or 6 ounces lasagna noodles

Brown onion in oil. Add meat and brown. Add all ingredients except pasta and simmer for at least an hour — the longer the better. Cook noodles as directed.

For vermicelli: Serve the sauce over the vermicelli.

For lasagna: in a greased 10 × 16 × 1½″ casserole, layer cooked lasagna noodles, meat sauce, grated mozzarella cheese, cottage cheese and Parmesan cheese. Repeat layering. Bake at 375° for 30 minutes. Let stand 15 minutes before serving.
Yield: 8 servings

 Let the sauce simmer for several hours if time permits.

Pasta Primavera

1	bunch broccoli flowerets	¼	cup parsley, chopped
1	small zucchini squash, sliced	2	tablespoons chopped fresh basil or I teaspoon dried
1	yellow squash, cubed		Tabasco sauce, to taste
2	carrots, thinly sliced	¼	cup chicken stock
½	cup frozen peas	¾	cup milk
1	cup sliced fresh mushrooms	⅔	cup Parmesan cheese
2	shallots, chopped (not green onions)		salt and pepper, to taste
¼	cup sliced red pepper	12	ounces vermicelli
¼	cup sliced green pepper		toasted pine nuts or sunflower seeds, optional
4	tablespoons margarine, divided		
¼	teaspoon garlic powder		

Cook or steam broccoli, squash and carrots al dente. Stir in peas for last minute of cooking. Drain and refresh under cold water. Set aside. This may be done well in advance. Sauté mushrooms, green onions, and peppers in 2 tablespoons margarine 2-3 minutes. Combine with vegetables, parsley, garlic powder, basil and Tabasco sauce. Melt remaining margarine. Add milk, chicken stock, cheese, salt and pepper. Cook vermicelli al dente. Drain. Add vegetables to sauce. Heat and toss gently with vermicelli. Garnish with sunflower seeds or pine nuts.
Yield: 4 servings

Vegetables & fruits

Artichoke and Cheese Bake

1	bunch green onions	1	garlic clove, crushed
1	6½-ounce jar marinated artichoke hearts	4	eggs, beaten
		8	ounces Cheddar cheese, grated
1	6½-ounce jar marinated artichoke bottoms	6	saltine crackers, finely crushed

Chop green onions with half the tops. Drain artichokes, reserving liquid. Cut hearts and bottoms in thirds. Sauté onions and garlic in reserved oil. Combine with all other ingredients. Put in a 2-quart casserole. Bake for 40 minutes at 350°.
Yield: 4-6 servings

Asparagus Casserole

1	19-ounce can asparagus	4	tablespoons butter, divided
1	17-ounce can English peas	1	10 ¾-ounce can mushroom soup
1	8-ounce can water chestnuts	¾	cup bread cubes or crumbs
1	2-ounce jar pimientos	¼	cup almonds

Drain peas, asparagus and water chestnuts. Into a greased casserole, put a layer of each vegetable with bits of pimiento on each layer. Dot with 2 tablespoons butter. Pour undiluted soup over. Mix cubes or crumbs and almonds with remaining butter and sprinkle on top. Bake in 350° oven until bubbly, about 20 minutes.
Yield: 6-8 servings

Hot Asparagus Mousse

Cream Sauce:

6	tablespoons butter	⅛	teaspoon white pepper
6	tablespoons flour	1	teaspoon Worcestershire sauce
2	cups milk	2	teaspoons onion juice
½	teaspoon salt		

Melt butter over low heat. Add flour and blend. Stir and cook on low heat about 5 minutes. Stir in milk slowly. Add seasonings. Cook and stir with a wire whisk until mixture is smooth and close to a boil.

Mousse:

2	cups cream sauce	1	15-ounce can asparagus tips, drained
1	cup mayonnaise		
1	tablespoon lemon juice	6	eggs, beaten
	a few drops green food color	½	cup fresh bread crumbs

To the cream sauce, add mayonnaise, lemon juice and food coloring. Stir in the asparagus tips and the eggs. Pour mixture into a buttered 10″ ring mold. Sprinkle bread crumbs on top and bake at 325° for 45 minutes or until firm.
Yield: 8 servings

Baked Beans

1 15-ounce can butter beans
1 15-ounce can lima beans
1 15-ounce can kidney beans
1 28-ounce can B & M baked
   beans
1 cup brown sugar

½ cup chopped onion
1 teaspoon salt
1 teaspoon dry mustard
6 slices bacon, chopped

Drain butter beans, lima beans and kidney beans. Place in a large bowl. Toss in undrained B & M baked beans. Add sugar, onion, salt and mustard. Mix well. Place in large casserole and top with chopped bacon. Bake at 300° for 2 hours.
Yield: 10-12 servings

Chili Beans

1 pound ground beef
1 green pepper, chopped
2 onions, chopped
2 garlic cloves, pressed
4 ribs celery, chopped
1 10-ounce can Ro-Tel tomatoes

4 15-ounce cans Van Camp's
   kidney beans, drained
   chili powder to taste
   salt, black pepper, red pepper,
   to taste
1 bean can of water

Cook beef, pepper, onions, garlic and celery until beef is browned and vegetables are soft. Drain grease. Add tomatoes, beans and seasonings. Stir in water. Cover and simmer 2 hours.
Yield: 10-12 servings

Santa Fe Pinto Beans

1 pound pinto beans, soaked in
   water overnight
3-4 cans beer
   salt and pepper, to taste
½ teaspoon cumin
1 bay leaf

2 garlic cloves, crushed
1 tomato, chopped
1 onion, chopped
3-4 jalapeño peppers, seeded and
   chopped
¼ cup chopped cilantro

Drain water from beans and replace with beer. Add salt, pepper, cumin, bay leaf and garlic. Simmer 1-1½ hours, until beans are tender. Add remaining ingredients and simmer approximately 45 minutes more.
Yield: 6-8 servings

 This is very hot. Reduce peppers to 1 or 2 if preferred.

South Louisiana Red Beans

3 or 4 small ham hocks
16 ounces dried beans, small red or pink preferred
2 tablespoons corn oil or safflower oil
2 cups finely chopped onions
2 cups finely chopped green pepper
1 cup chopped celery
1 4-ounce can mild green chilies
1½ teaspoons minced garlic
¼ cup chopped parsley
1 teaspoon Tabasco sauce
¼ teaspoon cayenne pepper
¼ teaspoon ground black pepper
1 teaspoon sugar
½ teaspoon thyme
1 bay leaf
1 tomato, quartered, or 1 cup diced canned tomatoes
1 pound smoked Polish sausage, cooked and cut into pieces

Remove skin from ham hocks. Add to beans and cover with water 2″ over beans. Soak overnight. Drain and reserve soaking water; add additional water to make 6 cups. Put back into pot with beans and ham hocks and cook slowly, uncovered. Heat oil in skillet and sauté onions, peppers, celery, chili and garlic. Cook, stirring until mixture is wilted, then add to beans. Add remaining spices and ingredients. About 30 minutes before serving, add cooked sausage. Serve over rice. Total time 4-6 hours.
Yield: 8 servings

Green Bean Casserole

5 tablespoons margarine, divided
2 tablespoons flour
1 teaspoon salt
¼ teaspoon pepper
½ teaspoon minced onion
1 teaspoon sugar
1 cup sour cream
2 16-ounce cans French-cut green beans, drained
2 cups grated Swiss cheese
12 Ritz crackers, crushed

Melt 2 tablespoons margarine over low heat. Stir in flour, salt, pepper, onion and sugar. Add sour cream and stir. Increase heat to medium and cook until sauce bubbles and thickens, stirring constantly. Remove from heat. Fold in beans and put into a 1½ quart greased baking dish. Sprinkle cheese and then crushed crackers on top. Pour 3 tablespoons melted margarine over crackers. Bake for 20 minutes at 400°
Yield: 8-10 servings

Green Bean and Mushroom Casserole

2	cups milk	1	teaspoon salt
1	cup light cream	½	teaspoon pepper
1	stick butter, melted	3	packages frozen French-style
1	pound fresh mushrooms, sliced		green beans, cooked just until
1	medium onion, chopped		tender
¾	pound sharp Cheddar cheese,	1	8-ounce can water chestnuts,
	grated		sliced and drained
⅛	teaspoon Tabasco sauce	¾	cup toasted, slivered almonds
2	teaspoons soy sauce		

Preheat oven to 375°. Heat milk and cream in top of double boiler, stirring constantly. Sauté mushrooms and onion in the butter. Add to the cream mixture. Add the cheese and seasonings. Simmer until the cheese melts. Add the drained beans and water chestnuts and mix well. Pour into a 3-quart casserole. Sprinkle with almonds and bake 30-40 minutes or until bubbly.
Yield: 8-l0 servings

Kaly's Broccoli Kasserole

4	boxes frozen chopped broccoli	1	teaspoon Worcestershire sauce
½	pound Velveeta cheese	½	teaspoon salt
½	10-ounce can Ro-Tel tomatoes	4	green onions, chopped

Cook broccoli according to package directions. Drain. Melt cheese in top of double boiler. Stir in tomatoes and seasonings. Add broccoli and mix well. Place in a buttered casserole and bake at 350° until bubbly for 20 minutes.
Yield: 8-10 servings

Sonia's Creole Cabbage

1	large head of cabbage	2-3	tomatoes, diced
5	tablespoons bacon grease or	1-2	green peppers, sliced
	salad oil		salt and pepper, to taste
1-2	large onions, sliced		

Cut cabbage into 1" slices and place in a large Dutch oven. Pour in bacon grease or salad oil, salt and pepper. Toss. Put onions, tomatoes and green peppers on top. Cover and cook slowly on top of the stove for about 40 minutes.
Yield: 6 servings

 Need an easy vegetable or appetizer? Brush fresh mushroom caps with melted butter. Fill with thawed Stouffer's spinach soufflé. Sprinkle with Parmesan cheese and bake at 400° for 20 minutes.

Cabbage au Gratin

1   head cabbage, cut in small pieces
1   10¾-ounce can cream of chicken soup
½   soup can of milk

¾   cup grated Cheddar cheese
    salt and pepper, to taste
1   cup bread or cracker crumbs
2   tablespoons butter, melted

Boil cabbage in water 10 minutes. Drain. Combine soup and milk. In a greased casserole, alternate layers of cabbage, soup mixture and cheese. Salt and pepper to taste between each layer. Top with crumbs mixed with butter. Bake at 350° for 30 minutes.
Yield: 6-8 servings

Rosie's Marinated Carrots

1   10¾-ounce can tomato soup
½   cup oil
¾   cup vinegar
1   large onion, chopped
1   large green pepper, chopped
1   cup sugar

1   teaspoon prepared mustard
1   teaspoon Worcestershire sauce
1   teaspoon salt
1   teaspoon pepper
1-2 pounds carrots, scraped and sliced

Heat all ingredients except carrots; bring to boiling point. Pour over raw carrots. Cool and store in refrigerator 2 days before serving.
Yield: 6-8 servings

Shoe Peg Corn with Green Chilies

1   8-ounce package cream cheese
1   stick butter, softened
1   4-ounce can diced green chilies, drained

2   garlic cloves, minced
16 ears shoe peg corn, scraped from cob, or 3 16-ounce cans white shoe peg corn, drained

Mix the cream cheese with butter, chilies and garlic. Add the corn. Put in a buttered 2 quart casserole and bake 20 minutes at 325°.
Yield: 8 servings

Celery Almondine

4   cups celery, strings removed, cut diagonally
½   cup butter, divided
1   garlic clove, crushed
2   tablespoons grated onion

2   tablespoons chopped green onion, with tops
2   tablespoons white wine
½-1 cup slivered almonds

Sauté celery in ¼ cup butter. Add garlic, onions and white wine. Cover and simmer 10 minutes. Sauté almonds in remaining butter and add to celery. Serve immediately.
Yield: 4-6 servings

Eggplant Broiled with Cheese and Bacon

1 large eggplant	1/3 cup peanut oil
1/2 tablespoon salt	4 slices American cheese
1 teaspoon paprika	4 slices tomato
1/2 cup flour	2 slices bacon, halved

Peel the eggplant and cut lengthwise into 1/2" slices. Sprinkle with salt and paprika. Dredge in flour and sauté in the oil until almost tender. Place the eggplant slices on a broiler rack. Cover each with a slice of cheese, then tomato, then bacon half. Broil until cheese is melted and bacon is crisp.
Yield: 4 servings

Bernice Beard's Grits Soufflé

1 cup yellow grits	4 eggs, separated, the whites
1 stick butter	beaten until stiff
1 8-ounce roll garlic cheese	

Cook the grits according to package directions. Combine with the butter, cheese and beaten egg yolks. Mix well in mixer or processor. Gently fold in the beaten egg whites. Pour into a greased baking dish and bake 25 minutes at 350°.
Yield: 8 servings

Creamed Onions with Peas

2 pounds small white onions	1 cup light cream
4 tablespoons butter	4 tablespoons grated Parmesan
4 tablespoons flour	cheese
1/2 teaspoon salt	sherry, to taste
1/8 teaspoon pepper	1 20-ounce package frozen green
1 cup chicken broth	peas, thawed and blanched

Peel the onions and put in saucepan. Cover with hot, salted water. Bring rapidly to a boil, cover and simmer over moderate heat until tender, about 30 minutes. Drain well in colander. Melt butter over low heat; blend in flour, salt and pepper, stirring constantly. Slowly stir in broth and cream, using a wire whisk. Stir until thickened and smooth. Add Parmesan cheese and sherry. Stir onions into the sauce. Add the peas. Pour into a 1 1/2 quart casserole. Bake at 350° for 20 minutes or until bubbly.
Yield: 6-8 servings

Vidalia Onion Casserole

5 large Vidalia onions, or any sweet onions	1 cup grated Parmesan cheese
1/2 cup butter	20 Ritz crackers, crumbled

Slice onions into thin rings. Melt butter in a large skillet and sauté onions until limp or opaque. Pour half the onions into a 2 quart greased casserole. Cover with half the cheese and half the cracker crumbs. Repeat layers. Bake at 325° uncovered for 30 minutes or until golden brown.
Yield: 6-8 servings

Tarte aux Poireaux (Green Onion Pie)

Crust:

1   cup sifted enriched flour
½   teaspoon salt

⅓   cup shortening
3-4 tablespoons cold water

Sift flour and salt together. Cut in shortening until size of peas. Sprinkle water over mixture while tossing and stirring lightly with a fork. Have dough just moist enough to hold together. Form into a ball. Roll out on floured pastry cloth to a circle 1-1½" larger than inverted 8" or 9" pie pan. Fit into pan, forming a standing rim. Flute and bake at 425° for 15 minutes.

Filling:

3   tablespoons butter, melted
3   cups sliced green onions,
     including tops
2   eggs, beaten

½   cup cream
1   teaspoon salt
     pinch of pepper

Sauté onions in butter until tender. Arrange in baked pie shell. Stir cream into beaten eggs. Add salt and pepper. Pour over onions and bake at 425° for 18-20 minutes until browned and knife comes out clean.
Yield: 6-8 servings

New Year's Black-Eyed Peas

6   slices bacon, cut into small
     pieces
2   cups chopped celery
2   cups chopped onions
1   cup chopped green pepper

2   16-ounce cans tomatoes with
     juice
2   16-ounce cans black-eyed peas
     with juice

Sauté bacon with celery, onion, and green pepper. Add tomatoes and peas. Simmer 40 minutes. Serve in soup bowls, or drain if serving on plates.
Yield: 6-8 servings

 Chopped green onions and/or chopped jalapeños may be added when served.

English Pea Casserole

1   stick butter, melted
⅓   cup chopped celery
⅓   cup chopped green pepper
⅓   cup chopped onion
1   4-ounce can mushrooms

1   17-ounce can peas
1   8-ounce can water chestnuts
¼   cup milk
¾   cup seasoned bread crumbs

Sauté the celery, green pepper and onion in the melted butter. Drain the mushrooms and peas. Drain the water chestnuts, reserving the liquid. Mix the milk and water chestnut juice. Add all the vegetables. Put into a greased casserole, top with the crumbs and bake 30 minutes at 350°.
Yield: 6-8 servings

Delmonico Potatoes

8	medium potatoes	1	teaspoon dry mustard
1	cup whipping cream	1	teaspoon salt
¾	cup milk		pepper to taste
½	pound sharp Cheddar cheese	3	dashes nutmeg

Boil the potatoes until almost done. Cool, peel and cut into chunks. Put them in a 1½ quart greased casserole. Heat the cream, milk and cheese until the cheese melts. Add seasonings. Mix well and pour over potatoes. Bake 1 hour at 325°.
Yield: 6-8 servings

Variation: Swiss or Monterey Jack cheese may be substituted for Cheddar.

Sweet Potato Casserole

1	29-ounce can yams	½	cup sugar
3	eggs, beaten	½-1	teaspoon cinnamon
½	stick butter, melted		Marshmallows, optional
1	8-ounce can crushed pineapple		

Mash drained yams in mixer. Add eggs and melted butter. Add pineapple with juice, sugar and cinnamon, blending thoroughly. Bake in a greased casserole at 350° for 30-40 minutes. If desired, top with marshmallows the last 10 minutes.
Yield: 6-8 servings

Praline Sweet Potatoes

6	medium yams or 3 16-ounce cans sweet potatoes	2	teaspoons cinnamon
1	stick margarine, melted	1	teaspoon nutmeg
1	teaspoon salt	½	of a 5-ounce can evaporated milk
2-4	tablespoons brown sugar	⅓	cup orange juice

Drain canned yams and reserve liquid to use if needed. Mix all ingredients until smooth, adding liquid if needed for consistency. Pour into greased casserole dish.

Topping:

2	tablespoons flour	2	tablespoons butter
⅓	cup firmly packed brown sugar	½	cup chopped pecans
½	teaspoon salt		

Mix dry ingredients. Cut in butter until crumbly and mix in nuts. Sprinkle on top of sweet potatoes. Bake 30 minutes at 350°.
Yield: 8 servings

Louisiana Dirty Rice

1   package of fresh or frozen
    chicken livers
½   pound ground beef
2   large onions, chopped
3   ribs celery, chopped
1   green pepper, chopped

4   garlic cloves, crushed
1   cup rice, cooked
¼   teaspoon poultry seasoning
½   teaspoon Worcestershire sauce
    cayenne pepper, to taste

Cook the chicken livers in microwave or in 1½ cup boiling water on top of stove. Brown beef in skillet. Add small amount of bacon grease to pan and stir in vegetables to sear. Add a small amount of water (from the livers, if cooked on stove) and cook slowly, 5-10 minutes. Mix in cooked rice and seasonings. Simmer for at least 15 minutes.
Yield: 6-8 servings

Rice Casserole

1   stick butter
1   10¾-ounce can onion soup
1   10½-ounce can beef broth
1   teaspoon oregano, optional

1   cup regular rice
1   4-ounce can sliced mushrooms
1   8-ounce can sliced water
    chestnuts

Melt butter in bottom of casserole. Stir in rest of ingredients, draining the mushrooms and water chestnuts. Cook covered for 1 hour at 350°.
Yield: 6-8 servings

Rice Ring

1   4-ounce jar whole pimientos
1   cup raw rice
2   teaspoons salt
1   teaspoon chopped onion
3   tablespoons melted butter

1½ cups cheese, Cheddar and
    American
    Dash of red pepper
    Dash of Worcestershire sauce
¾   cup evaporated milk
    parsley

Grease a ring mold with cooking oil. Slice pimientos and arrange in bottom of mold. Cook rice according to directions. Mix in all ingredients. Set mold in pan of hot water for 30 minutes in a 350° oven. Turn out onto serving platter and garnish with parsley.
Yield: 6-8 servings

Variation: Add ¼ cup diced red bell pepper and ¼ cup chopped green onions. Fill the center with creamed chicken or a green vegetable if desired. Double this recipe for a large ring to serve 12-16.

Red, White and Green Rice

3 cups leftover white rice
1 tablespoon olive oil
¾ medium green pepper, chopped
4-5 green onions, chopped

2 tomatoes, diced
1½ cups grated Cheddar cheese
salt and pepper, to taste

Add olive oil to rice, stirring to separate the grains. Mix in vegetables. Top with cheese and bake in greased casserole 30-35 minutes at 350° until cheese is melted.
Yield: 6-8 servings

Spinach and Artichokes

4 10-ounce packages chopped spinach
2 14-ounce cans artichoke hearts, halved
2 cups sour cream
1 1⅓-ounce envelope onion soup mix

2 10¾-ounce cans cream of mushroom soup
½ cup Parmesan cheese
2 or 3 slices cooked bacon, crumbled

Cook spinach and drain well. Cut artichoke hearts in half; put in a buttered 9 × 13″ baking dish. Toss spinach with sour cream and soup mix. Mix in mushroom soup and Parmesan cheese. Top with crumbled bacon. Bake 40 minutes at 350°.
Yield: 8-10 servings

Cheese-Stuffed Zucchini

2 medium zucchini
¼ cup minced onion
1 tablespoon butter
⅛ cup Italian bread crumbs
⅛ teaspoon salt

¼ teaspoon pepper
2 tablespoons Parmesan cheese
2 tablespoons bacon, fried crisp and crumbled
¼ cup grated Cheddar cheese

Wash zucchini and cut off ends. Drop into boiling water to cover for 10 minutes. Drain and slice zucchini lengthwise. Scoop out pulp to make zucchini boats. Chop the pulp finely. Sauté the onion in butter until golden. Add zucchini pulp, bread crumbs, salt, pepper and Parmesan cheese. Cook until soft and some of the liquid has evaporated. Add crumbled bacon to pulp mixture and fill zucchini boats. Cover with cheese and bake at 450° about 10 minutes, until boats are hot and cheese is melted.
Yield: 3-4 servings

Stuffed Acorn Squash

2 acorn squash
4 tablespoons butter or margarine, divided
Salt and cinnamon to taste

2 tart apples
1 tablespoon lemon juice
½ tablespoon grated lemon rind
½ cup brown sugar, packed

Cut squash in half. Remove seeds. Cook cut side down in ½″ of water at 375° for 30-35 minutes. Melt 2 tablespoons of butter and brush on the squash. Sprinkle with seasonings. Peel and cut the apples into small pieces. Add to them the remaining butter, lemon juice, rind and brown sugar. Mix well and fill the squash. Bake at 325° for 20-25 minutes.
Yield: 4 servings

Squash and Corn Casserole

1 stick margarine, melted	1 7-ounce can of shoe peg corn, drained
1 large onion, chopped	
6 medium yellow squash, sliced	1 cup grated cheese
¼ cup water	½ cup buttered cracker crumbs

Sauté the onion in melted margarine. Add squash and water, steaming with lid on until squash is tender. If necessary, remove lid to cook down the water. Add corn and cheese. Put into a greased casserole and top with crumbs. Bake at 350° until top is brown.
Yield: 4 servings

Gefüllte Rüben (Stuffed Turnips)

8 medium-sized turnips	1 1¼-ounce package McCormick cheese sauce mix
2 tablespoons butter, melted	
1 onion, diced	1 cup milk
	1 4¼-ounce can deviled ham

Peel, halve crosswise and hollow out the turnips. Cook in a little water until tender. Sauté the onions in melted butter until clear. Prepare sauce according to package directions; combine with onions. Place turnips in a baking dish and stuff with deviled ham. Cover with sauce and brown in broiler.
Yield: 8 servings

 This dish is served at one of the top restaurants in Salzburg, Austria.

Marinated Vegetable Tray

1 head cauliflower, separated into flowerets	1 bunch broccoli, separated into flowerets
½ pound green beans, ends snipped off	2 tablespoons lemon juice
6 carrots, scraped and cut into sticks	1 12-ounce bottle Italian salad dressing

Steam all vegetables 5-8 minutes or until slightly tender but still crunchy. Cool. Place in a large bowl and pour on salad dressing mixed with lemon juice. Cover and refrigerate 3 hours or overnight. Drain and arrange on serving tray.
Yield: 8-10 servings

Variation: For lower calories, use Italian diet dressing or make any vinaigrette dressing. Sprinkle vegetables with sesame seeds.

To preserve the color in a boiled green vegetable, add a few spoonfuls of oil to the water immediately before lifting the vegetable out of the water.

Ratatouille (Vegetable Stew)

1/4 cup olive oil	1 teaspoon oregano
4 garlic cloves, crushed	1 medium zucchini, cubed
1 bay leaf	1 medium green pepper
1 medium onion, chopped	1 medium red bell pepper
1 small eggplant, cubed	Salt and pepper, to taste
6 tablespoons Burgandy or dry red wine	2 medium tomatoes, in chunks
1/2 cup tomato juice	2 tablespoons tomato paste
1 1/4 teaspoon basil	parsley, chopped black olives
1/4 teaspoon marjoram	and grated white cheese for
1/4 teaspoon rosemary	garnish

Heat olive oil in large cooking pot. Add garlic, bay leaf and onion. Sauté over medium heat until onion turns transparent. Add eggplant, wine and tomato juice. Add herbs. Mix well, cover and simmer 10-15 minutes over low heat. Add zucchini and peppers, cut into strips. Cover and simmer 10 minutes. Add salt, pepper, tomatoes and tomato paste. Mix and continue to stew until all vegetables are tender. Serve over rice or in a bowl with garnish.
Yield: 4 servings

Spicy Vegetable Casserole

3 medium sized potatoes, peeled	1/2 teaspoon nutmeg
2 large white onions	1 tablespoon sugar
6 carrots, scraped	1/4 cup dry vermouth
1-1 1/2 teaspoons salt	6 tablespoons butter or margarine
1/2 teaspoon white pepper	minced parsley
1/2 teaspoon coriander powder	

Slice the vegetables thinly into a well-greased baking dish. Mix them well; do not layer. Mix the dry ingredients and stir into the vegetables. Pour the vermouth over and dot with butter. Cover the casserole and bake at 350° for 45-50 minutes. Sprinkle with parsley before serving.
Yield: 6 servings

Delicious Corn Casserole

2 17-ounce cans cream style corn	1/2 onion, chopped
1 17-ounce can whole kernel corn, drained	1 tablespoon butter
1 2-ounce jar diced pimiento, drained	1 tablespoon sugar
3 eggs, beaten	salt and pepper, to taste
1/2 cup milk	2 cups grated Cheddar cheese
	buttered bread crumbs

Mix all ingredients except the cheese and bread crumbs. Put into a buttered casserole. Stir in 1 cup grated cheese. Top with the remaining cheese and then add bread crumbs. Bake at 375° for 35 minutes.
Yield: 10-12 servings

Jalapeño Spinach

2   packages frozen chopped
    spinach
4   tablespoons butter or margarine
½   cup chopped onion
2   tablespoons flour
½   cup vegetable liquor
½   cup evaporated milk
1   teaspoon Worcestershire sauce

½   teaspoon pepper
½   teaspoon celery salt
½   teaspoon garlic salt
1   6-ounce roll jalapeño cheese, cut
    into cubes
3-4 slices bacon, fried crisp and
    crumbled, optional

Cook spinach and drain well, reserving ½ cup vegetable liquor. Melt butter and sauté onion lightly. Remove onion and stir in flour, then vegetable liquor and milk. Cook until thickened. Add seasonings, then cheese. Stir cheese until it is melted. Combine with the spinach and put into greased 1½ quart casserole. Chill 6 hours or longer. (Flavor improves with age.) Bake at 350°, uncovered, for 25-30 minutes. Top with crumbled bacon just before serving.
Yield: 6-8 servings

Variation: If you prefer less hot, use half a roll jalapeño and half a roll of Cheddar with bacon or plain Cheddar.

Bean and Corn Casserole

½   cup chopped onion
½   cup chopped celery
½   cup chopped green pepper
½   cup sour cream
½   cup grated Cheddar cheese

1   10¾-ounce can cream of celery
    soup
1   16-ounce can shoe peg corn,
    drained
1   16-ounce can French-style green
    beans, drained
¼   cup butter, melted
1   cup crush cheese crackers

Mix onion, celery, green pepper, sour cream, cheese and soup. Stir in corn and beans and put into a greased casserole. Combine butter and crackers and sprinkle over mixture. Bake at 350° for 45 minutes.
Yield: 6-8 servings

Squash Medley

6   zucchini squash, sliced
6   yellow squash, sliced
4   tomatoes, sliced
2   onion, sliced

¼   teaspoon oregano
    salt and pepper to taste
1   stick of butter
    Parmesan cheese

Layer vegetables in a greased casserole. Sprinkle with seasonings and dot generously with butter. Repeat layers. Sprinkle Parmesan cheese over top of casserole and bake, covered, at 350° for 45 minutes.
Yield: 6 servings

Scalloped Pineapple

4	cups bread cubes	2	cups sugar
1	20-ounce can pineapple chunks, drained	1	cup butter, melted
3	eggs, beaten		

Toss bread cubes with pineapple chunks and pour into greased 2 quart casserole. Combine remaining ingredients and pour over pineapple. Bake at 350° for 30 minutes.
Yield: 6-8 servings

 Can be made ahead and refrigerated overnight before baking. Reheats well.

Tipsy Watermelon

5	cups watermelon balls	½	cup dry sherry
½	cup sugar		

Combine all ingredients and refrigerate at least 2 hours before serving.
Yield: 6-8 servings

Tropical Freeze

1½	cups water		juice of 3 lemons
1½	cups sugar	3	bananas
	juice of 3 oranges		

Heat water and sugar until sugar dissolves. Add orange and lemon juices. Mash bananas and mix well into juice mixture. Pour into loaf pan and freeze.
Yield: 6-8 servings

Cranberries au Grand Marnier

1	16-ounce package fresh cranberries	½	cup Grand Marnier
2	cups sugar		

Wash and cull cranberries. Spread berries in a single layer in a 9 × 13″ ovenproof dish. Sprinkle sugar over cranberries. Cover tightly with foil. Bake at 350° for 1 hour. Cool covered. Then add Grand Marnier and mix well. Store in glass container in refrigerator.
Yield: 1½ cups

 Do not double the recipe; make separate recipes.

Curried Hot Fruit

1	16-ounce can peach halves	½	teaspoon each — nutmeg,
1	16-ounce can apricot halves		cloves, cinnamon, curry
1	8¾-ounce can pear halves	⅓	cup brown sugar
1	15¼ can pineapple tidbits	½	cup butter
1	16-ounce can light sweet	1½	cups canned seedless grapes,
	cherries		drained
4	Winesap apples, pared, cored,	2	large bananas, sliced thickly
	cubed		
	juice of one lemon		

Drain and mix syrups from all fruits except grapes, reserving 1½ cups syrup. Toss drained fruits and apples with lemon juice. Pour into 1½ quart casserole. Combine spices, brown sugar, butter and reserved syrup in a saucepan. Heat and stir until butter is melted. Pour over fruit. Bake at 350° for 20 minutes. When ready to serve, stir in grapes and bananas.
Yield: 16 servings

Baked Pineapple

1	20-ounce can crushed pineapple	2	tablespoons flour
1	cup grated Cheddar cheese		bread crumbs
1	cup sugar	1	tablespoon butter

Drain pineapple, reserving juice. Mix drained pineapple with cheese and pour into 1½ quart casserole. Combine sugar and flour with reserved juice and pour over pineapple-cheese mixture. Sprinkle bread crumbs on top. Dot with butter. Bake uncovered at 350° for 45 minutes.
Yield: 6 servings

Loquat Chutney

4	quarts loquats	2	teaspoons allspice seasoning
2	large onions, minced	2	teaspoons ground ginger
1	large green papaya or mango,	2	teaspoons ground cloves
	peeled and chopped	1-2	jalapeños, chopped
1	cup raisins		sugar, as needed
4	tablespoons vinegar		sterilized jars and lids

Cook loquat with 2-3 tablespoons water until tender. Remove seeds. Measure fruit. Add 1 cup sugar per 1 cup fruit. Stir in onions, mango, raisins and spices. Boil rapidly, stirring constantly until fruit forms a slight wrinkle or crustiness. Remove from heat and put into prepared jars and seal.
Yield: 3-4 quarts

Main Dishes

Apricot Chicken au Vin

2½-3 pounds chicken, cut up
3 tablespoons butter
1 cup chopped celery
1 cup sliced water chestnuts
½ teaspoon rosemary
½ teaspoon salt, divided

2 cups cooked rice
¾ cup dry white wine, divided
1 cup grated Swiss or Monterey Jack cheese
1 16-ounce can apricot halves
4 teaspoons cornstarch

Brown chicken in butter, season to taste and set aside. In same pan sauté celery, water chestnuts, rosemary and ¼ teaspoon salt. Add rice and one-half cup wine. Turn into greased casserole and top with cheese. Bake at 375° for one hour. Drain apricots, reserving syrup. Combine syrup, cornstarch and ¼ teaspoon salt in pan, cooking and stirring until thickened. Add ¼ cup wine to form a glaze. Pour over chicken. Bake uncovered at 375° for 10 minutes. Serve as soon as possible to prevent drying out.
Yield: 4-6 servings

Baked Almond Chicken

3 cups chopped cooked chicken
1½ cups sliced celery
1 cup mayonnaise
½ cup slivered almonds, divided
1 cup chopped Swiss cheese

¼ cup chopped onions
2 tablespoons chopped pimiento
2 tablespoons chopped green pepper
1 teaspoon salt
dash of pepper

Combine all ingredients except ¼ cup almonds. Pour into greased 11×7″ ovenproof dish. Sprinkle remaining almonds on top. Bake at 350° for 25 minutes.
Yield: 2-4 servings

Chicken Chow Mein

¼ cup chopped onion
1 cup bias-cut celery
1 tablespoon butter
⅓ cup chicken broth
1 10¾-ounce can cream of mushroom soup

1 tablespoon soy sauce
½ teaspoon black pepper
2 cups diced, cooked chicken
1 cup chow mein noodles
⅓ cup almonds

Sauté onions and celery in butter. Stir in broth, soup, soy sauce and pepper. Add chicken. Pour into casserole. Cover top with noodles. Sprinkle with almonds. Bake at 350° for 20 minutes.
Yield: 4 servings

Chicken Crêpes

4 eggs	¾ cups milk, divided
1½ cups flour	¾ cups chicken broth
½ teaspoon salt	2 tablespoons melted butter

Beat the eggs 1 minute at medium speed in mixer. Combine flour and salt. Add half the dry mixture to the eggs. Mix well, then add the other half. Add half the milk, a little at a time. Pour in remaining milk and chicken broth, beating until smooth. Add the melted butter and mix well. Cover the batter and set aside at room temperature for I-2 hours.

Filling:

2 cups chopped cooked chicken	3 cups chicken broth, strained
1 tablespoon chopped fresh parsley	1 egg yolk
	large pinch of sage
1 teaspoon grated onion	3 strips of bacon, cooked crisp and crumbled
½ cup plus 2 tablespoons light cream	½ cup Swiss cheese, shredded
6 tablespoons melted butter	½ cup Parmesan cheese, shredded
6 tablespoons flour	

Simmer the chicken, parsley and onion in the cream for about I0 minutes. Make a cream sauce with the butter, flour and broth. Mix the egg yolk with half of the cream sauce. Add sage; then add to the chicken mixture. Cook over low heat for a few minutes until mixture thickens a little more. Stir in crumbled bacon and half of each cheese. Fill and roll the crêpes and put seam side down in a greased oblong baking dish. Stir 2 tablespoons cream into the remaining sauce to thin slightly. Pour over the crêpes. Mix the remaining cheeses and sprinkle over the top. Bake at 350° for 20-30 minutes.
Yield: 16 6″ crêpes.

 Romanoff MBT instant chicken broth can be substituted. Crêpes can be made and stored between sheets of waxed paper, wrapped tightly in foil and frozen until ready to fill.

Chicken Deluxe

3 tablespoons unflavored gelatin	2 cups diced cooked chicken
½ cup cold water	1 cup chopped celery
1½ cups seasoned chicken broth, heated	1 17-ounce can LeSueur peas
1 cup mayonnaise	3 hard-cooked eggs, chopped
	½ cup sliced almonds

Dissolve gelatin in cold water and mix with hot broth until blended. Cool. Stir in mayonnaise and chill to thicken slightly. Add chicken and rest of ingredients and pour into oiled mold or 9×13″ glass dish. Refrigerate overnight or at least several hours. To serve, unmold or cut into squares and place on a lettuce leaf.
Yield: 8-10 servings

Chicken Livers and Mushrooms

3 slices bacon	⅓ cup white wine
¼ cup finely chopped onion	½ teaspoon salt
1 4-ounce can mushroom caps or stems and pieces	dash pepper
	dash Tabasco
8 ounces chicken livers, quartered	

Sauté bacon until crisp, reserving grease. Sauté onion in grease. Add mushrooms and livers. Cook 5 minutes. Add wine and seasonings. Simmer 2-3 minutes. Serve over cooked rice and crumble bacon on top.
Yield: 2 servings

Chicken Loaf with Sauce

4 tablespoons butter	1 cup mayonnaise
1 cup cooked rice	4 cups diced cooked chicken
1 cup chicken broth	1 cup sliced almonds
1 cup milk	1 cup Chinese noodles
2 eggs, beaten	

Melt butter. Add rice, broth, and milk. Add eggs and stir in mayonnaise. Fold in chicken and almonds. Pour into greased casserole. Sprinkle noodles on top and press in. Bake at 325° for 50-60 minutes.

Sauce:

2 tablespoons butter	1 10¾-ounce can cream of celery soup
2 tablespoons flour	
1 4-ounce can mushrooms and liquid	1 cup chicken broth

Melt butter and blend in flour. Add rest of ingredients. Simmer until heated, stirring constantly.
Yield: 4-6 servings

Chicken Piccata

6 chicken breasts, skinless flour, salt and pepper	1 cup chicken broth
	juice of one lemon
2 tablespoons butter	lemon slices
2 tablespoons olive oil	parsley

Pound chicken with smooth side of mallet. Dredge in mixture of flour, salt and pepper. Sauté in butter and olive oil until lightly browned. Remove chicken and add broth to pan. Deglaze pan. Add lemon juice to taste. Return chicken to pan. Add lemon slices and parsley for garnish. Simmer 5 minutes until chicken is tender.
Yield: 6 servings

 Can be prepared ahead and heated quickly before serving.

Chicken Spinach Casserole

5 pounds stewing chicken or 2 fryers
5 ounces fine egg noodles
¼ cup butter
½ cup flour
1 cup milk
1 cup chicken broth
2 cups sour cream
⅓ cup lemon juice
1 10-ounce package frozen chopped spinach, cooked and drained
1 6-ounce can mushrooms with juice
1 8-ounce can sliced water chestnuts, drained
1 4-ounce jar chopped pimientos, drained
½ cup chopped onion
2 teaspoons seasoning salt
½ teaspoon cayenne
1 teaspoon paprika
1 teaspoon salt
2 teaspoons pepper
1½ cups grated Monterey Jack cheese

Cook chicken, reserving broth, and cut into bite-sized pieces. Cook noodles and drain. Melt butter; slowly stir in flour until blended. Add milk and broth. Cook over low heat, stirring constantly until thick. Add all other ingredients except chicken, noodles, and cheese. Mix well. Fold in noodles. In a very large buttered casserole, layer ⅓ of vegetable/noodle mixture, then ½ of chicken; repeat, ending with vegetable/noodles. Top with cheese. Bake at 300° for 25-30 minutes until bubbly.
Yield: 6-8 servings

Chicken Tamale Pie

2 7-ounce cans shoe peg corn, drained
2½ pounds cooked chicken, cut into bite-sized pieces
24 tamales
1 4-ounce can chopped green chilies
⅔ cup sliced ripe olives
⅓ cup sliced almonds
2 tablespoons corn oil
1 large onion, chopped
1 1.58-ounce package chili mix (Gebhart or McCormick preferred)
1 16-ounce can whole tomatoes, cut up
10 ounces Monterey Jack cheese, grated

In a 13½×8½×7″ baking dish, layer corn, chicken, tamales, chilies, olives, and almonds. Sauté onions in oil. Stir chili mix with tomatoes and blend well. Pour over almonds. Top with cheese. Bake at 350° for 30 minutes until bubbly.
Yield: 8-10 servings

 When poaching chicken breasts, it's important not to let the liquid boil; boiling will toughen the meat. Cook over low heat, tightly covered, for 5 minutes. Turn off heat and let sit 5 minutes more. Remove the lid and let cool uncovered in the liquid for 10 minutes.

 Chicken broth can be strained and frozen for later use. It will keep up to 3 months.

Chicken Scallion

1   10¾-ounce can cream of celery soup
⅓   cup sour cream
⅓   cup buttermilk
½   cup chopped scallions, including some green tops
2   teaspoons Lawry's baconion or Hormel's real bacon bits
1   4-ounce can sliced mushrooms, drained
3   tablespoons butter or margarine
3   whole chicken breasts, cooked, boned and cubed
4   ounces flat noodles, cooked and drained
    salt and pepper, to taste
    buttered bread crumbs
    paprika

Mix soup, sour cream and buttermilk. Sauté scallions, bacon and mushrooms in butter. Combine with soup mixture. Add chicken and noodles. Pour into 1 quart greased casserole. Top with bread crumbs. Sprinkle paprika over crumbs. Bake at 350° for 35-40 minutes until bubbly and slightly browned.
Yield: 5-6 servings

 Recipe can be doubled or tripled to serve a crowd.

Chinese Chicken

8   chicken thighs or breasts, cut into 1" pieces
¼   cup cornstarch
¼   cup corn oil
1   large tomato, cut into chunks
⅓   cup sliced water chestnuts, drained
1   4-ounce can sliced mushrooms, drained
1   cup chopped green onions
1   cup bias-cut celery
⅛   teaspoon garlic powder
¼   cup soy sauce
2   cups shredded iceburg lettuce

Roll chicken pieces in cornstarch. Heat oil in skillet or wok; brown chicken quickly. Add tomato, water chestnuts, mushrooms, onions and celery. Sprinkle with garlic powder. Stir in soy sauce. Cover; reduce heat and simmer 5 minutes. Remove from heat. Add lettuce and toss.
Yield: 6 servings

Cornish Hens a l'Orange

2	rock Cornish game hens	1	teaspoon grated orange peel
	sherry	1½	cups dry bread cubes
¼	cup chopped onion	2	tablespoons orange juice
2	tablespoons chopped celery		paprika
2	tablespoons margarine	1	tablespoon orange marmalade
2	tablespoons chopped walnuts	1	teaspoon bottled steak sauce

Rub insides of hens with sherry. Sauté onions and celery in margarine. Add walnuts, orange peel and bread cubes. Stir in orange juice. Place stuffing inside hens and sprinkle with paprika. Put breast side up in casserole and microwave 10 minutes on high or bake at 350° for 1 hour. Combine marmalade and steak sauce and brush on hens. Microwave 1 minute on high or bake at 350° for l5 minutes more. Hens are done when juices run clear. Let stand 5 minutes before serving.
Yield: 2 servings

 Cornish hens are very bland little birds (though adaptable to many occasions). Be sure to season highly and butter well!

Cornish Hens in Rice

2	Cornish hens	2	cups cooked wild rice or wild
½	cup butter		and white rice
½	cup dry white wine	2	tablespoons lemon juice
½	cup chopped green onions	1	tablespoon Worcestershire
½	cup chopped mushrooms		sauce
½	cup chopped green olives	½	cup hot water

Roast hens at 350° for 30 minutes, basting with butter and wine. In same pan, sauté onions, mushrooms, and olives. Stir in rice and bury the hens under the rice. Cover and simmer on top of stove until hens are done. Mix lemon juice, Worcestershire sauce, and water. Pour over hens and rice. Heat and serve.
Yield: 2 servings

Green Chili Chicken Enchiladas

4	large chicken breasts or 1 fryer	2	4-ounce cans chopped green
1	medium onion, chopped		chilies
2	tablespoons margarine	2-3	cups grated Cheddar cheese,
1	10¾-oz can cream of chicken		divided
	soup	24	corn tortillas
1	cup small curd cottage cheese		chicken broth, heated
1	cup sour cream		

Cook chicken, reserving broth. Debone and chop. Sauté onion in margarine. Add soup, cottage cheese, sour cream and chilies. Simmer 15 minutes to make a sauce. Mix chicken with ½ of the cheese and ½ of the sauce to make the filling. Soften each tortilla in hot broth. Place 2 tablespoons of chicken filling in center of each tortilla and roll up. Arrange tortillas seam side down in a 3 quart casserole. Top with remaining sauce and cheese. Bake at 350° for 30 minutes.
Yield: 6-8 servings

Freezes well.

Grilled Sesame Chicken

½ cup white grape juice	¼ teaspoon garlic powder
¼ cup soy sauce	¼ teaspoon ground ginger
¼ cup dry white wine	4 skinned chicken breasts,
1 tablespoon sesame seeds	preferably boneless
2 tablespoons vegetable oil	

Combine first 7 ingredients in a shallow dish and mix well. Add chicken. Cover and marinate 2 hours. Remove chicken, reserving marinade. Grill 4-5" from medium hot coals 15 minutes, turning and basting frequently with marinade until done.
Yield: 4 servings

 Can be cooked in a skillet.

Herb-Marinated Chicken

3 pounds chicken pieces	1½ teaspoons crushed rosemary
½ cup vegetable oil	leaves
⅓ cup cider vinegar	1½ teaspoons salt
¼ cup water	½ teaspoon minced garlic
¼ cup minced onion	¼ teaspoon black pepper

Pierce chicken on all sides and put into bowl. Combine rest of ingredients and pour over chicken. Turn to coat on all sides. Cover and refrigerate for at least 2 hours or overnight, turning occasionally. Place marinade and chicken, skin side up, in a shallow pan. Bake and baste, uncovered, at 350° for 50 minutes.
Yield: 6 servings

Comment: Can be broiled. Start skin side down, 6" from broiler, for 20 minutes. Turn and broil 20 minutes more. Baste throughout cooking. Cooking on a grill is also possible.

Little Red Chick

1 fryer, cut up	¼ teaspoon cayenne
½ cup onion, coarsely chopped	1¾ cups tomato sauce
½ cup green pepper, coarsely	3 tablespoons brown sugar
chopped	2 tablespoons prepared mustard
1 clove garlic, pressed	1 teaspoon salt
1 bay leaf	¼ teaspoon pepper
2 tablespoons parsley, finely	¼ cup vinegar
chopped	1 tablespoon Worcestershire
½ teaspoon oregano	sauce

Lay chicken pieces in bottom of Dutch oven. Mix all other ingredients and pour over chicken. Simmer 1 hour on top of stove, until tender. The chicken will have a barbeque taste.
Yield: 6 servings

Opulent Chicken

4	chicken breasts,split		pinch of tarragon
	paprika, salt, and pepper	3	tablespoons flour
1	stick butter, divided	⅓	cup sherry
1	15-ounce can artichoke hearts,	1½	cups chicken bouillon
	drained	1	6-ounce box Uncle Ben's wild
8	ounce fresh mushrooms,sliced		and white rice, cooked

Season chicken with paprika, salt, and pepper. Sauté in ½ stick butter until golden brown. Arrange chicken and artichokes in a large casserole. Sauté mushrooms in remaining butter with tarragon. Sprinkle the flour gently into the mushrooms and butter and mix in. Add sherry and bouillon. Stir while simmering 5 minutes. Pour over casserole, cover, and bake at 375° for 45 minutes. Serve over cooked rice.
Yield: 4 servings

Patty's Chicken

2	thick slices bacon	1	chicken bouillon cube, dissolved
4	whole boneless chicken breasts		in water
	lemon pepper	½	cup red wine
	garlic salt	1	pound fresh mushrooms, sliced
	flour	1	large tomato, chopped
¼	cup oil	1	14-ounce can artichoke hearts,
3	tablespoons butter		drained, optional
1	medium green pepper, sliced		cooked rice or pasta
1	large onion, sliced		

Cook bacon until crisp. Drain on paper towel, reserving drippings in skillet. Clean breasts and sprinkle with lemon pepper and garlic salt. Put flour into plastic bag and add breasts. Shake to coat. Add oil and butter to bacon drippings. Brown chicken on both sides. Add green pepper and onion; sauté with chicken. Stir bouillon and red wine into chicken mixture. Top with mushrooms and tomato. Cover and continue to cook on medium heat. Crumble bacon and add. Continue cooking, stirring occasionally, until it forms a rich sauce. Keep covered. Add artichoke hearts and cook 10 more minutes. Serve over rice or pasta.
Yield: 4 large servings

Rolled Chicken Supremes

8	large boned chicken breasts	3	cups Italian seasoned bread
8	slices imported Swiss Cheese		crumbs
8	slices boiled ham	1	stick butter
3	eggs, beaten		

Wrap 1 slice of cheese and 1 slice of ham around each breast. Secure with wooden toothpicks. Dip each wrapped breast in the eggs, then roll it in bread crumbs. In shallow baking dish, melt butter and add chicken rolls. Place on low oven rack and bake at 350° for 35 minutes, turning only once. Baste often with more butter, if necessary.
Yield: 8 servings

R. L.'s Company Chicken

1   2½-ounce jar dried beef
8-10 chicken breasts, skinned and
    deboned
8-10 slices of bacon
2   3-ounce packages cream cheese

1   cup sour cream
2   10¾-ounce cans cream of
    mushroom soup
    paprika

Spray large casserole with Pam. Place beef in single layer on bottom. Wrap each breast with slice of bacon and place on top of beef. Heat cream cheese, sour cream and soup until cheese is melted and well blended. Pour over chicken. Sprinkle with paprika. Bake covered at 275° for 3 hours.
Yield: 8-10 servings

Spicy Chicken

½   cup melted margarine
¼   cup sugar
2   tablespoons flour
½   teaspoon chili powder
¼   teaspoon dry mustard
¼   teaspoon pepper

½   teaspoon salt
2   tablespoons Worcestershire
    sauce
3   tablespoons hot water
½   cup vinegar
4   chicken breasts

Combine all ingredients except vinegar and chicken. Bring to simmer. Cool. Stir in vinegar. Bake chicken without sauce, covered, at 300° for 1 hour and 45 minutes. Pour off juices. Pour sauce over chicken. Bake uncovered 15 minutes.
Yield: 4 servings

Rosie's Chicken Veronique

¼   cup flour
1   teaspoon salt
½   teaspoon pepper
8   chicken breasts, skinned and
    deboned

½   cup butter or margarine
1   tablespoon currant jelly
⅔   cup Madeira wine
1½ cups seedless grapes

Combine flour, salt and pepper. Dredge breasts in flour mixture. Sauté breasts in butter until brown. Cover; reduce heat; cook 20 minutes or until tender. Remove chicken to a serving dish. Stir jelly and wine into reserved pan drippings and cook until heated. Stir in grapes. Pour over chicken.
Yield: 8 servings

For easy oven-fried chicken, dip pieces in either melted margarine or evaporated milk. Then roll in a mixture of 1 cup Pepperidge Farm herb dressing, 1 teaspoon salt, 1 teaspoon flavor enhancer, ½ teaspoon paprika, ¼ teaspoon thyme and ½ teaspoon sesame seeds. Bake at 350°.

Alcohol-Is-Good-for-Your-Liver

1½ pounds calves liver, sliced
1   large sweet onion, thinly sliced
3   tablespoons oil
2   tablespoons cognac
1   garlic clove, minced
1   8-ounce can tomato sauce

1   cup Cabernet Sauvignon
2   tablespoons Dijon mustard
½   teaspoon pepper
1   8-ounce package fresh
     mushrooms, coarsely sliced

Rinse liver and pat dry. Stack slices; wrap in plastic and place in freezer until firm but not frozen, about 30 minutes. Then slice the stack into approximately ½" strips. Sauté onion in oil. Raise heat to high and add liver, stirring continuously until liver begins to brown. Add cognac and ignite. Combine remaining ingredients and add to liver. Cover and simmer for 3-5 minutes.
Yield: 4 servings

Variation: Use chicken livers, halved

Apple Glazed Brisket

4-5 pound beef brisket
1   medium onion, quartered
2-3 garlic cloves, halved
10   whole cloves
1   10-ounce jar apple jelly
1/3 cup dry white wine
3   tablespoons Dijon mustard

3   tablespoons minced green
     onions
¾   teaspoon coarsely ground black
     pepper
1   teaspoon salt
¾   teaspoon curry powder

Place brisket, onion, garlic and cloves in large Dutch oven. Add water to cover. Bring to a boil; reduce heat; cover and simmer 2½-3 hours or until tender. Drain brisket; cover and refrigerate up to 24 hours. To prepare the glaze, combine the remaining ingredients and heat until jelly melts, stirring occasionally. Place brisket on the grill for 30 minutes, basting often with glaze. Carve brisket into thin slices and serve with glaze.
Yield: 8 servings

Variation: May also be cooked in a 325° oven for 45 minutes, basting with glaze.

Beef Burgundy

1   pound beef stew meat, trimmed
     and cubed
2   tablespoons butter
2½   tablespoons flour
½   cup Burgundy wine

8-10 small boiling onions
3-4 carrots, peeled and cut into 1"
     slices
1   10½-ounce can beef consommé
     cooked noodles, buttered

Melt butter in large heavy skillet. Brown meat; then sprinkle with flour. Cook and stir until flour gains color. Add remaining ingredients. Cover and bake at 300° for 3 hours. Add more wine or water if needed. Serve over cooked noodles.
Yield: 4-6 servings

Beef Tenders

5-6 pound untrimmed beef
    tenderloin, trimmed

Marinade:

3   tablespoons butter, melted
½   pound fresh mushrooms, sliced
3   tablespoons butter
3   tablespoons brown sugar

juice of 1 lemon
½   cup red wine
½   cup soy sauce
1   bunch scallion tops, chopped

Sauté mushrooms in melted butter; then remove. Add the remaining marinade ingredients and simmer 15 minutes. Add mushrooms again and pour over meat. Marinate for 3 hours at room temperature in foil-lined roasting pan. Fold the foil up around the meat with the sauce inside. Open the foil and bake at 400° for 45 minutes to 1 hour. Check at 40 minutes for rare.
Yield: 8 servings for dinner or 18-20 for cocktail buffet

Crescent Italiano Casserole

1½ pounds ground beef
½   cup chopped onion
½   teaspoon salt
½   teaspoon pepper
1   8-ounce can tomato sauce
1   4-ounce can sliced mushrooms,
    drained

4   ounces shredded Cheddar
    cheese
1   can Pillsbury crescent dinner
    rolls
½   cup sour cream
¼   teaspoon oregano
¼   teaspoon rosemary or basil

Brown beef and onions, then drain. Add salt, pepper, tomato sauce and mushrooms. Spread in a greased 8×12″ baking dish. Sprinkle with cheese. Separate rolls into 8 triangles. Combine sour cream with herbs and spread evenly over each triangle. Roll crescents beginning at the widest end. Arrange rolls on top of casserole. Bake at 375° for 25-30 minutes until golden brown.
Yield: 4-6 servings

Dilly Beef

⅓   cup flour
2   teaspoons salt
1   teaspoon pepper
1   pound sirloin, cubed
2   tablespoons shortening
1⅔ cup hot water

1   bay leaf
¾   teaspoon dill weed
4   teaspoons paprika
¾   cup sour cream
    cooked rice

Mix flour, salt and pepper; roll cubed meat to coat. Brown the meat in the shortening. Add water, bay leaf and dill. Cover and simmer 1½-2 hours. When ready to serve, add paprika and sour cream. Serve over rice.
Yield: 4 servings

Fajitas

1½ pounds skirt steak (not flank steak)

cider vinegar, as needed
soy sauce, as needed

Remove as much membrane from the meat as possible — time-consuming but very important. Marinate meat with equal parts of vinegar and soy sauce, enough to cover the meat. Cover meat with foil and marinate for at least 8 hours or up to 3 days in refrigerator. Grill over a hot fire, close to the coals, for 5-10 minutes or until well done and tender. Slice across the grain into thin slices. Serve with heated flour tortillas and Louise's Pico de Gallo or Dallas Picante Sauce.

Louise's Pico de Gallo

2   avocados
1   large ripe tomato
4   scallions, minced
½   cup cilantro, minced
     pickled jalapeños, to taste,
     seeded and finely minced

juice of 2 fresh limes
garlic salt, to taste
seasoned salt, to taste
seasoned pepper, to taste

Cut avocados and tomato into ¼″ dice. Combine all the above ingredients. Serve with fajitas or chips. Keeps several days refrigerated.
Yield: 2 cups

Dallas Picante Sauce

3   chilies del arbol (2″ long dried red chilies)
2   cups canned tomatoes (not tomato sauce)
1½ teaspoons salt

1   tablespoon vinegar
2   tablespoons oil
1   clove garlic
1   teaspoon oregano

Remove seeds from dried red chilies. Grind finely or soak in boiling water for 5 minutes, then drain. Blend in blender with the vinegar and oil to make a paste. Put garlic through a press, then add to paste. Add remaining ingredients and chop in a food processor until tomatoes are finely chopped. Serve hot or cold. Yields 2 cups. Keeps for weeks in refrigerator. Very good with meat or eggs.
Yield: 4-5 servings

Southwest Casserole

12 corn tortillas
1   pound ground chuck
1   large onion, chopped
1   garlic clove, diced, optional
¼   teaspoon oregano
2   teaspoons chili powder
     salt and pepper, to taste

1   15-ounce can Ranch Style beans
1   1-pound box Velveeta cheese, sliced
1   10-ounce can Ro-Tel tomatoes with green chilies
1   10¾-ounce can cream of chicken soup

Grease a 3 quart casserole. Line with 6 tortillas torn into pieces; set aside. Brown meat and pour off drippings. Add onion, garlic, oregano, chili powder, salt, pepper and beans. Spoon this evenly over tortillas in casserole; cover with a layer of cheese slices and remaining tortillas. Combine tomatoes and soup. Spoon evenly over casserole. Run a fork through the layers to mingle the soup mixture. Place remaining cheese on top. Bake at 300° for 30-40 minutes.
Yield: Serves 8-10.

Hungarian Goulash

2½ pounds beef, rump or round
⅓ cup suet, chopped
¾ cup chopped onions
1 garlic clove, crushed
2½ cups water, divided
1 cup catsup
½-1 teaspoon prepared mustard

1 tablespoon paprika
2 tablespoons brown sugar
2 teaspoons salt
1 tablespoon Worcestershire sauce
1 teaspoon vinegar
2 tablespoons flour
1 8-ounce package fine noodles

Cut meat into 1″ cubes. Brown meat in suet with onion and garlic. Add water, catsup and seasonings. Cover and cook at low heat until tender, about 2 hours. Mix flour with ½ cup of water and add to mixture, stirring constantly until thickens. Cook noodles in boiling salted water. Drain and mix some of the sauce from the meat and serve with meat on top.
Yield: 4 servings

Hungarian Pot Roast

5-6 pound roast
2 teaspoons salt
¼ teaspoon pepper
1 cup chopped onion
2 tablespoons oil
1½ tablespoons paprika

1 10½-ounce can bouillon
1 bay leaf
1 teaspoon caraway seeds
½ cup water
3 tablespoons flour
1 cup sour cream

Season meat with salt and pepper. Sear meat on all sides; then remove from pan. Sauté onions in oil, then add paprika. Return meat to pot, adding bouillon, bay leaf and caraway seeds. Cover and simmer for 3 hours. Mix flour and water and add to make a gravy. Just before serving, add the sour cream.
Yield: 8 servings

Spanish Delight

2 large onions, chopped
1 garlic clove, minced
4 tablespoons margarine
2 pounds ground meat
1 8-ounce can tomato sauce
1 6-ounce can tomato paste
1 10¾-ounce can tomato soup
1 10½-ounce can Green Giant niblet corn

1 4-ounce can mushroom pieces, drained
1 4-ounce can sliced ripe olives, drained
1 teaspoon each salt and pepper
1 8-ounce package medium egg noodles, cooked and drained
1-2 cups grated sharp Cheddar cheese, optional

Brown onions and garlic in margarine and set aside. Brown meat; drain well and mix with onions and garlic. Add the remaining ingredients, except cheese, and mix well. Pour into greased 9×13″ casserole. Top with cheese and bake at 350° for 30 minutes until bubbly.
Yield: 10-12 servings

 Can be made ahead and heated in oven before serving. Freezes well. Thaw before baking.

Steak Diane

4	sirloin strip steaks, ½" thick
	salt, to taste
	freshly ground black pepper, to taste
4	teaspoons dry mustard

4	tablespoons butter
3	tablespoons lemon juice
2	teaspoons chopped chives
1	teaspoon Worcestershire sauce

Pound steaks to ⅓" thick. Sprinkle both sides with salt, pepper and mustard; pound into meat. Heat butter in a skillet. Cook steak for 2 minutes per side. Transfer to a hot serving dish. Add remaining ingredients to the skillet. Bring to a boil, then pour over meat.
Yield: 4 servings

Variation: You can use Burgundy instead of the lemon juice in the sauce or make sauce flambe: Add 2 tablespoons sherry and 1 tablespoon brandy at the last minute. Flame and then pour over steaks.

Butterfly Barbecued Lamb

1	leg of lamb, deboned
½	cup soy sauce

1	8-ounce bottle garlic salad dressing
6	onions, sliced

Combine soy sauce and salad dressing. Top lamb with onion slices. Pour soy mixture over lamb and marinate 1 hour or longer. Drain meat, saving marinade. Cook over charcoal about 15 minutes per side, basting as you cook.
Yield: 8-10 servings

Variation: Broil or bake lamb at 400° until it reaches an internal temperature of 160°-165° for slightly rare, or 175°-180° for well done.

Roast Leg of Lamb

1	leg of lamb, deboned and tied
⅓	cup flour
3	teaspoons salt
1	tablespoons paprika
2	tablespoons butter
2	tablespoons olive oil
1	cup Madeira wine
2	garlic cloves, minced
½	teaspoon thyme
1	teaspoon basil

2	teaspoons Dijon mustard
1	16-ounce can tomatoes, coarsely chopped
1	6-ounce can tomato sauce
1	10-ounce basket pearl or boiling onions
12-15	pitted ripe olives
1	8-ounce package fresh mushrooms

Put flour, salt and paprika into a bag. Shake lamb in mixture until coated. Sear in butter and olive oil on all sides. Transfer to non-metallic casserole for roasting. Add wine, tomatoes, tomato sauce, garlic, thyme, basil and mustard to skillet in which lamb was seared, scraping to incorporate brown bits. Pour over lamb. Add onions and bake at 350° for 20-25 minutes per pound. Add olives and mushrooms for the last 15 minutes of baking. Let cool for 10-15 minutes before slicing. Serve with sauce.
Yield: 6 servings

 Accompanied by a green salad with a vinaigrette dressing and crusty bread for soaking up the sauce, it's a feast!

Ham Casserole

6 tablespoons butter, divided	1 cup half and half
1 cup fresh mushrooms, sliced	2 cups paper-thin slices of cooked
1 tablespoon lemon juice	ham
4 tablespoons flour	1 13¾-ounce can artichoke hearts
1 cup milk	¼ cup Parmesan cheese

Melt 2 tablespoons of butter and sauté the mushrooms. Add the lemon juice. Melt the remaining 4 tablespoons butter in another pan, adding flour, milk and cream to make a cream sauce. Stir and cook until smooth and thick. Fold in mushrooms and ham. Drain the artichoke hearts, cut in half and arrange, cut side down, in the bottom of a buttered casserole. Cover with ham mixture. Sprinkle with Parmesan cheese and bake at 350° for 20-30 minutes until bubbly.
Yield: 4-6 servings

 This casserole can be made ahead and frozen.

Ham and Swiss Roulades with Dill Sauce

4 slices cooked ham	1 10-ounce package frozen
4 slices Munster or baby Swiss	broccoli spears or fresh broccoli,
cheese	slightly cooked

Top each slice of ham with a slice of cheese. Place 1-2 pieces of broccoli on cheese with the top of the broccoli past the edge. Roll up and secure with wooden toothpicks. Place the cheese rolls in a buttered baking dish. Top each with Dill Sauce. Bake at 350° for 15-20 minutes or until bubbly.

Dill Sauce:

2 rounded tablespoons flour	1 tablespoon prepared mustard
2 tablespoons butter	¼-½ teaspoon dill weed
1 cup milk	¼ cup sour cream

Melt butter; add flour and milk. Stir until slightly thickened. Add dill and mustard, blending well. Add sour cream, blend, and heat for a minute. Pour over ham roulades.
Yield: 4 servings

 The dill sauce is also excellent on fish.

Ham Soufflé

16 slices white bread, divided	½ cup green onion, finely chopped
12 ounces canned ham, diced	6 eggs, beaten
1 10-ounce package chopped	3½ cups milk
broccoli, well drained	1 teaspoon salt
¾ pound sharp cheese, diced	1 teaspoon pepper
1 2-ounce jar pimiento, drained	½ teaspoon dry mustard

Remove crust from the bread. Place 8 slices on the bottom of a buttered 9 × 13″ baking dish. Scatter ham, broccoli, cheese, pimientos, and onion over bread. Place the remaining bread slices on top. Combine remaining ingredients and pour over bread. Cover and refrigerate overnight or at least 6 hours. Bake uncovered at 325° for 1 hour.
Yield: 8-10 servings

Variation: Crumbled bacon, shrimp, crab meat or oysters may be substituted for ham.

Pork Chops à la Orange

4   pork chops, 1" thick
     seasoned salt, to taste
2   tablespoons water
5   tablespoons sugar
1½   teaspoons cornstarch
¼   teaspoon cinnamon

10   whole cloves
2   teaspoons orange rind
½   cup orange juice
1   navel orange, peeled and
     sectioned

Brown pork chops; sprinkle with seasoned salt. Add water; cover and simmer for 1 hour or until tender. A few minutes before the pork chops are done, combine the remaining ingredients in a small saucepan. Heat until boiling, clear and slightly thickened. Spoon over chops and serve.
Yield: 4 servings

Pork Chops Paprika

2-4 lean pork chops
⅓   cup flour
2   teaspoons paprika
2-4 tablespoons butter
½   cup consommé
3   tablespoons water

2   tablespoons capers
2   tablespoons chopped onions
2   tablespoons prepared mustard
½   teaspoon cracked pepper
¾   cup sour cream

Dredge chops in flour mixed with paprika. Brown meat in butter. Add consommé and water; then add the next four ingredients. Simmer, covered, for 1 hour. Add more liquid if needed. Stir in sour cream just before serving.
Yield: 2-4 servings

Souvlaki
(Shish Kabob)

1   tablespoon oregano
1½   teaspoons salt
     garlic powder, to taste
3   garlic cloves, chopped
2   cups chopped onions
½   teaspoon pepper

2   cups Mogen David red wine
1   cup vegetable oil
1   cup olive oil
1   cup wine vinegar
4-5 pounds pork tenderloin, cut into
     cubes

Combine the first 10 ingredients and add to the tenderloin. Marinate in a sealed container for at least 24 hours. Grill on skewers over charcoal for 20-30 minutes.
Yield: 8-10 servings

Variation: The tenderloin can be marianated whole and sliced after cooking. Cook 30-45 minutes and baste with marinade while grilling.

Polish Sausage and Vegetable Dinner

¾	pound Polish sausage	1	onion, quartered
4	medium potatoes	1	medium cabbage, cored and quartered
1	medium green pepper, cut into strips		salt and pepper, to taste
4	medium carrots, cut into 3″ slices	1	cup water
1	16-ounce can French-style green beans, drained		

Slice sausage diagonally into ½″ pieces. Slice potatoes with skins into ⅓″ pieces. In a large Dutch oven layer ingredients in order given. Salt and pepper each layer. Add water and bring to a boil. Cover; reduce heat and simmer for 35-45 minutes or until vegetables are tender.
Yield: 4-6 servings

Chinese Spareribs

½	cup honey	4	teaspoons salt
½	cup tomato pureé	1	tablespoon dry mustard
½	cup soy sauce	3	tablespoons onion soup mix
2	cups chicken stock	6	pounds spareribs
¼	cup vinegar	2	tablespoons cornstarch
5	garlic cloves, crushed		

Combine the first 9 ingredients, mix well, and spread on ribs. Marinate for several hours or overnight. Roast in a 450° oven for 10 minutes; reduce heat to 300° and cook for 1 hour or longer. Thicken sauce with cornstarch.
Yield: 6 servings

Variation: The ribs can be cooked over charcoal. The sauce is also very good with chicken.

Lemon Veal

1	pound veal scallopini	2	tablespoons lemon juice
⅓	cup flour	1	tablespoon chopped scallions
1½	teaspoons salt	1	tablespoon minced parsley
	freshly ground pepper, to taste	2	sprigs fresh rosemary or 1 tablespoon dry (fresh is best)
3	tablespoons butter	1	lemon, sliced paper thin
¼	cup chicken stock		
2	tablespoons dry vermouth		

Cut veal into 3″ squares. Dredge veal in mixture of flour, salt and pepper. Melt butter and brown veal over moderately high heat. Add remaining ingredients. Cover and gently simmer 3-4 minutes.
Yield: 3-4 servings

Veal Cutlets in Sherry

1 pound veal cutlets	½ cup sherry
¼ cup flour	2 tablespoons chopped parsley
salt and pepper, to taste	4 thin slices cooked ham
2 tablespoons butter	4 thin slices Swiss cheese
½ cup consommé	
½ cup water	

Dust cutlets with flour, salt and pepper. Sauté lightly in butter; cover with consommé, water and sherry. Sprinkle with parsley; cover and bake at 350° for 1 hour. Uncover, place slices of ham and cheese on top of each cutlet and return to oven until cheese melts. Serve at once.
Yield: 4 servings

Veal Scallopini

¼ cup flour	2 tablespoons olive oil
½ cup grated Parmesan cheese	2 large garlic cloves
1 teaspoon salt	½ cup dry white wine
⅛ teaspoon pepper	½ cup consommé
1½ pounds veal cutlets, sliced ¼" thick and cut into 2" strips	parsley

Mix flour, cheese, salt, and pepper together. Wipe meat dry; sprinkle with flour mixture and pound into meat. Heat olive oil with garlic and brown meat lightly on both sides. Remove garlic; add wine and consommé. Cover and simmer slowly for about 30 minutes. Sprinkle with chopped parsley.
Yield: 6 servings

 Serve over buttered noodles if desired.

Jalapeño Sauce

4 cups fresh jalapeños, seeded and chopped	1½ teaspoons salt
2 large onions, chopped	1 teaspoon cumin
5 garlic cloves, chopped	½ teaspoon oregano
4 teaspoons black pepper	½ cup cider vinegar

Put all the ingredients into the blender and blend for a few seconds.
Yield: 5-6 cups

 Prepare 4-5 days ahead.

Slang Jang

1⅔ cups chopped tomatoes	½ cup vinegar
1 cup chopped green pepper	3 tablespoons Accent
2 cups chopped onion	salt and pepper, to taste
⅓ cup sugar or less, to taste	

Do not use blender or processor. Mix all the ingredients; cover and refrigerate.
Yield: 3 cups

 Very good with black-eyed peas or ham or other meats. Keeps for several weeks.

Mustard Sauce

4 ounces Coleman's dry mustard	4 eggs
1 cup vinegar	1 cup sugar

Combine mustard and vinegar and refrigerate overnight. In the top of a double boiler add the eggs and sugar to the mustard/vinegar mixture. Cook until it thickens. Store covered in the refrigerator.
Yield: 3 cups

 The sauce thickens quickly when cooked, and for it to be most pungent it should be removed from the heat quickly. The longer it cooks, the milder and sweeter it becomes.

Mexican Doves

12-18 doves (whole)	6-9 strips of bacon
6-9 jalapeño peppers	salt and pepper, to taste.

Clean and pick doves, clipping wings and feet at first joints and cutting backs open with poultry shears. Wash thoroughly and drain. Split peppers lengthwise into halves. Cut bacon strips in half. Place one pepper half inside each dove, securing the open side of the pepper firmly against the underside of the breastbone with a toothpick pushed through the breast of the bird. Wrap each dove with a half bacon strip, secured to the same toothpick. Season with salt and pepper. Grill over charcoal or mesquite for 30 minutes.
Yield: 4-6 servings

Rio Grande Whitewing Doves

16 whitewing doves	1 5-ounce bottle Worcestershire
salt and pepper, to taste	sauce
garlic powder, to taste	1 cup cream sherry
1½ cups flour	1½ cups water
1 pound butter	parsley, chopped

Season birds with salt, pepper and garlic powder. Dredge birds heavily in flour and then brown in the butter in a heavy skillet. Place birds in an ungreased 9 × 13″ baking dish. Pour butter from skillet over birds. Mix Worcestershire, sherry and water, adding more salt, pepper and garlic powder. Bake uncovered at 300° for 2-3 hours until tender. Sprinkle with parsley before serving.
Yield: 16 servings

Birds Paprika

1	cup chicken broth	1	cup flour
1	sprig fresh dill or 2 pinches dried	½	cup butter
2	sprigs fresh rosemary or ¼	2	shallots, chopped
	teaspoon dried	1	tablespoon chopped parsley
½	cup of chopped celery with	4	ounces dry sherry
	leaves	1	cup sour cream
8-10	quail or doves		salt and pepper, to taste
	salt and pepper, to taste	1½	teaspoons paprika

Place chicken broth, dill, rosemary and celery in saucepan,. Bring to a boil; then reduce to a simmer. Split birds lengthwise and rub with salt and pepper and dust with flour. In large skillet melt butter and add shallots; sauté 2 minutes. Add birds and brown well. Pour in broth mixture and add parsley. Place lid on skillet and simmer for 20 minutes. Add sherry and simmer 5 more minutes. Add sour cream, salt, pepper and paprika. Remove to serving platter.

Yield: 4-5 servings

 May be cooked ahead of time through sherry stage. At last minute heat thoroughly; then add sour cream and paprika.

Deep-Fried Quail or Dove

8-12	quail or dove, cleaned	½	cup Bisquick
6	eggs, beaten	2	cups flour
1	quart milk		salt and pepper, to taste
	peanut oil		

Marinate birds in mixture of eggs and milk for 3 hours. In deep fryer, preheat enough oil to cover birds. Heat oil to 375°. In paper bag mix Bisquick, flour, salt and pepper. Put birds in bag and shake to coat. Fry approximately 5 minutes, until birds are golden.

Yield: 3-4 servings

Mary Anne's Baked Quail

8-10	quail, lightly salted	¾	cup sliced mushrooms
⅓	cup salad oil	2	tablespoons flour
1	carrot, finely chopped	2	cups chicken broth, heated
1	onion, finely chopped	⅓	cup white wine
1	tablespoon finely chopped green pepper		

Brown birds in oil. Remove to heated casserole. Sauté carrots, onions, pepper and mushrooms in same oil until tender. Blend in flour; gradually add heated chicken broth. Add wine and pour over quail. Cover and bake at 325° for 2 hours or until tender.

Yield: 4-6 servings

Chirp: Serve applesauce with lots of horseradish stirred in as an accompaniment to pork or game.

Savory Baked Quail or Dove

12 quail or 24 dove, cleaned	1 onion, chopped
½ cup butter or margarine, melted	1 green pepper, chopped
1 cup flour	1 10¾-ounce can cream of
½ teaspoon sage	chicken soup
½ teaspoon thyme	½ of a 10¾-ounce can cream of
2 teaspoons salt	celery soup
¼ teaspoon pepper	2 teaspoons Worcestershire sauce
1 teaspoon paprika	2 teaspoons Kitchen Bouquet
½ cup cooking oil	1½ cups water
	½ cup sherry

Coat birds with melted butter and shake well in a bag containing flour and seasonings. Brown quickly in hot oil and move to a shallow baking pan. Sauté onion and green pepper in the remaining oil. Add soups and all other ingredients, mixing well. Pour the sauce over the birds and bake, covered, at 350° for 1½ hours. Uncover the last 10 minutes.
Yield: 4-6 servings

Smothered Quail or Dove Breasts

4-6 quail or dove breasts	½ cup white wine or Madeira
salt and pepper, to taste	1 cup consommé
1 cup flour	½ cup heavy cream
½ cup butter, melted	1 tablespoon chopped fresh
¼ cup chopped white onion	parsley
½-¾ cup chopped fresh mushrooms	cooked wild rice or brown rice

Clean breasts thoroughly; dry well. Salt, pepper and roll each breast in flour. Sauté in butter until browned. Add onions and mushrooms and cook until tender. Add wine and consommé. Cover and cook very, very slowly, checking frequently, until done; or bake, covered, at 325° for about 1½ hours until done. Dust with parsley before serving with rice.
Yield: 2 servings

Stuffed Quail

12 quail	1 cup butter or margarine
2 apples, cut into small pieces	12 thin slices bacon
3 ribs celery, cut into small pieces	2 cups red wine
2 cups flour, as needed	3 tablespoons grape jelly
salt and pepper, to taste	

Stuff quail with the apples and celery. Season flour with salt and pepper. Roll the quail in the seasoned flour and brown in margarine. Remove quail and wrap each bird with a slice of bacon. Place in a deep baking dish. Stir enough flour into the pan drippings to make a brown gravy. Stir in wine and jelly. Pour over quail; cover with foil and bake at 250° for 1½-2 hours.
Yield: 6 servings

Variation: May use Cornish game hens.

 In a hurry? Marinate quail breasts in prepared Italian salad dressing, adding black or red pepper to taste. Grill over charcoal for 8-10 minutes, basting with marinade. Legs can be used, too — cooked 4-5 minutes and served as hors d'oeuvres.

Duck and Oyster Gumbo

⅔ cup vegetable oil
3-3½ pounds wild ducks, split in half
⅔ cup flour
2 cups chopped onion
⅔ cup chopped green pepper
½ cup thinly-sliced shallots with tops
1 tablespoon finely minced garlic
2 quarts cold water, divided
½ pound lean baked ham, cut in ½" cubes
1 pound smoked sausage (creole, Polish, French or garlic), sliced ¼" thick and divided

2 tablespoons finely minced parsley
1 quart fresh oysters with juice
1¼ teaspoon freshly ground black pepper
⅛ teaspoon cayenne pepper
salt, to taste (up to 3½ teaspoons)
1 teaspoon dried thyme
3 bay leaves
⅛ teaspoon mace
2½-3 tablespoons filé powder
cooked rice

Heat oil in a heavy 7-8 quart pan over high heat. Brown ducks in the hot oil, turning several times. Remove browned ducks and set aside. Make a roux by gradually adding the flour to the oil, stirring constantly over medium heat until dark brown. Quickly add onion, green pepper, shallots and garlic. Stir thoroughly and add ¼ cup water, ham and ½ of the sausage. Mix well and continue browning for 10 minutes over low heat, stirring constantly. Add parsley, the juice from the oysters, the ducks, the remaining sausage and all seasonings except the filé powder. Gradually add the remaining water. Bring to a boil, lower heat and simmer 1 hour or longer, stirring frequently. Remove ducks, debone them, and return duck meat to the gumbo. Ten minutes prior to serving, add oysters and cook 4-5 minutes. Remove pan from heat and add filé powder. Let stand 5 minutes before serving over rice.
Yield: 8 servings

Duck and Wild Rice Casserole

2 wild ducks
3 ribs celery, cut in 2" pieces
1 onion, halved
1½ teaspoons salt
¼ teaspoon pepper
1 6-ounce package long grain and wild rice mixture
½ cup chopped onion

½ cup butter, melted
1½ cups chicken broth
¼ cup flour
1 4-ounce can mushrooms, drained
1½ cups half and half
1 tablespoon chopped parsley
½ cup slivered almonds

Put ducks, celery, onion, salt and pepper in a saucepan. Cover with water and bring to a boil. Reduce heat and simmer 1 hour. Remove ducks; strain stock and reserve. Remove meat from ducks and cut into pieces. Cook rice according to directions and set aside. Sauté onion in butter and add flour. Brown flour and add chicken broth slowly, stirring until smooth. Add mushrooms, half and half, parsley and almonds, stirring constantly until thick and bubbly. Stir in duck meat. Place rice mixture into greased casserole and pour duck mixture over rice. Cover and bake at 350° for 15-20 minutes. Uncover and bake 5-10 minutes longer.
Yield: 8 servings

Jalapeño Ducks

6	duck breasts	2	4-ounce cans chopped green
½	cup flour		chilies
½	cup butter, melted	1	onion, finely chopped
	salt and pepper, to taste	2	garlic cloves, crushed
2	15-ounce cans stewed tomatoes	2-3	canned jalapeño peppers,
1	15-ounce can water		seeded and sliced
1	6-ounce can tomato paste	12	flour tortillas
1	cup red wine	1	cup oil
			parsley, fresh or dried

Slowly brown ducks in a heavy deep pot in butter. Add salt and pepper. Add next 7 ingredients. The ducks need to be covered with liquid; add more stewed tomatoes if necessary. Cover and cook very slowly until skin comes off. Remove skin and continue cooking until the meat comes off the bones. Remove bones. Add jalapeño peppers and taste to correct seasonings. Cover and remove from heat. Quarter the flour tortillas and fry in oil until they puff and are brown. Layer the tortillas on a warm platter and spoon duck meat and juices over tortillas. Dust with parsley flakes and serve immediately. Be sure to have plenty of extra fried tortillas.
Yield: 6 servings

Oven-Barbecued Ducks

4	ducks	1	teaspoon black pepper
2	2-ounce bottles onion juice	1	tablespoon parsley
⅓	cup olive oil	2	cups sherry
1	cup water		salt and pepper, to taste
½	pound butter	4	bay leaves
½	teaspoon cayenne pepper		

Pick and clean ducks. Make sauce using next 9 ingredients. Baste ducks with sauce and broil under medium heat, turning frequently until ducks are lightly browned. Place ducks in a roasting pan and pour some sauce over them. Place a bay leaf on each duck breast. Cover and cook at 325° until tender, approximately 45 minutes. Then pour remaining sauce over ducks and simmer gently until completely done and ready to serve.
Yield: 4 servings

Roasted Wild Ducks

4	small ducks	1-2	tablespoons olive oil
2	ribs celery, halved		salt and pepper, to taste
1	onion, quartered	1½	cups chicken broth
2	carrots, halved	1½	cups red wine
1	apple, quartered	1-2	tablespoons cornstarch,
			dissolved in a little water

Wash and dry ducks well. Into each cavity put a slice of celery, onion, carrot and apple. Brush ducks with olive oil and salt and pepper to taste. Place in a large casserole and add the chicken broth and wine. Cover and bake at 300° for 3 hours. When tender, remove ducks and keep warm. Remove the vegetables and discard. Thicken the sauce with the cornstarch and serve over the ducks.
Yield: 4 servings

Variation: 1 – 2 dashes of Tabasco sauce may be added to the broth.

Wild Ducks

4	wild ducks		cloves, ground
	pinch of each of the following:		thyme
	garlic	1	10½-ounce can beef bouillon
	parsley	¼	cup butter
	celery salt		juice of one lemon
	peppercorns, ground	1	cup port wine
	bay leaves, ground		

Take the backs off the ducks. Place backs in a pan and cover with water. Add the spices and bouillon. Cook until meat falls off bones. Remove from fire and reserve stock. Wash and dry duck breasts. Melt butter in a heavy skillet and fry breasts until golden brown. Lower heat. Add lemon juice and wine. Simmer for a few minutes. Add stock from backs. Bake covered in 400° oven for 1-1½ hours.
Yield: 4 servings

Wild Rice Stuffed Ducks

1	4-ounce package wild rice	3	ducks
1	cup chopped celery	6	slices bacon
1	pound mushrooms, sliced	½	cup butter
1	cup chopped onion	2	cups port wine
½	teaspoon thyme		

Cook rice according to package directions. Add celery, mushrooms, onion and thyme. Stuff ducks with rice mixture. Place bacon strips over breast of ducks in an ''X'' with bacon extending over legs. Melt butter in wine and pour a little over the ducks. Baste ducks often with the remainder of the sauce while baking in a 350° oven for 1½ hours or until tender.
Yield: 6-8 servings

Fried Venison Fingers

1	cup milk		pepper, to taste
1	egg		corn oil
1	venison roast	1	lemon, cut in wedges
1	cup flour		parsley
1	cup finely crushed saltine		
	crackers		

Mix milk and egg. Slice venison roast into fingers 4-5″ long and ½″ thick. Dip venison in milk mixture and roll in flour and cracker crumbs. Season with pepper. Fry in oil in heavy skillet, then drain. Squeeze a lemon wedge over the fingers and dust with parsley. Serve with remaining lemon wedges.
Yield: 6 servings

Venison Cutlets à la Mandarin

	Venison cutlets or small steaks	1	11-ounce can mandarin oranges
	salt and pepper, to taste	1	tablespoon cognac
4	tablespoons butter	1	10-ounce jar currant jelly

Salt and pepper venison, Sauté cutlets in butter until brown on both sides. Remove cutlets. Drain oranges and reserve juice. Add ¼ cup juice, cognac and jelly to pan drippings. Bring to a boil and simmer 2 minutes. In a saucepan heat oranges in remainder of juice. Arrange cutlets and oranges on a platter. Pour the heated sauce over.
Yield: 4 servings

Venison with Sauce Poivrade

1	cup raw rice	2	cups bouillon, heated
6	tablespoons butter, divided	6	venison steaks or chops
3	tablespoons chopped onion	¼	cup cream
2	tablespoons chopped candied ginger	1	tablespoon currant jelly
½	teaspoon salt		

Cook rice as directed. Stir in 2 tablespoons butter. Sauté onion in 1 tablespoon butter until limp and add to rice. Add ginger, salt and bouillon; cover and simmer 10-15 minutes. Remove to heated platter and keep warm in oven. Fry steaks in 3 tablespoons butter until browned on both sides. Arrange on top of rice and return to warm oven. In the skillet heat the cream, jelly and Sauce Poivrade. Pour part over the top and serve the rest in a sauce boat.

Sauce Poivrade:

3	tablespoons butter, divided	½	cup finely chopped onions
1½	tablespoons flour	¼	cup olive oil
2	cups beef consommé	¼	cup tarragon vinegar
½	cup finely chopped carrots	6	whole peppercorns, crushed

Make a roux using 1½ tablespoons butter and 1½ tablespoons flour. Cook until brown, stirring constantly. Add consommé and boil 4 minutes, stirring. Reduce heat and simmer 30 minutes. Sauté carrots and onions in olive oil. Drain oil and add vinegar. Cook over high heat, stirring constantly, until reduced by ⅓. Add roux and simmer 30 minutes. Add crushed peppercorns and simmer 10 minutes more. Strain and add the remaining butter, stirring until butter has melted.
Yield: 6 servings

Venison Pâté

2	pounds deer steaks	1	teaspoon salt
1	beef bouillon cube	¼	cup brandy
1	tablespoon hot water		bacon slices
	pinch of thyme, marjoram, and sage	2	pounds deer sausage
1	bay leaf		

Grind steaks in a food processor until very fine. Dissolve bouillon cube in hot water. Add spices and brandy and blend into ground deer meat. Place slices of bacon on bottom of an 8½ × 4½" loaf pan and add alternate layers of ground meat and sausage. Finish with ground meat on top, then additional bacon slices. Set pâté pan in a larger pan of cold water. The water level should be half-way up the sides of the pâté pan. Bake at 300° for 1½ hours. Remove from oven and from the water bath. Place a weighted pan on top of meat and allow to cool.
Yield: 10-12 servings

Crab Casserole

¾	cup butter, melted	1	cup milk
2	cups finely chopped onions	1	8-ounce can sliced mushrooms, drained
2	cups chopped celery		
2	teaspoons Worcestershire sauce	1	8-ounce can sliced water chestnuts, drained
	Tabasco sauce, to taste		
2	pounds crab meat	2	cups Hellmann's mayonnaise, slightly thinned with milk
2	cups Pepperidge Farm herb dressing mix, divided		
		¼	cup butter

Sauté the onions and celery in butter until clear. Add Worcestershire and Tabasco. Add crab meat and 1 cup of dressing, softened with the milk. Add mushrooms, water chestnuts and mayonnaise. Mix well. Put into a greased 2 quart casserole. Sprinkle with remaining dry dressing. Dot with remaining butter. Bake at 375° for 20 minutes or just until hot.
Yield: 8 servings

 Can be served in individual shells.

Albert's Baked Stuffed Fish

2½ pounds red snapper or red fish	3 tablespoons unsalted butter,
butter	melted
salt and pepper, to taste	¼ cup chopped onion
paprika	2 tablespoons chopped parsley
2 slices wheat or white bread	¼ cup chopped celery
¼ cup (or more) white wine	1 tablespoon chili sauce

Slit a pocket for stuffing on the back of fish. Rub fish with butter, salt and pepper and sprinkle with paprika. In a very slow oven dry out bread. Crumble and soak in white wine for 10 minutes. Sauté onion, parsley and celery in butter and add to crumbs. Add chili sauce. Season to taste with salt and pepper. Add more wine or milk to make stuffing consistency. Stuff fish, stomach and back cavities. Place in baking dish. Bake at 325° for 50-60 minutes, basting often.

Basting Mixture:

¼ cup unsalted butter	juice of 1 lemon
¼ cup white wine	

Melt butter; add wine and lemon juice. Baste fish.
Yield: 4 servings

Crab Meat Casserole

8 slices day-old bread, divided	4 beaten eggs
2 pounds crab meat	1 teaspoon salt
¾ cup mayonnaise	1 teaspoon seafood seasoning
1 onion, finely chopped	1 10¾-ounce can cream of
1 green pepper, finely chopped	mushroom soup
1 cup celery, finely chopped	1 cup grated American cheese
3 cups milk	paprika, to taste and color

Trim the crusts and dice the bread. Put half the diced bread in a buttered 16″ baking dish. Mix crab meat, mayonnaise, onion, pepper and celery; place the mixture over the bread. Put remaining diced bread on top of crab mixture. Mix milk, eggs and seasonings and pour over casserole. Refrigerate overnight so the bread will absorb the milk. When ready to bake and serve, pour undiluted soup over the top and sprinkle with cheese and paprika. Bake at 325° for 1 hour.
Yield: 10-12 servings

Variation: You may use diced cooked shrimp combined with crab meat.

Crab Meat Remick

1¼ pounds lump crab meat	½ teaspoon Tabasco sauce
7 strips bacon, fried crisp and crumbled	½ cup chili sauce
1 scant teaspoon dry mustard	1 teaspoon tarragon vinegar
½ teaspoon paprika	1½ cups mayonnaise
½ teaspoon celery salt	

Pick crab meat well for shell. Divide into buttered individual shells or ramekins. Heat in 350° oven until warm. Top with crumbled bacon. Mix together mustard, paprika, celery salt and Tabasco. Add chili sauce, vinegar and mayonnaise. Spread the warm crab with the sauce and glaze under the broiler.
Yield: 6 servings

Baked Fish Fillets with Topping

2 pounds thick fillets	lemon juice
salt and lemon pepper	½ cup chopped onion
¾ cup sour cream	¼ cup chopped parsley
¼ cup mayonnaise	

Sprinkle fillets with salt and lemon pepper. Mix sour cream and mayonnaise with a few drops of lemon juice in a separate bowl. Place seasoned fillets in a buttered oven-proof pan or dish. Top with a sprinkling of chopped onions. Spread the sour cream and mayonnaise mixture evenly over the fillets. In a preheated 350° oven, bake the fillets for 30 minutes. Sprinkle with fresh parsley when serving.
Yield: 4 servings

Dolphin Cozumel

4   pounds dolphin fillets
1   cup lemon juice, divided
1   cup mayonnaise

1   tablespoon garlic powder
1   tablespoon Lawry's seasoned
    salt
1   tablespoon dill weed

Marinate fish in ½ cup lemon juice for at least 1 hour. Slice fillets ½″ deep but not completely through. Pour on remaining lemon juice. Spread mayonnaise on entire surface of fish. Sprinkle with garlic powder, seasoned salt and dill. Barbecue for 20 minutes or bake at 350° for l5 minutes, and then brown under broiler.
Yield: 4-6 servings

Variation: Sole, flounder or snapper may be used.

Fiesta Fish

1   l6-ounce box frozen fish (cod,
    perch, etc.)
1   cup small shell macaroni
1   l6-ounce can tomatoes, cut into
    small pieces

½   cup chopped onion
2½ tablespoons taco seasoning mix
1   medium green pepper, cut into
    strips
¼   cup shredded Cheddar or
    Velveeta cheese

Thaw unwrapped fish at room temperature for 20 minutes. Cook macaroni and drain. In medium pan heat undrained tomatoes, onion and taco mix. Add macaroni and green pepper strips and bring to a boil. Pour ⅔ of tomato mix into a l0 × 6 × 2″ baking dish. Fold each fish portion as necessary to fit pan. Spoon remaining sauce over fish. Bake covered at 350° for 35 minutes. Sprinkle cheese over fish and bake for 5 minutes or until cheese melts.
Yield: 3-4 servings

Hauchinango à la Veracruz (Red Snapper)

4   pounds red snapper fillets with
     skin
1½   teaspoons salt, divided
2   tablespoons fresh lime juice
1   large onion, finely sliced
1   minced garlic clove
⅓   cup plus 3 tablespoons olive oil,
     divided

3   pounds fresh tomatoes, peeled,
     seeded and chopped
2   large bay leaves
⅓   teaspoon oregano
16   pitted green olives, halved
3   tablespoons capers
2   canned jalapeños, cut into strips

Preheat oven to 350°. Prick skin of fillets with a fork and rub with 1 teaspoon salt; add the lime juice. Let stand for 20 minutes. Sauté the onion and garlic in ⅓ cup oil. Add the remaining ingredients; simmer for 10 minutes. Place fillets in baking dish and top with sauce. Sprinkle 3 tablespoons oil over sauce and bake for 15-20 minutes or until fish flakes.
Yield: 6 servings

Mustard Trout

6 trout fillets	¼ cup butter
salt and pepper, to taste	1 tablespoon minced parsley
Dijon mustard	juice of 1 lemon
¼ cup cooking oil	lemon wedges

Salt and pepper trout. Spread both sides of fish with mustard. Place trout on greased broiler pan. Bake at 350° for 5-10 minutes. Then baste with oil and broil for 5-10 minutes, depending on thickness of fillets. Cream butter; beat in parsley and lemon juice. Arrange fish on platter and spread with the butter. Garnish with lemon wedges.
Yield: 6 serving

Our Favorite Fish

2 trout fillets	2 tablespoons vegetable oil
3-4 chopped green onions, some	2 tablespoons soy sauce
tops included	

Place fish on a steam tray in a skillet with 1-2″ of water below; cover and steam for approximately 10 minutes. While the fish is steaming, heat the oil. When fish is done, sprinkle the onions over and then pour remaining hot oil over the fish and onions. Quickly pour soy sauce over fish and serve immediately.
Yield: 2 servings

Variation: Can substitute red fish or red snapper.

Redfish à la Winston

4 redfish or snapper fillets	1 8-ounce can artichoke hearts,
3 tablespoons butter	drained
salt and pepper, to taste	juice of 2 lemons
8-l0 fresh mushrooms, sliced	1 teaspoon Worcestershire sauce

Pre-soak fish in lemon water. Skin, dredge in flour and shake off excess. Melt butter in skillet, then sauté until fish is brown on one side. Turn and lightly salt and pepper. When fish flakes, remove from skillet and place on warmed serving platter while completing preparation. Add mushrooms and artichokes to the butter in the bottom of the skillet and heat. Sprinkle lemon juice over all and add Worcestershire. When blended, place mushrooms and artichokes over fillets. Add a little hot water to remaining juices in skillet and pour over fish.
Yield: 4 servings

Baked Oysters

2 dozen large oysters	½ teaspoon onion salt
1 cup Italian bread crumbs	dash cayenne pepper
½ teaspoon garlic salt	½ cup margarine

Pat oysters dry. Combine crumbs and seaonings. Dip oysters in mix and let set 5-10 minutes. Melt margarine and dribble over oysters. Bake at 400° for 12 minutes.
Yield: 2 servings

Chicken-Oyster Bake

1   3-3½ pound chicken, cut into
    pieces
    salad oil
2   tablespoons chopped onion
1   garlic clove, minced
1   cup water
1   4-ounce can sliced mushrooms,
    undrained
1   tablespoon Worcestershire
    sauce

1   10¾-ounce can cream of
    mushroom soup, undiluted
½   cup sour cream
½   teaspoon red pepper
2   pints oysters, drained
    cooked rice
4-6 slices bacon, fried crisp and
    crumbled

Lightly brown chicken pieces in oil in a skillet. Remove and place in a shallow 2 quart casserole. Sauté onion and garlic in pan drippings until tender. Remove from heat and add remaining ingredients except oysters and bacon. Pour mixture over chicken. Cover and bake at 350° for 45 minutes. Uncover and stir in oysters. Bake for 15 minutes. Serve over rice and top with bacon.
Yield: 6 servings

Salmon Croquettes

1   16-ounce can red salmon,
    drained
½   cup buttermilk
½   cup flour
2   eggs, beaten

1   small onion, finely chopped
¼   teaspoon soda
1   cup cracker crumbs
    salt and pepper, to taste

Remove bones and skin from salmon and flake well. Add rest of ingredients. Shape into croquettes and roll in additional cracker crumbs. Fry in hot grease.
Yield: 6 servings

Salmon Loaf with Dill Sauce

1   16-ounce can red salmon with
    liquid
1   10¾-ounce can cream of celery
    soup
1   cup dry bread crumbs

2   eggs, slightly beaten
½   cup chopped onion
1   tablespoon lemon juice

Debone and flake salmon. Mix celery soup, bread crumbs, eggs, chopped onion and lemon juice. Place in greased 4½ × 8½″ loaf pan. Bake at 350° for 1 hour.

Sauce:

1   10 ¾-ounce can cream of celery
    soup

⅓   cup sour cream
1-2 teaspoons dill weed

Mix soup and sour cream. Add dill weed and heat gently. Serve over salmon loaf.
Yield: 6 servings

Scallops Provencal

¼	cup minced onion	1	tablespoon chopped fresh parsley
1	garlic clove, minced		freshly ground pepper, to taste
¼	cup olive oil	1½	pounds bay scallops
¼	cup quartered black olives	½	cup white wine
1¼	cups diced fresh tomatoes	2	tablespoon capers, optional
1	teaspoon fresh thyme or ½ teaspoon dried pinch of rosemary		

Sauté onion and garlic in oil. Add ingredients through pepper. Bring to a boil. Put scallops in greased shallow baking dish. Stir wine into sauce and pour over scallops. Bake covered at 375° for 15 minutes. Sprinkle with capers before serving.
Yield: 4 servings

 Can be done in a skillet, simmering for about 10-12 minutes.

Artichoke and Shrimp Supreme

2	cans artichoke hearts, drained	2	tablespoons Worcestershire sauce
1½	pounds cooked shrimp	½	cup dry sherry
10	tablespoons butter, divided		salt and pepper, to taste
½	pound mushrooms, sliced	½	cup grated Parmesan cheese
6	tablespoons flour		paprika
2	cups half and half		

Layer artichokes in a buttered baking dish. Put shrimp on top of artichokes. Melt 4 tablespoons of butter and sauté the mushrooms. Put on top of shrimp. Make a cream sauce with remaining butter, flour and half and half. Add Worcestershire, sherry, salt and pepper. Pour over the shrimp-artichoke mixture. Top with Parmesan and paprika. Bake at 375° for 30-40 minutes.
Yield: 8-10 servings

Baked Stuffed Shrimp

16	large raw shrimp	2	teaspoons parsley, chopped
½	pound fresh crab meat	¼	teaspoon Worcestershire sauce
3	slices stale bread, finely crumbled	3-5	drops Tabasco sauce
¼	cup finely chopped celery	2½	tablespoons mayonnaise paprika
1	tablespoon pimiento, finely chopped	½	cup butter
		2	garlic cloves, minced

Clean and butterfly shrimp. Combine crab meat, bread crumbs, celery, pimiento, parsley, Worcestershire, Tabasco and mayonnaise. Place a heaping tablespoon on top of each shrimp. Sprinkle each with paprika. In a small skillet, melt butter and add minced garlic. Sauté for 3 minutes. Place shrimp in baking dish and pour garlic butter over and around shrimp. Bake in 400° oven for 12 minutes. Spoon garlic butter on shrimp and serve.
Yield: 4 servings

Broiled Shrimp

½ teaspoon salt
¼ teaspoon cayenne pepper
1 tablespoon Pickapeppa sauce
½ cup melted butter

2 tablespoons Worcestershire sauce
3 tablespoons lemon juice
2 pounds shrimp, peeled and deveined

Simmer all ingredients but shrimp for 5 minutes. Pour over shrimp in a baking dish. Broil for 16-18 minutes, turning once.
Yield: 6 servings

Shrimp Creole

5 pounds cleaned and cooked shrimp
4 tablespoons fresh bacon drippings
2 large onions, chopped
1 large green pepper, chopped
4 rounded tablespoons flour
1 17-ounce can Del Monte tomato wedges with juice

1 12-ounce bottle Heinz chili sauce
2 tablespoons Worcestershire sauce
1 15-ounce can tomato sauce
½ teaspoon salt
   ground pepper, to taste
   Tabasco sauce, to taste
1-2 pinches of basil
1 7-ounce can tomato sauce

Sauté onions and green pepper in bacon drippings until soft and clear. Add flour and mix, adding more grease if necessary. Cook briefly but do not brown flour. Add remaining ingredients except for shrimp and small can of tomato sauce. Blend and simmer gently for 30-40 minutes. Add shrimp and continue to cook for 2-3 minutes. Add more tomato sauce if it is too thick.
Yield: 8-10 servings

Shrimp à la New Orleans

5 pounds raw shrimp
1 cup salad oil
1 cup vinegar
1½ teaspoons salt
2 teaspoons celery seed

1 garlic clove, crushed
2 tablespoons capers
2 tablespoons horseradish
7 bay leaves
2 large onions, sliced

Boil shrimp in salted water for 10 minutes. Clean and devein. Mix next eight ingredients to make sauce. Layer shrimp and sliced onion in a large bowl. Pour sauce over shrimp. Cover and marinate for 3-4 days in refrigerator. Drain before serving.
Yield: 6-8 servings

Zat's Barbecued Shrimp

5 pounds medium raw shrimp	2 heaping tablespoons Cavender's
1 pound butter or margarine, melted	Greek Seasoning
2 heaping tablespoons black pepper	2 tablespoons soy sauce
	3 tablespoons Worcestershire sauce
	juice of 2 lemons

Place shrimp in a large shallow baking dish. Combine remaining ingredients and pour over shrimp. Bake at 350° for 20-30 minutes.
Yield: 6 servings

 Shrimp are served hot in sauce and peeled at table. Dip hot French bread into sauce.

Shrimp and Crab Coquille

½ cup green onions, chopped	1 cup dry white wine
1 garlic clove, minced	1½ pounds shrimp, boiled and cleaned
1 cup celery, chopped	1 pound crab meat
12 tablespoons butter, melted and divided	1 cup bread crumbs
½ cup flour	8 tablespoons Swiss cheese, grated
3 cups light cream	8 tablespoons parsley, chopped

Sauté vegetables in 4 tablespoons butter until limp. Add flour and stir for 2 minutes. Remove from heat and stir in cream all at once. Return to heat and stir constantly as you bring the mixture to a boil. Boil one minute, continuing to stir. Add wine, shrimp and crab meat. Put in individual buttered shells or 9×13" casserole. Combine bread crumbs, cheese, parsley and remaining butter. Top seafood with crumb mixture. Bake at 350° for 20 minutes.
Yield: 8-10 servings

Seafood Quiche

1 unbaked deep-dish pie shell	½ cup green onions, finely chopped
1 6½-ounce can tuna, drained	3 eggs
2 6½-ounce cans crab meat or fresh crab	¾ cup mayonnaise
1½ cups shredded Swiss cheese	¾ cup milk
1 4-ounce can sliced mushrooms, drained	

Preheat oven to 400°. Thaw pie shell for 20 minutes if using a frozen shell. Bake for 10-12 minutes. Remove from oven and lower temperature to 375°. Toss tuna, crab, cheese, mushrooms and onions; spoon into shell. In medium bowl, beat eggs, mayonnaise and milk until smooth. Gradually pour over cheese/seafood mixture. Bake for 45-50 minutes until golden and knife inserted into center is clean.
Yield: 6-8 servings

Variation: Shrimp or scallops may be used.

Seafood au Gratin

1 large onion, chopped	6-8 drops Tabasco sauce
1 bunch green onions, chopped	4 tablespoons Worcestershire
1 cup chopped celery	sauce
½ cup chopped green pepper	1 teaspoon salt
2 cups fresh mushrooms, sliced	cayenne pepper, to taste
6 tablespoons melted butter	2 pounds shrimp, cooked and
1 10¾-ounce can cream of	cleaned
mushroom soup	1 pound lump crab meat
1 10¾-ounce can cream of	1 I6-ounce can artichoke hearts,
chicken soup	drained
2 cups mayonnaise	8 ounces sharp Cheddar cheese,
1 cup cream	grated

Sauté onions, celery, green pepper and mushrooms in melted butter. Stir in soups, mayonnaise, cream and seasonings. Cook and stir until well blended. Add shrimp, crab meat and artichokes, stirring gently. Pour into large greased casserole and cover with cheese. Bake at 325° for 30-45 minutes. Serve over rice.
Yield: I2 servings

Shrimp Quiche

1 bay leaf	2 tablespoons of oil
½ teaspoon thyme	½ cup chopped onions
1 garlic clove	4 eggs, beaten
1 teaspoon white peppercorns	¼ teaspoon white pepper
2½ teaspoons salt	salt, to taste
2 thin slices of lemon	9″ pie shell, partially baked
1 dried red pepper	2 tablespoons grated Parmesan
4 quarts of water	cheese
1 pound shrimp, unpeeled	½ cup grated Gruyère cheese
1½ cups whipping cream	1 cup watercress

Preheat oven to 375°. Put the first 8 ingredients into a large saucepan and boil for 5 minutes. Add the shrimp. When the water returns to a boil, turn off heat; cover and let stand for 3-5 minutes. Drain; rinse under cool water and peel. Reserve 3 whole shrimp and coarsely chop the remaining shrimp. Mix the shrimp and cream in a glass bowl; cover and refrigerate for 2-3 hours. Heat oil and sauté onions for 4-5 minutes. Stir onion into shrimp mixture and add eggs. Season with pepper and salt. Pour into pie shell and sprinkle cheeses on top. Place on a baking sheet on the bottom shelf of the oven and bake for 25-30 minutes. Let stand for 10 minutes before cutting. Garnish with reserved whole shrimp and watercress.
Yield: 8 servings

Quiche Brotagne

½	cup mayonnaise	3	ounces small shrimp, cooked and peeled
2	tablespoons flour	1	small celery rib, sliced
2	eggs, beaten	5	green onions, chopped
½	cup white wine	2	cups grated Swiss cheese
1	6½-ounce can crab meat, drained	1	9" baked pie shell

Blend mayonnaise, flour, eggs and wine. Stir in crab meat, shrimp, celery, onions and cheese. Pour into crust and bake at 350° for 35 minutes or until done. May be prepared ahead and frozen.
Yield: 6 servings

Seafood Casserole

½	cup butter or margarine melted	1	teaspoon Worcestershire sauce
1	medium onion, finely chopped		dash of cayenne pepper and black pepper
1	green pepper, finely chopped	1	8-ounce package Pepperidge Farm dressing mix
½	cup mayonnaise	1	pound cooked and cleaned shrimp
1	10¾-ounce can cream of mushroom soup	1	pound crab meat
1½	soup cans of water		
1	tablespoon prepared mustard		

Sauté onion and green pepper in butter. Mix in mayonnaise, soup, water, mustard, Worcestershire, cayenne pepper and black pepper. Carefully add the dressing mix, shrimp and crab meat. Put into a 2 quart casserole and bake at 350° for 35-40 minutes with foil laid loosely on top.
Yield: 8-10 servings

Sherried Seafood

6	tablespoons butter	12	ounces fresh or frozen crab meat
7	tablespoons flour	½	pound shrimp, cooked and peeled
3	cups milk	1	14-ounce can artichoke hearts, drained
6	tablespoons dry sherry	3	tablespoons lemon juice
1¼	teaspoons salt	1	cup grated sharp Cheddar cheese
⅛	teaspoon pepper		
1	tablespoon Worcestershire sauce		

In saucepan, melt the butter and blend with flour. Gradually stir in milk and cook until thickened. Stir in sherry, salt, pepper and Worcestershire. Layer crab, shrimp and artichokes in a greased 11 × 7" baking dish. Sprinkle with lemon juice. Top with sauce and cover with grated cheese. Bake at 350° for 30 minutes.
Yield: 8 servings

 May be prepared ahead.

Rémoulade Sauce

6 hard-boiled egg yolks, finely mashed
4 garlic cloves, finely chopped
3 tablespoons Zatarain's creole mustard
1 quart mayonnaise
4 tablespoons prepared mustard
3 tablespoons horseradish
2 tablespoons Worcestershire sauce
dash of Tabasco sauce
4 tablespoons vinegar
4 tablespoons chopped parsley

Blend well and store in the refrigerator.
Yield: 1½ quarts

Instant Rémoulade Sauce

mayonnaise   Zatarain's creole mustard

Combine equal parts of mayonnaise and mustard. Mix well. Good over boiled, peeled cold shrimp.

Desserts

Chocolate Chess Pie

3 cups sugar	pinch of salt
6 tablespoons cocoa	2 5-ounce cans evaporated milk
1 stick butter, melted	Cool Whip or whipped cream,
4 eggs, beaten	optional
2 teaspoons vanilla	

Preheat oven to 350°. Prepare 2 8" unbaked pie shells. Mix sugar and cocoa; stir in butter; add eggs and mix well. Add vanilla, salt and milk. Pour into pie shells. Bake for 45 minutes. Use a dollop of Cool Whip or whipped cream for garnish, if desired.
Yield: 2 pies

 These freeze well.

Chocolate Layered Pie

1 baked 9" pie shell	1 teaspoon vinegar
2 egg whites	½ cup sugar
¼ teaspoon cinnamon	

Meringue Layer:

Preheat oven to 325°. Beat egg whites, cinnamon and vinegar until foamy. Gradually add sugar, beating until stiff peaks form. Spread this on sides and bottom of pie shell. Bake until browned, about 15 minutes. Let cool.

Filling:

1 6-ounce package chocolate chips, melted	1 cup whipping cream
2 egg yolks, beaten	¼ cup sugar
¼ cup cold water	¼ teaspoon cinnamon

Combine chocolate, egg yolks and water, beating until smooth. Spread 3 tablespoons of mixture over meringue. Whip cream until thick, slowly adding sugar and cinnamon until stiff. Spread ½ of it over the chocolate. Fold the remaining chocolate into the reserved whipped cream and spread on top. Refrigerate for 4 hours before serving. Store in refrigerator.
Yield: 8-10 servings

Green Parrot Fudge Pie

1 9" unbaked pie shell	6 tablespoons butter, melted
4 eggs	1 teaspoon lemon juice
2 cups sugar	1 cup pecans, coarsely chopped
3 squares unsweetened chocolate, melted	

Preheat oven to 360°. Beat eggs; slowly blend in sugar. Add chocolate, butter, lemon juice and pecans. Pour into pie shell; bake for 30 minutes. Pie should be "shaky" when removed from oven. Do not chill.
Yield: 8-10 servings

Chocolate Mousse Pie

1   **15-ounce package Keebler Fudge Cookies**   ½   **stick butter, melted**

Preheat oven to 350°. Chop cookies in blender, add butter and mix well. Press mixture on bottom of 10" springform pan. Bake for 10 minutes.

Filling:

1   **12-ounce package Nestle's semi-sweet chocolate chips, melted**
4   **egg yolks**
2   **eggs**

3   **egg whites**
3   **cups whipping cream, divided**
1   **teaspoon vanilla, rum or Kahlúa**
    chocolate shavings

Beat egg yolks and whole eggs together; slowly add to melted chocolate. Beat egg whites until stiff peaks form. Whip 2 cups cream; add flavoring. Fold together the egg whites, cream and chocolate mixture. Pour into crust. Whip 1 cup cream, spread over pie, garnish with chocolate shavings and refrigerate.
Yield: 10-12 servings

Chocolate Walnut Pie

1   **10" pie shell, unbaked**
1   **cup brown sugar**
2   **tablespoons flour**
3   **tablespoons butter, softened**
1   **cup light corn syrup**
3   **eggs, beaten**

¼-½   **teaspoon salt**
1   **teaspoon vanilla**
1   **generous cup walnut pieces**
1   **ounce square Baker's chocolate, grated, or 6-ounce package of semi-sweet chocolate chips**

Preheat oven to 325°. Mix sugar and flour; cream butter into sugar mixture. Add corn syrup and eggs; beat until frothy. Add salt, vanilla, nuts and grated chocolate; pour into pie shell and bake for 40 minutes. If chocolate chips are used, sprinkle over bottom of pie shell and pour pie mixture over.
Yield: 10-12 servings

Variation: ½ cup sugar, ½ cup packed brown sugar, ½ cup flour, 1 cup melted butter or margarine, 1 cup chocolate chips, 1 cup chopped pecans and 2 eggs in a 9" pie shell. Bake at 350° for 1 hour.

Dewberry Cream Pie

1 unbaked 10″ pie shell	1-1½ pints dewberries or blackberries to fill crust

Mound berries in unbaked crust. Preheat oven to 325°-350°.

Filling:

2 eggs, beaten	½ cup heavy cream or sour cream
1½ cups sugar	or crème fraîche
½ cup flour	pinch of salt

Combine ingredients in order, mixing thoroughly. Pour over berries.

Topping:

8 tablespoons flour	4 tablespoons butter
8 tablespoons sugar	

Mix ingredients until crumbly. Sprinkle over top of berries. Bake pie on a cookie sheet for 30-45 minutes.
Yield: 10-12 servings

Peanut Butter Pie

1 10″ baked pie shell	½ cup crunchy peanut butter
1 cup powdered sugar	

Preheat oven to 325°. Mix sugar and peanut butter well. Spread ½ cup of this mixture on pie shell.

Filling:

¼ cup corn starch	2 tablespoons butter
⅔ cup sugar	¼ teaspoon vanilla
¼ teaspoon salt	3 egg whites, beaten
2 cups milk, scalded	1½ tablespoons sugar
3 egg yolks, beaten	

In top of double boiler, mix cornstarch, sugar and salt. Slowly add milk, mixing well. Gradually pour small amount over egg yolks, then return to milk mixture. Cook over boiling water until it thickens; add butter and vanilla. Cook until thick. Pour into pie shell over peanut butter layer. Beat egg whites and gradually add sugar until stiff peaks form. Top pie with meringue. Sprinkle remainder of peanut butter mixture over meringue. Bake until brown.
Yield: 10-12 servings

Pineapple Ice Box Pie

1 baked 9" pie shell or 8 tart shells	1 tablespoon sugar
	2 cups sour cream
1 8-ounce can crushed pineapple with juice	1 5.5-ounce box Jello instant vanilla pudding

Mix all ingredients in order, stirring well after each entry. Pour into cold pie shell or tart shells.
Yield: 8 servings

Raleigh House Buttermilk Pie

1 stick butter or margarine, softened	1 cup buttermilk
	dash of nutmeg
2 cups sugar	1 teaspoon vanilla
3 eggs	1 unbaked 9" pie shell
3 rounded tablespoons flour	

Preheat oven to 350°. Mix margarine and sugar well; add eggs and flour, mixing well. Add buttermilk, nutmeg and vanilla. Pour into an unbaked pie shell and bake for 45 minutes. Freezes well.
Yield: 8-10 servings

Sour Cream Peach Pie

2 cups crushed vanilla wafer crumbs	6 tablespoons butter, melted
	¼ cup sugar

Mix all ingredients and press into 9" pie pan.

Filling:

2 16-ounce cans Elberta peach halves, drained	¼ cup brown sugar
	1 heaping tablespoon flour
1½ cups sour cream	freshly ground nutmeg
¼ cup sugar	

Preheat oven to 300°. Arrange peach halves, pit side up, over crust. Mix sour cream, sugar and flour together. Put a dollop of the mixture in each peach half. Pour remainder of mixture over all. Grate nutmeg over top of pie. Bake for 45 minutes. Serve warm.
Yield: 6-8 servings

Blackberry Wine Cake

1 Duncan Hines white cake mix
1 3-ounce box blackberry Jello
½ cup salad oil
4 eggs

1 cup Mogen David blackberry wine
½ cup chopped pecans

Preheat oven to 325°. Combine all ingredients except pecans. Mix on low speed until moistened, then on high for 2 minutes. Grease and flour a 10″ bundt pan. Sprinkle pecans on bottom and sides of pan. Spoon batter over pecans. Bake for 1 hour.

Glaze:
½ cup butter
1 cup powdered sugar

½ cup Mogen David blackberry wine

Combine butter, sugar and wine; bring to a boil. Punch holes in cake with ice pick and pour half of glaze over cake while still in pan. Let stand 30 minutes. Turn out and pour remaining glaze over cake.

Chocolate Cake

1 Duncan Hines butter cake mix
1 4-ounce box instant chocolate pudding mix
1 cup sour cream
½ cup Wesson oil

1 tablespoon vanilla
4-5 tablespoons rum
4 eggs
6 ounces chocolate chips
1 cup chopped nuts

Preheat oven to 325°. Combine cake mix, pudding mix, sour cream, oil, vanilla and rum. Add eggs one at a time, beating after each. Add chocolate chips and nuts. Pour into a well-greased and floured bundt pan. Bake for 1 hour or until done.

Chocolate Fleck Cake

1 yellow or white cake mix

⅓ cup chocolate sprinkles

Prepare cake according to box directions; fold in chocolate sprinkles. Bake in two 8″ or 9″ prepared cake pans. Cool before frosting.

Frosting:
1½ cups heavy cream
⅔ cup Nestle's instant cocoa

¼ cup chopped pecans or walnuts

Combine cream and cocoa; chill, then whip. Frost cake, sprinkling nuts between layers. Chill.

3-5 Day Coconut Cake

1   white cake mix

Follow directions to bake two layers. Cool, then cut the two layers in half to make four layers.

Filling:

1   cup sugar
1   12 or 16-ounce package frozen coconut

2   cups sour cream
1   12-ounce carton Cool Whip

Blend well the sugar, coconut and sour cream. Set aside one cup of filling. Spread filling generously on three layers. To the one cup of reserved filling, add the Cool Whip. Ice top and sides generously. Cover with cake cover and store in refrigerator 3-5 days before serving.

Coconut Pound Cake

1   Pillsbury yellow cake mix
¼   cup salad oil
3   eggs, beaten
8   ounces cream of coconut

2   teaspoons vanilla
1   cup sour cream
1   cup angel flaked coconut, slightly chopped

Preheat oven to 325°. Combine cake mix, salad oil, eggs, cream of coconut, vanilla and sour cream; mix well. Add coconut. Pour into well-greased and floured bundt pan. Bake for 1 hour and 15 minutes or until tests done. Cool before removing from pan.

Hot Milk Sponge Cake

6   eggs
2   cups sugar
2   teaspoons vanilla

2   cups flour
2   teaspoons baking powder
⅔   cup milk, heated

Preheat oven to 350°. Beat eggs in an electric mixer on high speed for 10 minutes until thick and lemon colored. Sift sugar and gradually add to eggs, continuing to beat vigorously. Add vanilla. Sift flour and baking powder together three times and gradually add to egg and sugar mixture. While mixing the other ingredients, heat the milk slowly; do not let it boil. Add milk to mixture gradually. Pour into a tube pan that is totally free of grease or oil. Bake for 1 hour. When done, turn upside down on a bottle until cool. Remove from pan and frost with favorite frosting, whipped cream, your favorite fruit or a combination of these.

Lemon Carrot Cake

1	9-ounce package condensed None Such mincemeat, crumbled	¾	cup vegetable oil
2	cups finely shredded carrots	¼	cup lemon juice
½	cup chopped nuts	3	eggs
2	cups unsifted flour, divided	2	teaspoons baking powder
1	cup light brown sugar, packed	1	teaspoon baking soda
		1	teaspoon salt

Preheat oven to 325°. Combine mincemeat, carrots and nuts. Toss with ½ cup flour. Set aside. In mixer bowl combine brown sugar, oil, lemon juice and eggs — one at a time, beating after each addition. Sift together remaining 1½ cups of flour, baking powder, soda and salt, gradually adding to batter and beating until smooth. Stir in mincemeat mixture and mix well. Pour into well-greased and floured 10″ bundt or tube pan. Bake for 1 hour. Cool 15 minutes. Remove from pan and drizzle glaze over top of cake.

Glaze:

2	tablespoons butter	1	cup powdered sugar
4	teaspoons ReaLemon lemon juice		

In a small saucepan melt butter; add lemon juice and sugar. Mix well.

Mace Pound Cake

1	cup butter	2	cups sifted flour
1⅔	cups sugar	1	teaspoon mace
5	eggs	1	teaspoon vanilla

Preheat oven to 325°. Cream butter and sugar until light and fluffy. Add eggs one at a time, mixing well. Add flour and mace; beat until batter is smooth. Add vanilla. Pour into a well-greased and floured tube pan. Bake for 30-40 minutes or until done.

Old Fashioned Shortcake

2	cups flour	3	tablespoons shortening
4	teaspoons baking powder	1	egg
½	cup sugar	½	cup milk
½	teaspoon salt		

Preheat oven to 350°. Sift together flour, baking powder, sugar and salt. Mix in shortening; beat egg and milk together and add to dry ingredients to make a soft dough. Pour into well-greased 8″ square pan. Bake for 20-25 minutes. Cool and cut into squares. Slice in half and fill with berries, crushed and sweetened.

Pound Cake

1	cup butter	1	teaspoon lemon extract
3	cups sugar	3	cups sifted cake flour
6	eggs	1	cup whipping cream
1	tablespoon vanilla		

Preheat oven to 315°. Cream butter and sugar until light and fluffy. Add eggs two at a time. Add vanilla and lemon extract. Alternate whipping cream and flour in three portions, beginning with cream. Pour into a well-greased and floured tube pan. Bake for 1 hour or until done.

Black Russian Cake

1	Duncan Hines deep chocolate cake mix	4	eggs, room temperature
½	cup salad oil	¾	cup strong coffee
1	4½-ounce box instant chocolate pudding mix	¾	cup Kahlúa and Crème de Cacao, combined

Preheat over to 350°. Combine cake mix, oil, pudding, eggs, Kahlúa and Crème de Cacao in a large bowl. Beat 4 minutes on medium speed until smooth. Spoon into a well-greased bundt pan. Bake for 45-50 minutes. Cool slightly before removing from pan.

Topping:

1	cup powdered sugar, sifted	2	tablespoons Kahlúa
2	tablespoons strong coffee	2	tablespoons Crème de Cacao

Combine all ingredients, beating well until smooth. Pour topping over warm cake.

Toffee Nut Cake

2	cups flour	1	teaspoon baking soda
½	teaspoon salt	1	cup sour cream
1	teaspoon cinnamon	1	egg
¼	teaspoon nutmeg	½	cup chopped nuts
2	cups brown sugar		sweetened whipped cream, optional
½	cup butter		
2	fresh Bartlett pears, cored, cut into eighths		

Preheat oven to 350°. Grease generously a 9″ square baking pan. Sift flour, salt, cinnamon and nutmeg. Mix in brown sugar. Cut in butter until crumbly. Spoon in half the flour-butter mixture and press evenly over bottom of pan. Arrange pear slices over flour-butter mixture. Mix soda and sour cream; add to remaining flour mixture. Mix in egg. Pour batter over pear slices and spread evenly. Sprinkle with nuts. Bake for 40-50 minutes. Serve warm with whipped cream, if desired.

White Chocolate Cake

4 ounces white chocolate	1 teaspoon soda
½ cup hot water	1 teaspoon salt
1 pound butter	1 cup buttermilk
2 cups sugar	4 egg whites, stiffly beaten
4 egg yolks	1 cup flaked coconut
1 teaspoon vanilla	1 cup chopped pecans
2½ cups sifted cake flour	

Preheat oven to 350°. Melt chocolate in the hot water. Cool. Cream butter and sugar and add egg yolks, one at a time. Add the cooled, melted chocolate and vanilla. Sift flour, soda and salt together and add alternately with buttermilk. Do not overbeat. Fold in stiffly beaten egg whites. Gently stir in coconut and pecans. Pour into 3 well-greased and floured 9″ cake pans. Divide batter evenly between pans. Bake for 25-30 minutes. Cool layers before frosting.

Icing:

⅔ cup evaporated milk	3 egg yolks, beaten
1 cup sugar	1 cup flaked coconut
¼ cup butter	1 cup chopped nuts
1 teaspoon vanilla	

Combine milk, sugar, butter, vanilla and egg yolks. Cook over low heat, about 15 minutes, stirring constantly. Remove from heat; add coconut and nuts. Beat until creamy. Spread between layers and over top of cake.

Bourbon Sauce

1 cup sugar	1 cup boiling water
1 tablespoon flour, well rounded	½-1 cup bourbon, or to taste
½ stick butter or margarine, melted	

Blend sugar, flour and butter thoroughly in saucepan; then pour in boiling water. Stir constantly while cooking over low heat until mixture thickens. Add bourbon to taste. Pour over slice of cake while warm.

Four-Minute Icing

2 unbeaten egg whites	¼ teaspoon cream of tartar
1½ cups sugar	1 tablespoon white corn syrup
3 tablespoons water	1 teaspoon vanilla

Fill bottom of double boiler with water and bring to boil. In boiler top combine egg whites, sugar, water, cream of tartar, corn syrup and vanilla. Turn off heat and with electric mixer, over the hot water, beat 4 minutes. Spread on 2 layers of 8 or 9″ cake.

Marsala Cream Liqueur

2 cups sugar	1¼ cups vodka
1 cup water	¾ cup Marsala or dry sherry
5 egg yolks	1 teaspoon vanilla
1 cup half and half	cinnamon stick, optional

In a saucepan mix sugar and water to make a simple syrup. Stir over medium heat until boiling. Reduce heat and simmer until sugar dissolves. Set aside to cool. Beat egg yolks in a double boiler over boiling water and slowly blend in cream, stirring constantly until mixture thickens — about 5 minutes. If mixture is not smooth, cool and beat in a blender until smooth. Stir in 1½ cups simple syrup, vodka, wine and vanilla. May be stored in refrigerator up to 6 weeks, shaking 2-3 times a week until there is no separation. Add cinnamon stick during storage. Use over cake, puddings or ice cream.

Ultimate Sour Cream Icing

1 stick margarine	2 1-ounce squares bitter chocolate
1 cup sour cream	dash of salt
1 cup brown sugar, packed	1 teaspoon vanilla
1 cup white sugar	2-3 tablespoons cream for thinning

Place margarine, sour cream, sugars, chocolate and salt in a pan that has a cover. Stir only until sugar dissolves. Bring to a boil and cook 3 minutes. Put lid on and cook 3 minutes longer. Remove from fire; put pan in cold water bath until cooled to 155°. Add vanilla and beat until ready to spread. If icing hardens too fast, add cream by teaspoons for thinning.
Yield: Frosting for two 9" layers

Fresh Strawberry Topping

1 quart fresh strawberries	juice of ½ lemon
4 cups sugar, divided	

Remove stems and halve strawberries. Add 2 cups sugar and lemon juice to strawberries. Let stand a few minutes to extract juice from berries. Place in a pan and bring to a full boil for 4 minutes. Slowly add 2 cups sugar; bring to rolling boil and cook 4 minutes. Pour into a crock. Let stand for 24 hours; "push down" frequently. Refrigerate in glass jars.
Yield: 1 quart

Oreo Cheesecake

1¼ cups graham cracker crumbs	¼ cup brown sugar, firmly packed
⅓ cup unsalted butter, melted	1 teaspoon cinnamon

Blend graham cracker crumbs, butter, brown sugar and cinnamon. Press into bottom and sides of 9" or 10" springform pan. Refrigerate until firm.

Filling:

4 8-ounce packages cream cheese, softened	⅓ cup whipping cream
1½ cups sugar, divided	2 teaspoons vanilla, divided
2 tablespoons flour	1½ cups coarsely crushed oreo cookies
4 extra large eggs	2 cups sour cream
2 large egg yolks	

Preheat oven to 425°. Use electric mixer. In a large bowl mix cream cheese and 1¼ cups sugar until well blended. Add flour and mix well. Add eggs and yolks, beating one at a time until smooth. Add cream and 1 teaspoon vanilla. Pour half of batter into prepared crust. Sprinkle with oreo cookie crumbs. Pour remaining batter over crumbs, smoothing with a spatula. Bake for 15 minutes. Reduce oven to 225°and bake for 50 minutes. Cover top with foil if it is browning too quickly. Remove cake from oven and increase heat to 350°. In a small bowl, blend sour cream, ¼ cup sugar and 1 teaspoon vanilla. Spread over cake. Bake for 7 minutes. Refrigerate immediately, covered with plastic wrap. Chill overnight.

Glaze:

1 cup whipping cream	1 teaspoon vanilla
8 ounces semi-sweet chocolate, chopped	5 oreo cookies, halved crosswise
	1 maraschino cherry, halved

Scald cream in heavy saucepan over high heat. Add chocolate and vanilla. Stir 1 minute; remove from heat and stir until chocolate is melted. Refrigerate 10 minutes. Set cake on platter. Remove from springform pan. Pour glaze over top. Arrange oreo halves, cut side down, around outer edge of cake. Place cherry halves in center.

 Prepare a day ahead; glaze shortly before serving.

Cheesecake Miniatures

20 vanilla wafers	2 eggs
2 8-ounce packages cream cheese, softened	1 teaspoon vanilla
¾ cup sugar	2 cans of cherry or blueberry pie filling

Preheat oven to 375°. Line 20 muffin cups with paper liners. Place a vanilla wafer on bottom of each liner. Beat cream cheese and sugar. Add eggs and vanilla. Beat until well blended. Fill muffin cups ¾ full and bake for 10 minutes. Can be frozen. When ready to use, top with pie filling and whipped cream.

Yield: 20 miniatures

Cream Cheese Squares

1   box yellow cake mix   1   stick butter, melted
1   egg, beaten

Preheat oven to 325°. Combine cake mix, egg and butter. Mix well. Spread mixture in buttered 9 × 13″ pan.

Filling:
1   8-ounce package cream cheese,   1¼ cups powdered sugar, divided
    softened   1   teaspoon vanilla
2   eggs, beaten   pinch of salt
1   cup brown sugar, packed

Combine cream cheese, eggs, brown sugar and 1 cup powdered sugar; beat until smooth. Pour cream cheese mixture over cake mixture. Bake for 45 minutes or until golden brown. Sift remaining powdered sugar over top and cut into squares.
Yield: Approximately 3 dozen squares

Light and Easy Cheesecake

1¼ cups graham cracker crumbs   ⅓ cup butter, melted

Preheat oven to 350°. Lightly spray 10″ springform pan with Pam. Mix graham cracker crumbs and butter. Press into bottom of pan.

Filling:
6   large egg whites   3   8-ounce packages cream
1   cup sugar   cheese, softened
1   teaspoon vanilla

Beat egg whites until stiff. Add sugar and vanilla. Add cream cheese and beat until smooth and creamy. Pour over crust and bake for 25 minutes. Remove from oven. Increase heat to 425°.

Topping:
2   cups sour cream   1½ teaspoons vanilla
2   tablespoons sugar

Mix sour cream, sugar and vanilla. Pour over cake, spread from outside to center. Return to oven for 5 minutes. Cool to room temperature. Cover and refrigerate overnight before serving.
Yield: 12-14 servings

 It is best to make this a day ahead.

New York Cheesecake

graham cracker crumbs, crushed
fine
16 ounces small curd cottage
cheese, dry as possible
2 8-ounce packages cream
cheese, softened
1½ cups sugar
4 eggs, slightly beaten
⅓ cup cornstarch
2 tablespoons lemon juice
1 teaspoon vanilla
½ cup margarine, melted
1 pint sour cream

Preheat oven to 325°. Grease 9″ springform pan; dust with graham cracker crumbs. Sieve cottage cheese into large mixing bowl; add cream cheese; beat on high speed of electric mixer until well blended and creamy. Add sugar and eggs; reduce speed to low. Add cornstarch, lemon juice and vanilla. Beat until blended; add margarine and sour cream. Pour into prepared pan and bake for about 1 hour and 10 minutes, or until firm around the edges. Turn off oven. Let cake stand in oven 2 hours. Remove; cool completely on wire rack. Chill before removing sides of pan.
Yield: 12 servings

Strawberry Brie Cake

1 32-ounce wheel of brie
2 cups hulled whole strawberries
mint leaves

Preheat oven to 350°. With wet knife, cut the brie in half horizontally, making two layers. Slice enough strawberries to make a rosette for the top. Spread bottom layer with whole hulled strawberries. Replace top layer and garnish with sliced strawberries and mint leaves. Bake for 7 minutes or until cheese is barely melted. Serve warm.
Yield: 8-10 servings

English Toffee

2	cups sugar	2	teaspoons vanilla
1	pound butter (no substitutes)	6	1.65-ounce Hershey bars
¾	cup water	½	cup pecans, chopped

In heavy pan, mix sugar, butter and water; cook until thermometer reaches 300° — about 20 minutes. Scrape sides once or twice during cooking, but do not stir. Remove from heat and add vanilla. Pour onto large lightly-buttered cookie sheet. While warm, add Hershey bars, broken up. Allow to soften on top; then spread over toffee. Sprinkle with chopped pecans. Let cool and sit several hours until chocolate is very firm. Remove from cookie sheet. Break into pieces. This may be stored in tins.
Yield: Approximately 2 pounds

Chocolate Fudge par Excellence

3	6-ounce packages semi-sweet chocolate chips	½	teaspoon vanilla
1	can Eagle Brand condensed milk	½	cup chopped nuts
	dash of salt		

Melt chocolate over low heat with condensed milk. Remove from heat and stir in salt, vanilla and nuts. Spread in waxed paper-lined, greased 8" square pan. Chill 2-3 hours until firm. Cut into squares.
Yield: 36 squares

Peanut Brittle

3	cups sugar	3	tablespoons butter or margarine
1	cup white corn syrup	1	teaspoon salt
½	cup water	1	teaspoon vanilla
12	ounces shelled raw Spanish peanuts	2	heaping tablespoons soda

Line 3 cookie sheets with foil. In deep heavy pan combine sugar, corn syrup and water. Boil until a thread spins; test 3 times — approximately 5 minutes or 230-234° on a candy thermometer. Add peanuts and stir constantly until golden brown and peanuts smell cooked — approximately 12-15 minutes or 300°-310° on thermometer. Remove pan from heat and stir in butter, salt and vanilla until blended. Add soda and stir in well. This will foam up high. Pour onto cookie sheets, spreading as thin as possible; candy will not cover entire sheets. When cool — about 15-20 minutes — peel off foil from back and break into pieces. Store in airtight container. Freezes well.
Yield: Approximately 3 pounds

Sour Cream Fudge

2 cups sugar	2 tablespoons butter
½ teaspoon salt	½ cup chopped nuts
1 cup sour cream	

Butter top inch of heavy cooking pot. Mix sugar, salt and sour cream. Cook, stirring occasionally, until temperature reaches 240° on candy thermometer or makes a soft ball in cold water. Remove from heat and add butter. Beat with mixer until fudge loses its gloss. Add nuts; pour into buttered 8″ square pan. Cool well before cutting.
Yield: 36-48 squares

Texas Candy

1 12-ounce package chocolate chips	1 cup cocktail peanuts
	1 cup chow mein noodles
1 12-ounce package butterscotch chips	

Melt chocolate and butterscotch chips together over low heat, stirring until well blended. Add cocktail peanuts and noodles. Drop by teaspoonfuls onto waxed paper. Let harden.
Yield: Approximately 25-30 pieces

Variation: 12 ounces chocolate chips, 6 ounces butterscotch chips, 12 or 16-ounce can salted Spanish peanuts.

Almond Cookies

1¼ cups Crisco	1 teaspoon baking powder
1 cup sugar	¼ teaspoon salt
1½ teaspoons almond extract	½ teaspoon baking soda
1 egg	36 almonds
2 cups flour	1 egg white

Preheat oven to 350°. Cream Crisco and sugar; add almond extract and egg. Sift together flour, baking powder, salt and soda; add to creamed mixture. Mix until dough forms. Roll dough into 1″ balls and place on well-greased cookie sheet 2″ apart. Place an almond in the center of each ball, pressing down gently. Brush each ball with beaten egg white. Bake for 12-15 minutes.
Yield: 3 dozen

Apricot Bars

12 ounces dried apricots, washed well	2 cups sifted flour
1¾ cups sugar, divided	½ teaspoon soda
¾ cup butter or margarine	3½ ounces coconut
	½ cup chopped pecans

Preheat oven to 350°. Cover apricots with water and bring to a boil. Simmer uncovered 15 minutes or until tender. Drain, reserving ¼ cup liquid. Chop apricots and set aside. Combine reserved liquid and ¾ cup sugar in saucepan; simmer 5 minutes after sugar dissolves. Stir in chopped apricots. Cream butter and 1 cup sugar. Combine flour and soda and add to butter and sugar mixture until crumbly. Stir in coconut and nuts. Put ¾ of coconut mixture in greased 9 × 13″ pan and press, covering bottom. Bake for 10 minutes. Spread apricot mixture evenly over crust and sprinkle on remaining coconut mixture. Bake for 30 minutes. Cool in pan and cut into bars.
Yield: 3 dozen.

Beatriz's Cookies

1 stick butter, softened	¼ teaspoon salt
⅓ cup granulated sugar	½ cup pecans, finely chopped
1½ cups flour	1 tablespoon vanilla
⅓ cup powdered sugar	1 tablespoon water

Preheat oven to 350°. Cream butter and sugar with a spoon — approximately 3 minutes. Sift flour, powdered sugar and salt together; add to creamed mixture and blend well with hands. Add pecans, vanilla and water. Continue to work with hands until well mixed. Make into a roll, wrap in waxed paper and refrigerate for at least 2 hours. Slice thin; bake on ungreased cookie sheet for 12-15 minutes. Remove from cookie sheet and let cool. Dip each into powdered sugar to coat well.
Yield: 3 dozen.

 These cookie rolls store well in the freezer. Thaw before baking.

Breakfast Cookies

1 cup butter or margarine	2 cups rolled oats
½ cup peanut butter	1 cup wheat germ
1 cup brown sugar	1 teaspoon baking powder
2 eggs	½ teaspoon baking soda
1 cup honey, corn syrup or molasses	1 cup coconut
	1 cup raisins
2 cups whole wheat flour	1 cup chopped nuts

Preheat oven to 375°. Cream butter, peanut butter and brown sugar. Add eggs one at a time, beating until fluffy. Add the remaining ingredients and mix well. Drop by teaspoons onto a greased cookie sheet. Bake for 10-12 minutes in a 375° oven.
Yield: 6 dozen

 Great for breakfast-on-the-run.

Brown Sugar Brownies

1 stick butter, melted	1 teaspoon baking powder
2 cups brown sugar	2 teaspoons vanilla
2 unbeaten eggs	1 cup chopped walnuts
1½ cups flour	1 cup coconut

Preheat oven to 350°. With a spoon, mix melted butter and sugar well. Add eggs and beat slightly. Add flour, baking powder and vanilla; mix well. Add nuts and coconut. Pour into greased 9×13″ pan and bake for 30 minutes.
Yield: 3 dozen

Calorie Bars

1 14-ounce package light caramels (50 caramels)	¾ cups butter or margarine, melted
	1 cup chopped nuts
⅔ cup sweetened condensed milk, divided	1 6-ounce package semi-sweet chocolate chips
1 yellow cake mix	

Preheat oven to 350°. In top of double boiler, melt caramels and ⅓ cup condensed milk; mix well and set aside, keeping warm over hot water. In large bowl, combine cake mix, butter, nuts and ⅓ cup condensed milk. Mix thoroughly until crumbly. Spread half the mixture in greased 9×13″ baking pan; bake for 6 minutes. Remove from oven and sprinkle chocolate morsels evenly over baked layer; spread caramel mixture over chocolate morsels, working quickly with broad spatula. Crumble remaining dough over the top and press lightly with spoon. Bake for 14-18 minutes until top is set. Cool and refrigerate until firm. Cut into small squares.
Yield: 3 dozen

Variation: Substitute ⅔ cup milk, white or Swiss chocolate cake mix and chopped walnuts.

Chocoholic Brownies

2 sticks butter	1 teaspoon vanilla
4 ounces unsweetened chocolate	½ cup flour
4 eggs	1 cup coarsely chopped pecans
2 cups sugar	

Preheat oven to 350°. Melt butter and chocolate. Cool. Beat eggs with sugar until thick and lemon colored. Add chocolate, butter and vanilla; mix well. Fold in flour and then pecans. Pour into a greased and floured 9×13″ pan. Bake for 25 minutes. Do not overbake.
Yield: 3 dozen

Cheese Date Dainties

1   7½-ounce package pitted dates,   ½   cup brown sugar
    chopped   ¼   cup water

In a saucepan, mix dates, sugar and water. Cook, stirring until soft. Cool.

Pastry:
½   cup butter or margarine   2   cups flour
½   cup grated Cheddar cheese

Preheat oven to 350°. Cream butter and cheese; cut in flour until texture of cornmeal. Chill. Form into rolls. Slice thin slices from pastry roll. Place date mixture on one slice and top with another slice. Press edges together with fork. Bake on cookie sheet for 15 minutes.
Yield: 3-4 dozen.

Energy Cookies

1   cup brown sugar   ½   cup wheat germ
¾   cup white sugar*   ½   cup powdered milk
⅔   cup corn oil margarine   ¼   cup milk
2   eggs   1½ cups uncooked quick-cooking
1   teaspoon soda   oatmeal
½   teaspoon salt   1½ cups chopped nuts
¾   teaspoon cinnamon   1   cup raisins
2   teaspoons vanilla   1½ cups chocolate chips, optional
2   cups whole wheat flour

Preheat oven to 350°. Cream sugars and margarine; add eggs and beat well. Add soda, salt, cinnamon, vanilla, flour, wheat germ, powdered milk and milk, mixing after each addition. Stir in oatmeal, adding more if needed to make a very stiff dough. Add nuts, raisins and chocolate chips, if desired. Drop by teaspoonfuls onto a well-greased cookie sheet, about 1-1½" apart. Bake for 10-15 minutes. Remove from sheet immediately.

*If adding chocolate, reduce white sugar to ½ cup.
Yield: 5-6 dozen

 Keeps well. Freezes well.

Ranger Cookies

1   cup margarine or Crisco   ½   teaspoon salt
1   cup sugar   1   teaspoon baking powder
1   cup light brown sugar, packed   2   teaspoons soda
2   eggs   1   cup shredded coconut
2   cups corn flakes   1   cup chopped pecans
2   cups oatmeal, uncooked   1   teaspoon vanilla
2   cups flour

Preheat oven to 325°. Cream margarine and sugars; add eggs, beating well. Add and mix well after each addition all the remaining ingredients. Roll into small balls the size of a walnut and place on a greased cookie sheet. Press down with a fork. Bake for 12-15 minutes until brown.
Yield: 8 dozen

 For easy Mexican cookies, fry 1" flour tortilla strips until crisp and shake in a mixture of 1 cup sugar and 1 teaspoon cinnamon. Cool and serve.

Golden Brownies

1 stick margarine, softened	1 cup sifted flour
½ cup brown sugar	

Preheat oven to 350°. Mix margarine, brown sugar and flour; put into 9″ square pan, pressing down well to cover bottom. Bake for 20 minutes. Remove and reduce oven temperature to 325°.

Filling:

2 eggs	1 teaspoon vanilla
1 cup brown sugar	1 cup nuts, chopped
2 tablespoons flour	1 6-ounce package semi-sweet
½ teaspoon baking powder	chocolate morsels, optional

As crust bakes, beat together all ingredients except nuts and chocolate morsels. Then fold in the nuts and the chocolate morsels, if desired. Spread over crust. Bake approximately 35 minutes. Cut into squares while warm.
Yield: 2 dozen

Grand Marnier Cookies

2 sticks margarine, softened	1 teaspoon vanilla
1 cup sugar	1 teaspoon almond extract
1 egg	2 tablespoons Grand Marnier
2⅓ cups unsifted flour	liqueur
2 teaspoons baking powder	powdered sugar

Preheat oven to 350°. Mix well margarine, sugar, egg, flour, baking powder, vanilla, almond extract and Grand Marnier. Cover and chill thoroughly. Take out a small amount and roll ⅛″ thick on a slightly-floured board. Cut with a cookie cutter or roll into balls the size of a walnut and press flat; or use a cookie press. Place on ungreased cookie sheet and bake for 12-15 minutes. Sprinkle with powdered sugar.
Yield: Approximately 3 dozen.

Variation: Triple Sec may be used instead of Grand Marnier

Jane's Ginger Crinkles

⅔ cups Wesson oil	2 teaspoons soda
1 cup sugar	½ teaspoon salt
1 egg	1 teaspoon cinnamon
4 tablespoons dark molasses	1 teaspoon ginger
2 cups flour	granulated sugar

Preheat oven to 350°. Mix oil and sugar well; add egg and molasses. Sift together flour, soda, salt, cinnamon and ginger. Gradually add to egg mixture. Chill dough. Form into balls the size of a pecan and roll in granulated sugar. Place on wax paper-lined cookie sheet. Bake for 12-15 minutes.
Yield: 4 dozen

Meltaway Cookies

1 cup butter	¾ cup cornstarch
5½ tablespoons powdered sugar	1 cup flour

Preheat oven to 375°. Cream butter and sugar; add cornstarch and flour. Refrigerate dough for 1-2 hours. Roll into small balls and place on ungreased cookie sheet; mash with bottom of glass that has been dipped in cold water. Bake for 10 minutes. While cookies are warm, glaze.

Glaze:

1 tablespoon butter, melted	1 tablespoon orange juice
1 cup powdered sugar	1 tablespoon lemon juice

Mix above ingredients well and spread on top of cookies.
Yield: 3 dozen

Mint Stick Brownies

2 squares chocolate	¼ teaspoon peppermint flavoring
½ cup butter	½ cup sifted flour
2 eggs, well beaten	⅛ teaspoon salt
1 cup sugar	½ cup chopped nuts

Preheat oven to 350°. Melt chocolate and butter in double boiler. Cool; add remaining ingredients and mix well. Pour batter into a greased 9″ square pan. Bake for 20-25 minutes. Cool. Ice with mint frosting; then spread with glaze.

Mint Frosting:

2 tablespoons butter, softened	½ teaspoon peppermint flavoring
1 cup sifted powdered sugar	green food coloring
1 tablespoon cream	

Beat butter and powdered sugar until smooth; add cream and peppermint flavoring; add green coloring a drop at a time to desired color.

Glaze:

1 square baking chocolate	1 tablespoon butter

Melt chocolate and butter over hot water and blend. Dribble glaze over frosted brownies, covering surface well. Refrigerate. Cut into finger-sized sticks.
Yield: 2 dozen

Scotch Shortbread

1 cup butter or margarine	2 cups unsifted flour
½ cup sugar	

Preheat oven to 250°. Mix butter and sugar with a fork. Add part of flour and mix; turn mixture onto board and work in remaining flour with your hands. Make marble-sized balls and place on an ungreased cookie sheet, 2″ apart. Flatten with bottom of small glass. Make designs on top with prongs of fork. Bake for 50-60 minutes. The cookies will be light in color.
Yield: 3 dozen

 These can be made larger.

Chocolate Riches

3 1-ounce squares unsweetened baking chocolate	1 cup light corn syrup
1/3 cup butter or margarine	1 1/2 teaspoons vanilla
4 eggs	dash cinnamon
1 1/2 cups sugar	1 1/2 cups pecan halves

Preheat oven to 350°. Melt chocolate and butter over low heat. Mix well and set aside. In a large bowl beat eggs; blend in sugar, syrup, chocolate mixture, vanilla and cinnamon. Stir in pecans. Turn into a greased two quart 2″ deep baking dish. Place in pan with 1/2″ hot water. Bake for 40-50 minutes until just set. Remove from water. Cool thoroughly on rack.

Yield: 8 servings

 Serve warm with French vanilla or vanilla bean ice cream.

Glazed Bananas

4 bananas	1/4 cup honey
1/2 cup butter, divided	2 tablespoons dark rum
1/4 cup orange juice	

Peel bananas and cut in halves lengthwise. Melt 1/4 cup butter in medium-sized skillet; sauté bananas, turning until very lightly browned. Remove bananas and add remainder of butter, orange juice, honey and rum. Stir and cook until thick; add bananas and heat until well glazed. Serve at once with ice cream if desired.

Yield: 4 servings

Flan

2 cups sugar, divided	1 teaspoon vanilla
8 eggs	1 teaspoon lemon extract
1/2 teaspoon salt	4 cups milk, scalded

Preheat oven to 315°. Caramelize I cup sugar in a heavy pan or skillet, being careful not to burn. Pour into warmed baking dish or mold and tilt until bottom is covered with the syrup. Cool. Beat eggs and add remaining sugar, salt and flavorings. Gradually add milk, stirring constantly. Pour into caramel-lined pan. Set in a pan of warm water and bake for 1 hour or until knife inserted into center comes out clean. Cool and refrigerate. To serve, unmold onto platter.

Yield: 8-10 servings

Golden Custard

2½ cups milk	1 teaspoon vanilla
4 eggs, lightly beaten	½ teaspoon cinnamon
½ cup honey	pinch of salt

Preheat oven to 350°. Bring milk to a slight simmer. Blend eggs with honey and slowly stir in milk; add vanilla, cinnamon and salt. Pour into 5 or 6 custard cups and place cups in pan with 1" hot water. Bake 25-30 minutes or until knife inserted into center comes out clean.
Yield: 6 servings

 Good served with fresh fruit or berries.

Grasshopper Torte

24 creme-filled chocolate cookies, crushed	¼ cup butter or margarine, melted

Combine cookie crumbs and butter; press onto bottom of 9" springform pan. Chill.

Filling:

¼ cup Crème de Menthe	2 cups heavy cream, whipped
1 7-ounce jar marshmallow creme	

Gradually add Crème de Menthe to marshmallow creme, mixing until well blended; fold in whipped cream. Pour over cookie crust. Refrigerate until firm. Garnish with whipped cream and mint leaves, if desired.
Yield: 8-10 servings

 Freezes well.

Martha's Black Raspberry Mousse

8 ounces semi-sweet chocolate	3 tablespoons sugar
2 tablespoons butter	½ cup whipping cream, whipped
2 eggs, separated	
¼ cup Chambord (raspberry liqueur)	

Melt chocolate over hot water. Add butter and stir until melted; add beaten egg yolks and Chambord; mix and cool. Beat egg whites until stiff, gradually add sugar and fold into chocolate mixture. Fold in whipped cream. Cover and refrigerate overnight.

Sauce:

1 10-ounce package frozen raspberries	¾ cup Chambord
	1 cup whipping cream, whipped

In blender combine raspberries and Chambord. Fold in whipped cream. Serve with Mousse.
Yield: 10-12 servings

 This is an elegant dessert served in wine glasses or brandy snifters.

Pat's Fruit Pizza

1   20-ounce package Pillsbury
    sugar cookies

Preheat oven to 350°. Slice cookies and put ½″ apart on a lightly-greased pizza pan. The cookies will run together, making a crust. Bake for 12 minutes. Cool.

Filling:

1	8-ounce package cream cheese	sliced strawberries
½	cup sugar	sliced white grapes
1	teaspoon vanilla	mandarin orange sections
2	tablespoons crushed pineapple	kiwi, peeled and sliced

Mix cream cheese, sugar, vanilla and pineapple. Spread on crust. Arrange fruit on filling in an artistic manner and so that when sliced, each wedge has some of all the fruit.

Sauce:

1	cup sugar	1	cup orange juice
¼	teaspoon salt	¾	cup water
2	tablespoons cornstarch		

In a saucepan mix all ingredients and cook over medium heat, stirring constantly until thick. Pour sauce over pizza. Chill.
Yield: 10 servings

Pavlova

4	large egg whites	¼	teaspoon vinegar
⅛	teaspoon salt	1	cup heavy cream, whipped
¼	teaspoon lemon juice	2	tablespoons sugar
1	cup sugar		strawberries and kiwi

Preheat oven to 250°. Line a cookie sheet with foil and set aside. Beat egg whites, salt and lemon juice until very stiff and dry. Add sugar gradually until meringue stands in shiny peaks. Fold in vinegar. Place on cookie sheet, in dome form. Bake for 75 minutes. Remove from oven. Cool. Do not remove from cookie sheet until completely cooled. Decorate top with whipped cream, strawberries and kiwi.
Yield: 6-8 servings

Swedish Cream With Fresh Berries

1	envelope unflavored gelatin	2	cups sour cream
¼	cup cold water	1½	teaspoons vanilla
2	cups whipping cream	3	cups fresh berries
1	cup sugar		

Soften gelatin in water. In a sauce pan heat the cream and sugar; add gelatin, heating until gelatin dissolves. Cool until slightly thickened; fold in sour cream and vanilla. Pour into a serving bowl to mold. When ready to serve, add a layer of fresh berries, slightly sugared. Strawberries should be sliced.
Yield: 8 servings

Pineapple "No Ka Oi" (The Best)

1   fresh ripe pineapple   other fresh fruits, as desired

Split pineapple in half, remove fruit, and turn over halves to drain. Chop the pineapple and mix with sliced strawberries, bananas, kiwi — any fruits desired. Fill each pineapple half with the fruit and cover with Italian Meringue.

Italian Meringue:
½   cup water   1   cup sugar
¼   teaspoon cream of tartar   3   egg whites

Preheat oven to 350°. In heavy saucepan mix water, cream of tartar and sugar, heating until sugar dissolves. Cover and boil over low heat until candy thermometer reaches 238°-240°. Pour gradually over well-beaten egg whites and continue beating as you pour, until thick. Spread over fruit in pineapple shells, place in oven to brown lightly. May be served as is but especially good with each serving placed on top of Crème Anglais bordered with raspberry sauce.

Crème Anglais:
3   egg yolks   1¼ cups milk
¼   cup sugar   1   teaspoon vanilla
    pinch of salt

In top of double boiler, beat egg yolks, sugar and salt; add milk and cook, stirring constantly until mixture coats spoon. Add vanilla and place waxed paper over top to prevent drying. Let cool. This can be made the day before.

Raspberry Sauce:
1   10-ounce package of frozen   a squeeze of lemon juice
    raspberries in heavy syrup,
    thawed

In blender mix raspberries and juice. Press through strainer to remove seeds. This can be done the day before. To serve, bring the two pineapple halves to the table. Have custard and sauce on the plates and put serving of fruit on top.
Yield: 6-8 servings

Coffee Ice Cream Dessert

1   stick margarine, melted   1   cup shredded coconut
2½ cups crushed Rice Krispies   ½   cup chopped nuts
1   cup brown sugar   ½   gallon coffee ice cream

Preheat oven to 300°. Mix margarine, Rice Krispies, brown sugar, coconut and nuts. Press ¾ of this mixture into a large oven-proof glass pie plate. Set aside ¼ of the mixture to be used on top. Bake this crust for 10 minutes. When cool, press ice cream into crust. Spread remaining crumbs on top of ice cream and place in freezer until ready to use.
Yield: 8-10 servings

Cranberry Sherbet

1 envelope unflavored gelatin	2 cups sugar
3 cups water, divided	1/3 cup lemon juice, fresh or frozen
4 cups fresh cranberries	

Soften gelatin in 1/2 cup water. Cook berries in 2 1/2 cups water until skins pop. Strain through sieve. Add sugar and gelatin and mix until dissolved and blended. Cool. Add lemon juice. Freeze in ice trays until hard; beat to break up. Pour into 1 1/2-quart mold and return to freezer.
Yield: 8-10 servings

Frozen Strawberry Dessert

1 cup flour	1/2 cup chopped pecans
1/4 cup packed brown sugar	1/2 cup butter, melted

Preheat oven to 350°. Combine all ingredients; put into a 9"square pan and bake for 20 minutes, stirring often. Let cool.

Fruit Layer:

1 10-ounce package frozen strawberries, thawed, or 1 1/2 cups fresh strawberries	2 teaspoons fresh lemon juice
	2 egg whites
1 cup sugar	1 cup whipping cream, whipped

Use electric mixer. Combine strawberries, sugar, lemon juice and egg whites. Beat at high speed for 20 minutes or until light and fluffy. Fold whipped cream into strawberry mixture. Remove 1/3 of crumb mixture from pan; pat remaining crumbs into a smooth layer. Pour strawberry mixture over crumbs in pan and sprinkle reserved crumbs over top. Freeze.
Yield: 8-10 servings

Grand Marnier Orange Ice

1 2"-square orange peel, cut in pieces	1 cup sugar
	1/3 cup Grand Marnier
4 cups freshly squeezed orange juice, divided	

With metal blade in place, add orange peel, 1 cup orange juice, sugar and Grand Marnier to beaker of food processor. Process until combined — about 15 seconds. Add remaining 3 cups orange juice and mix. Pour into two ice cube trays; freeze. Just before serving, with metal blade in place, add frozen cubes to beaker of food processor, one tray at a time. Process, turning on and off rapidly, until it is a fine ice, free of lumps but still firm — about 2-3 minutes. Spoon into sherbet dishes and serve immediately. If desired, add a sprig of mint to each serving.
Yield: 4-6 servings

Variation: Triple Sec may be substituted for Grand Marnier.

 This can be stored in sherbet glasses until ready to serve.

Lemon Ice Cream

2 eggs	1 cup whipping cream
½ cup sugar	¼ cup lemon juice
½ cup light corn syrup	2 teaspoons grated lemon peel
1¼ cups milk	

Beat eggs until light and lemon colored. Gradually add sugar, beating constantly. Add corn syrup, milk, cream, lemon juice and grated lemon peel. Mix well. Freeze in ice trays until firm. Turn out into chilled bowl; beat until light. Return to freezer tray and freeze until firm.
Yield: 6 servings

Lemon Milk Sherbet

1¼ cups sugar	¼ teaspoon lemon extract
⅓ cup lemon juice	2 cups milk
1 lemon rind, grated	

Combine all ingredients and mix well. Pour into tray and freeze. Remove and beat with chilled beaters in a chilled bowl until light and fluffy. Return to freezer.
Yield: 6 servings

Mike's Orange Delight

6 10-ounce bottles Orange Crush	1 can Eagle Brand condensed milk
1 20-ounce can crushed pineapple	

Combine and mix ingredients well and put in ice cream canister. Freeze until not quite firm. Pack with more ice and leave in the canister to "age" or place canister into freezer for 1 hour.
Yield: 10 servings

Orange Alaskas

6 large oranges	2 teaspoons grated orange rind
1 pint orange sherbet, softened	4 egg whites
2 8-ounce cartons lowfat peach yogurt	½ teaspoon vanilla
⅓ cup orange-flavored liqueur	¼ teaspoon cream of tartar
	¼ cup sugar

Cut a small slice from the top of each orange. Clip membrane and carefully remove pulp. (Do not puncture bottom). Strain pulp, reserving ½ cup juice. Combine orange juice, sherbet, yogurt, liqueur and orange rind in a large bowl. Pour into orange shells. Place shells on a baking sheet. Freeze about 4 hours. Beat egg whites, add vanilla and cream of tartar until foamy. Gradually add sugar, 1 tablespoon at a time, beating until stiff peaks form. Spread meringue over top opening of each orange shell, making sure edges are sealed. Freeze. When ready to serve, broil orange shells 6″ from heat for 1-2 minutes until meringues are golden brown.
Yield: 6 servings

Pistachio Treat

40 Ritz crackers, crushed   ½ stick butter, melted
¾ cups chopped walnuts

Mix all ingredients. Press into a 9 × 13″ pan.

Filling:
2 3-ounce boxes pistachio instant   ½ gallon vanilla ice cream,
   pudding   softened
2 cups milk   2 cups whipping cream, whipped

Mix pudding and milk, according to package directions. Add this to softened ice cream and mix thoroughly. Pour on top of crumb layer; cover and freeze. Top with whipped cream when ready to serve.
Yield: 12 servings

Velvet Hammer Dessert

½ gallon Blue Bell vanilla ice   ½ cup brandy
   cream, softened   ¼ cup white Crème de Cacao

In a large mixing bowl, blend all ingredients. Put into a plastic container with a sealed lid and freeze or put into individual parfait glasses and freeze.
Yield: 8-12 servings

the GATHERING

Luncheon for a Gathering

Ham Loaf with Sweet Mustard Sauce
Shoe Peg Corn Salad
Wine Apples
Savory Cheese Muffins
Rosina's Seafoam Cookies
Ginger Krinkles*

Ham Loaf with Sauce

2 pounds cured ham	2 eggs
1 pound lean fresh pork	1 medium onion, chopped
1 cup toasted bread crumbs	½ cup chopped green pepper

Grind the ham and pork together. Add the remaining ingredients. Pour into a greased ring mold and bake at 325° for 1-1¼ hours.

Sauce:

½ cup tomato soup	½ cup vinegar
½ cup prepared mustard	1 stick butter or margarine
½ cup sugar	3 egg yolks

Combine all ingredients except egg yolks and cook over low heat for 5-7 minutes, stirring continuously. Add beaten yolks; cook for 1 minute more. Serve over ham loaf.
Yield: 12 servings

Variation: This can be tripled and baked in a 9×13″ baking dish. Test after 50-60 minutes.

Shoe Peg Salad

1 17-ounce can LeSueur peas, drained	1 bunch green onions, diced
1 15-ounce can shoe peg corn, drained	1 cup diced celery
	1 2-ounce jar diced pimientos, drained
1 8-ounce can sliced water chestnuts, drained	½ cup diced green pepper

Marinade:

½ cup sugar	⅓ cup cider vinegar
1 teaspoon salt	2 tablespoons oil

Mix marinade and pour over vegetables. Marinate 3-4 hours
Yield: I2-15 servings

*Refers to recipes found in other sections.

Wine Apples

10 apples, Jonathon or Rome Beauty	½ cup tarragon vinegar
2 cups sugar	2 sticks cinnamon, broken
½ cup dry red wine	¼ cup red hots
	red food coloring, as needed

Peel, core and slice apples into about 5 round pieces each. Mix remaining ingredients in a large flat pan and bring to a boil. Add half of the apple slices. Turn and cook at a fast boil until edges turn clear — about 5-10 minutes. Remove cooked apples. Cook remaining slices in the same sauce. Put apples into wide-mouth jars, pouring strained sauce over. Store in refrigerator.
Yield: 50 slices

Savory Cheese Muffins

1 cup whole wheat flour	¾ cup (3 ounces) grated Provolone cheese
¾ cup flour	2 tablespoons grated Romano cheese
3 tablespoons sugar	1 cup milk
1 tablespoon baking powder	1 egg, beaten
¾ teaspoon Italian seasoning	3 tablespoons butter, melted
½ teaspoon salt	

Combine dry ingredients. Stir in cheeses. Add combined milk, egg and butter. Stir just until dry ingredients are moistened. Fill buttered muffin cups ⅔ full. Sprinkle 1 teaspoon almond topping over the top of each. Press into batter. Bake at 400° for 15 minutes. Serve warm.

Almond Topping:

⅓ cup chopped blanched almonds	1 teaspoon Worcestershire sauce
2 tablespoons butter, melted	¼ teaspoon garlic salt

Combine all ingredients.
Yield: 12 muffins

Rosina's Sea Foam Cookies

½ cup butter, softened	1 teaspoon vanilla
½ cup shortening, softened	1 16-ounce package coconut
½ cup sugar	powdered sugar
2 cups flour, sifted	

Preheat oven to 300°. Cream butter, shortening and sugar; add flour and vanilla; then fold in coconut. Drop by teaspoonfuls onto a greased cookie sheet and bake for 15 minutes or until cookies are lightly browned. While still warm, roll in powdered sugar.
Yield: 5 dozen

Luncheon for a Gathering

Turkey and Stuffing Casserole
Green Bean Casserole*
Frozen Cranberry Salad
Toasted Pita Triangles
Chocolate Mint Meringues

Turkey and Stuffing Casserole

1	8-ounce package seasoned corn bread stuffing mix	½	cup flour
½	cup chopped onion	¾	cup margarine, divided
½	cup chopped celery	¼	teaspoon salt
1	jalapeño, finely chopped	⅛	teaspoon pepper
3	cups cooked and cubed turkey	3	cups cannned chicken broth
		4	eggs, slightly beaten

Prepare stuffing according to package directions. Sauté onion and celery in ¼ cup margarine. Combine stuffing, onions, celery and jalapeño. Spread in a greased 9×13″ casserole. Sprinkle turkey over stuffing. Melt remaining butter in a skillet and blend in flour and seasonings. Add broth, cooking and stirring until thickened. Add eggs and pour over turkey. Using a fork, pierce the stuffing so that broth mixture soaks through. Bake at 325° for 40-45 minutes. Cut into squares and serve with sauce.

Sauce:

1	10¾-ounce can cream of mushroom soup	1	cup sour cream
¼	cup milk	¼	cup chopped pimiento

Mix all ingredients. Heat and serve over squares.
Yield: 15 servings

 May be baked at 325° for 25 minutes, cooled, cut and frozen. To serve, thaw and bake at 325° for 20 minutes.

Frozen Cranberry Salad

1	8-ounce package cream cheese	½	cup chopped pecans
2	tablespoons mayonnaise	1	20-ounce can crushed pineapple, drained
2	tablespoons sugar		
1	16-ounce can whole cranberry sauce	1	13-ounce carton Cool Whip

Soften the cream cheese and blend in the mayonnaise and sugar. Add cranberry sauce, pecans and pineapple. Fold in Cool Whip. Pour into muffin papers and freeze. Store in a Ziploc bag. To serve, unwrap and place on lettuce leaves.
Yield: 20 servings

Chocolate Mint Meringues

2	egg whites, room temperature	¼	teaspoon peppermint extract, or to taste
¼	teaspoon cream of tartar		green food coloring, as desired
⅔	cup sugar		
1	6-ounce package chocolate morsels		

Preheat oven to 350°. Beat egg whites until foamy. Add cream of tartar gradually. Add sugar as you continue to beat egg whites until stiff peaks hold their shapes. Stir in chocolate morsels, extract and green food coloring. Cut a brown paper bag to fit the cookie sheet. Drop by teaspoonfuls onto the paper-covered cookie sheet. Put meringues in the preheated oven and turn it off. Leave meringues in oven until cold — at least 4 hours or overnight. Take meringues off paper gently. Store in an airtight tin.
Yield: 3 dozen

 Split pita bread in half and brush each piece generously with melted butter. With scissors cut each half into 8 triangles. Place buttered side up on a cookie sheet and bake at 200° for 1 hour. Cool completely on paper towels before storing in an airtight container.

Variation: May sprinkle on grated Parmesan cheese before baking.

Luncheon for a Gathering

Stuffed Shells Florentine
Antipasto Salad*
Caesar Crisps
Tortoni

Stuffed Shells Florentine

1	16-ounce package jumbo macaroni shells	1	teaspoon salt
2	9-ounce packages frozen creamed spinach	½	teaspoon pepper
1	15-ounce carton ricotta cheese	1	pound ground beef
8	ounces Mozarella cheese, shredded	1	15½-ounce jar spaghetti sauce

Prepare macaroni shells and creamed spinach according to package directions. Place spinach in a large bowl and cool slightly. Stir in cheeses and seasonings. Stuff each shell with 1 tablespoon of mixture. Place in a 9×13″ well-greased casserole. Brown meat and drain excess grease. Mix with spaghetti sauce. Spoon meat sauce over shells. Cover and bake at 350° for 30 minutes.
Yield: 10-12 servings

Caesar Crisps

2	cans refrigerated Pillsbury crescent dinner rolls	2	6-ounce boxes seasoned cheese and garlic croutons, crushed
1	8-ounce bottle Caesar salad dressing		

Press each 2 triangles of dough into a rectangle and brush generously with Caesar salad dressing. Sprinkle with crushed croutons and cut each rectangle into 4 squares. Bake on a greased cookie sheet. Bake at 375° for 12 minutes.
Yield: 32 squares

Variation: Sprinkle with sesame seeds or poppy seeds.

Tortoni

22	hard macaroons,crushed and divided	½	teaspoon vanilla
1½	cups coffee cream	1	teaspoon almond extract
2	cups whipping cream	½	cup almonds, ground

Mix 1 cup macaroons with coffee cream to soften. Whip cream and add almond and vanilla extracts. Fold in macaroon mixture. Spoon into dessert dishes or stemware. Mix remaining macaroon crumbs with almonds and sprinkle over top. Chill.
Yield: 16 servings

Luncheon for a Gathering

Tuna Salad Loaf
Three Green Salad
Strawberry Muffins
Pineapple Coconut Cake

Tuna Salad Loaf

3 tablespoons unflavored gelatin	3 hard-boiled eggs, chopped
3/4 cup cold water	2 1/4 cups chopped celery
3/4 cup boiling water	1/2 cup finely chopped onion
2 cups mayonnaise	1/2 cup chopped pimientos
2 tablespoons prepared mustard	1 1/2 cups small canned peas, drained
1/2 cup lemon juice	salt, to taste
3 7-ounce cans tuna, drained and flaked	

Soften gelatin in cold water, then add boiling water to dissolve. Set aside to cool. Mix mayonnaise, mustard and lemon juice. Add to gelatin; stir in rest of ingredients and mix well. Pour into greased mold or glass loaf pan. Chill until set. Serve with dilled mayonnaise.
Yield: 12-14 servings

Three Green Salad

2 10-ounce packages frozen French-style green beans	1 1-ounce package Hidden Valley Ranch dressing mix, prepared
2 10-ounce packages frozen chopped broccoli	1 teaspoon anchovy paste
2 15-ounce cans artichoke hearts, drained and chopped	

Cook green beans and broccoli al dente. Drain well. Add chopped artichoke hearts. Mix 2 cups, or less, of dressing with the anchovy paste and add to vegetables. Mix well and refrigerate overnight.
Yield: 12-14 servings

Variation: Use frozen mixed vegetables.

Strawberry Muffins

1	10-ounce package frozen strawberries
1	cup sugar
½	teaspoon cinnamon
½	teaspoon soda

1½	cups flour
½	cup corn oil
2	eggs, beaten
½	cup finely chopped nuts, optional

Thaw and drain strawberries, reserving juice. Mix sugar, cinnamon, soda and flour. Add ½ cup strawberry juice, oil, eggs, strawberries and nuts. Do not use a mixer; blend with a spoon. Pour into greased small muffin tins. Bake at 350° for 10-12 minutes.

Yield: Approximately 72 small muffins

 This may be made in a greased loaf pan and baked 40-45 minutes.

Pineapple Coconut Cake

1	yellow cake mix
4	eggs
1	cup Wesson oil

1	20-ounce can crushed pineapple, divided
1	teaspoon almond extract

Preheat oven to 325°. Mix cake mix, eggs, oil, 1 cup of pineapple with juice and almond extract; beat 3 minutes. Pour into a greased 10x15" pan. Bake for 25-30 minutes or until golden brown. Remove from oven and ice in pan while hot. Cool completely before slicing.

Icing:

	remaining pineapple and juice
½	stick margarine, melted

2	heaping cups powdered sugar
1	13½-ounce can shredded coconut

Mix all ingredients except coconut and pour over hot cake. Sprinkle coconut on top of cake icing and press in.

Yield: 24 slices

 Freezes well.

Luncheon for a Gathering

Pasta Primavera
Crispy Sesame Sticks
Lemon Carrot Cake*

Pasta Primavera

4	bunches broccoli, flowerets only
4	small zucchini, sliced
4	summer squash, cubed
8	carrots, thinly sliced
1	cup frozen peas
4	cups sliced mushrooms
8	shallots, chopped (not green onions)
1	cup red and green pepper strips
1	cup chopped parsley
1	teaspoon garlic powder
½	cup chopped fresh basil or 1 teaspoon dried

½-1 teaspoon red pepper flakes or Tabasco sauce, to taste, optional
½ cup diet margarine, melted
1 cup chicken stock
3 cups 2% lowfat milk
2⅔ cups grated fresh Parmesan cheese
salt and pepper, to taste
48 ounces vermicelli
toasted pine nuts or sunflower seeds, optional

Steam broccoli, zucchini, squash and carrots, or cook in boiling water 3 minutes. Drop peas in at last minute; then drain. Refresh under cold water. Drain and set aside. This may be done well in advance. Sauté mushrooms, shallots and peppers 2-3 minutes until just tender. Combine with vegetables, parsley, garlic powder, basil and red pepper flakes. Make sauce of melted margarine, stock, milk, cheese, salt and pepper. Cook vermicelli al dente. Drain. Add vegetables to sauce only to heat. Then gently toss with vermicelli. Garnish with pine nuts or sunflower seeds. Serve extra cheese on the side.
Yield: 12 servings

 This is a low cholesterol recipe.

Crispy Sesame Sticks

1 loaf Pepperidge Farm very thin white sandwich bread
1 stick butter, melted

sesame seeds
grated Parmesan cheese

Preheat oven to 250°. Cut bread lengthwise into 4 strips. Brush each side with butter. Sprinkle both sides with sesame seeds and Parmesan cheese. Bake for 20-30 minutes until crisp.
Yield: 65 sticks

 These can be baked ahead of time and frozen.

Luncheon for a Gathering

Chicken Tetrazzini
Winter Fruit Bowl
Monkey Bread
Coconut Pound Cake*

Chicken Tetrazzini

2   5-6 pound chickens
8   ounces fresh green noodles
8   ounces fresh white noodles
1   stick margarine
1   onion, chopped
¾   tablespoons flour
2   10¾-ounce cans cream of
    mushroom soup
½   cup milk
1   4-ounce jar chopped pimientos
    garlic powder, to taste

1   tablespoon Lawry's lemon
    pepper
½   cup white wine, divided
1   8-ounce can sliced mushrooms,
    liquid reserved and divided
1   pound Velveeta cheese
1   4½-ounce can chopped ripe
    olives
1   8-ounce can sliced water
    chestnuts, drained

Cook chicken, reserving broth. Cut chicken into bite-size pieces. Cook noodles in broth; drain well. In a large skillet, sauté the onion in margarine. Add flour, soup, milk, pimiento, the garlic powder, lemon pepper, ¼ cup wine and ½ of the mushroom liquid. Cut the cheese into small cubes and add to the sauce. Mix chicken, olives, water chestnuts, ¼ cup wine, mushrooms and remaining mushroom liquid. Combine the sauce and chicken mixture in two 3 quart casseroles. Bake uncovered at 350° for 30 minutes or until completely hot and bubbly.
Yield: 24 servings

Winter Fruit Bowl

8   medium grapefruit
2   cups sugar
1   cup orange marmalade

4   cups fresh or frozen whole
    cranberries
6   medium bananas

Peel and section grapefruit, reserving juice. Set sectioned fruit aside. Add enough water to the juice to measure 1 cup and combine with sugar and marmalade in a saucepan. Heat to boiling, stirring to dissolve sugar. Add cranberries; cook and stir until skins pop (about 5 minutes). Remove from heat and cool. Add grapefruit to cooled mixture; cover and chill. When ready to serve, slice bananas and add to chilled mixture. Serve in small bowls.
Yield: 20 servings

Monkey Bread

⅔ cup Crisco
¾ cup sugar
1 cup unsalted mashed potatoes
   (not too moist)
1 teaspoon salt

1¼ cups scalded Vitamin D milk
1 package yeast
½ cup lukewarm water
3 extra-large eggs, well beaten
6-7 cups flour
1 stick butter, melted

Mix first 4 ingredients. Add scalded milk and beat well. Dissolve yeast in the water. Add yeast and eggs to mixture and beat thoroughly. Gradually mix in ½ cup flour at a time. Mixing thoroughly is the secret to good bread. Knead in flour by hand or heavy-duty mixer until dough blisters. Shape dough in large ball and put into a large greased bowl. Cover with dry cloth and let rise 3-4 hours until dough rises and triples in size. Roll out dough to approximately ½" thick and 18 × 13" wide. Divide into 4 equal parts. Cut into 2" squares and pull lightly into diamond shapes. Dip one side into butter and place unbuttered side down with tips touching in a buttered ring pan. Make 3 layers. Cover again with dry cloth and let rise until it doubles in size. Preheat oven to 350°. Uncover and bake for 30 minutes until golden brown.
Yield: 10-12 servings

Luncheon for a Gathering

Mushroom Chive Bisque*
Veggie Sandwiches
Peanut Brittle Dessert

Veggie Sandwiches

6 zucchini	½ cup pecans
20 small carrots, peeled	½ teaspoon lemon juice
2-3 green onions	½-1 teaspoon dry oregano
1 small tart apple	mayonnaise, as needed

Grind all ingredients except mayonnaise in food processor. Mix with just enough mayonnaise to moisten. Spread onto whole wheat bread.
Yield: 10 sandwiches

Peanut Brittle Dessert

2 13-ounce cartons Cool Whip or	1 12-ounce box peanut brittle
1 pint whipping cream, whipped	

Crush peanut brittle with a rolling pin to the size of peas. (Do not use a processor or blender.) Mix peanut brittle with Cool Whip. Lightly spray a 9×13″ pyrex dish with Pam and pour whipped mixture into pan. Cover tightly and freeze. Before serving, let stand at room temperature a few minutes. Cut into squares and top with chocolate sauce.

Chocolate Sauce:

1 12-ounce package semi-sweet chocolate chips	1 cup white Karo syrup
1 12-ounce can evaporated milk	1 teaspoon vanilla

In a double boiler melt chocolate chips. Stir in remaining ingredients. Blend well and refrigerate.
Yield: 12 servings

Luncheon for a Gathering

Elmo's Curry Soup
Gouda and Apple Sandwiches*
Apricot Bavarian Salad
Meltaway Cookies*

Elmo's Curry Soup

4	10¾-ounce cans beef bouillon	6	cups milk
4	10¾-ounce cans green pea soup	4	teaspoons curry powder, or to taste

Combine all ingredients and serve hot or cold for an easy, delicious soup.
Yield: 12-14 servings

Apricot Bavarian Salad

1	cup sugar	⅓	cup lemon juice
3	envelopes unflavored gelatin	1	unbeaten egg white
	dash of salt	1	cup heavy cream, whipped
2	12-ounce cans apricot nectar		

Combine sugar, gelatin and salt. Heat 1 can apricot nectar to boiling. Add to gelatin mixture and stir to dissolve. Add remaining apricot nectar and lemon juice. Pour ¾ cup of mixture into a 1½ quart mold. Chill until firm. Cool remaining mixture to room temperature. Add unbeaten egg white. Chill until partially set; then beat until fluffy. Fold in whipped cream and pour over first gelatin mixture. Chill until firm. Remove from mold and trim with mint sprigs.
Yield: 12 servings

Luncheon for a Gathering

Tortillas de la Hacienda
Tomato Slices with Classic Guacamole
Wonderful Creamy Pralines

Tortillas de la Hacienda

5	tablespoons oil	5	teaspoons lemon juice
10	cups cubed cooked chicken or turkey	5	cups mayonnaise
2½	cups chopped onion	2½	teaspoons each ground cumin, paprika and black pepper
2½	cups chopped celery	10	garlic cloves, minced
2½	cups chopped cilantro or parsley	40	flour tortillas
5	2-ounce jars diced pimiento, drained		

Preheat oven to 350°. Heat oil in skillet; cook chicken, onion and celery 3-5 minutes until onion is transparent and celery softens slightly. Remove from heat and add cilantro, pimiento, lemon juice, mayonnaise, cumin, paprika, pepper and garlic. Stir well. Place ½ cup chicken mixture on each tortilla and roll up. Place seamside down in lightly buttered baking dishes.

Sauce:

5	10¾-ounce cans cream of chicken soup	2½	teaspoons each ground cumin, paprika and garlic powder
2½	soup cans water	10	large mushrooms, sliced, or 5 2-ounce cans sliced mushrooms, drained
5	cups grated Cheddar cheese		

Pour soup into a pan and stir vigorously until smooth. Add water and stir until blended. Heat until barely simmering. Add cheese and remaining spices, stirring until cheese melts and is blended. Pour over tortillas. Bake at 350° for 20 minutes. Arrange mushrooms on top and bake 3 minutes more.
Yield: 25-30 servings

Classic Guacamole

12	ripe avocados, peeled	4	teaspoons salt
8	small tomatoes, peeled and finely chopped	8	teaspoons lemon juice
4	medium onions, finely chopped	2	teaspoons Tabasco sauce, or to taste

Mash avocados with a fork. Set seeds aside. Add tomatoes and onions. Season with salt, lemon juice and Tabasco. Put seeds into the bowl with the mixture and cover with plastic wrap to keep from discoloring. Refrigerate up to 3 hours.
Yield: 24-26 servings

 The coarse texture and no mayonnaise makes this the traditional guacamole.

Wonderfully Creamy Pralines

2	cups white sugar	2	tablespoons butter
1	teaspoon soda	2	teaspoons vanilla
2	tablespoons light corn syrup	1½	cups chopped pecans
1	cup buttermilk		

Line a cookie sheet with foil; grease or spray with Pam. In a heavy saucepan combine sugar, soda, corn syrup and buttermilk. Cook over medium heat, stirring often to soft ball stage, or 234°-240°on a candy thermometer. Remove from heat; add butter, vanilla and pecans. Beat 1-3 minutes until slightly creamy. Drop by tablespoons onto cookie sheet.

Yield: Approximately 30

Spring Brunch for 12

Strawberry Daiquiries
Cheesy Sausage Crêpes
Green Grape Salad*
Texas Pecan Oatmeal Rolls*
Cinnamon Bread Sticks

Cheesy Sausage Crêpes

6 eggs	2 cups milk
2 cups all purpose flour	2 tablespoons oil

Put all ingredients in a processor and blend 1 minute. Scrape sides of container with rubber spatula and process 15 seconds more. Refrigerate batter 1 hour. Brush bottom of a 6" crêpe pan with oil. Pour in 2 tablespoons of batter when the pan is hot and quickly tilt in all directions to cover pan bottom with a thin film of batter. Cook 1 minute; turn over and cook 30 seconds more. Stack the crêpes between waxed paper until ready to fill.

Filling:

2 pounds bulk sausage (Owens or Jimmy Dean)	2 3-ounce packages cream cheese, softened
½ cup chopped onion	2 4-ounce cans mushrooms, drained and chopped
1 cup grated cheese (Cheddar or Monterey Jack)	

Cook sausage and onion in a skillet until brown, stirring to crumble. Drain off the grease and stir in other ingredients. Put about 2 tablespoons sausage mixture in each crêpe. Roll up and place seam side down in a greased 9 × 13" baking dish. Cover and bake at 350° for 25 minutes.

Topping:

½ cup sour cream	½ cup soft margarine

Combine and spoon over crêpes before serving.
Yield: 14-16 servings

Cinnamon Bread Sticks

1 4½-ounce package of plain bread sticks	½ cup sugar
¼ cup butter or margarine, melted	1 teaspoon cinnamon

Preheat oven to 350°. Break bread sticks to desired length. Roll sticks in the butter. Mix sugar and cinnamon and roll buttered sticks in the mixture. Place on a cookie sheet and bake for 10 minutes.
Yield: 15 sticks

Brunch Buffet

Kir
Serbian Soufflé
Beet Salad*
Blueberry Muffins*
Chafing Dish Ham Balls

 Kir makes a refreshing change for an aperitif: a glass of white wine with 1 ounce Crème de Cassis added.

Serbian Soufflé

6 eggs	1 pound Monterey Jack cheese, cubed
1 cup milk	
½ teaspoon salt	1 3-ounce package cream cheese, cubed
½ cup flour	
1 teaspoon baking powder	1½ cups small curd cottage cheese
	¾ stick butter, melted

Preheat oven to 350°. Beat eggs well. Add milk, salt, flour and baking powder. Fold in cheeses. Add butter. Pour into a well-greased 2 quart soufflé dish. Place in a pan and add hot water to a depth of 1″. Bake for 60 minutes.
Yield: 4 servings

 This soufflé can be tripled and baked in a 9 × 13″ baking dish. It can be used for a buffet and will not fall.

Chafing Dish Ham Balls

2 pounds ham, ground	1 cup plain bread crumbs
1 pound pork, ground	1 cup milk
3 eggs	½ teaspoon salt

Mix ingredients well and roll into small cocktail-size balls.

Cooking sauce:

4 cups dark brown sugar	2 cups white vinegar
4 cups water	

Mix well. Divide the ingredients equally between 2 large pots and bring to a boil. Place half the ham balls in each pot of boiling sauce and cook, uncovered, on top of the stove for 1 hour. Serve in a chafing dish with the following mustard sauce in a bowl on the side.

Mustard sauce:

1 small can Coleman's dry mustard	½ cup sugar
	1 egg, beaten
½ cup white vinegar	

Mix the first 2 ingredients and let stand overnight. Add sugar and egg. Heat to boiling on low heat and cook 1 minute.
Yield: 94-100 balls

Dinner Party for Ten

Sophia's Tirotrigona
Cornish Hens on Rice*
Squash Casserole
Stuffed Lettuce*
Raleigh House Orange Rolls with Orange Butter
Black Raspberry Mousse*

Sophia's Tirotrigona (Cheese-Filled Triangles)

1 pound phyllo pastry sheets	½ pound feta cheese, crumbled
½ pound butter, melted	½ cup grated Parmesan or Romano
½ pound small curd cottage	cheese
cheese	2 eggs, slightly beaten

Preheat oven to 325°. Blend all cheeses and mix thoroughly. Add eggs and mix well. Refrigerate 1 hour. Cut pastry sheets into 2″ wide strips. Keep covered with a damp cloth. Brush each strip with melted butter. Place 1 teaspoon of filling in the bottom right-hand corner of strip and fold over into triangle shape. With each fold, be certain that the bottom edge is parallel with the alternate side edge. Lightly butter finished triangle. Continue in this manner until all the cheese mixture and/or phyllo strips are used. Bake for 20-25 minutes or until golden brown. Allow to cool 5 minutes. Serve warm.
Yield: 25-30 servings

 May be frozen. Thaw and bake as directed.

Squash Casserole

8-10 yellow squash, cut up	1 cup sour cream
1½ sticks margarine, divided	1 8-ounce can sliced water
1 large carrot, grated	chestnuts, drained
1 large white onion, chopped	1 2-ounce jar chopped pimiento
1 10¾-ounce can cream of	salt and pepper, to taste
chicken soup	1 8-ounce package Pepperidge
	Farm herb dressing mix

Cook squash in small amount of water until tender. Drain well and mash squash. Melt 1 stick margarine and sauté the carrot and onion. Mix the soup and sour cream. Add water chestnuts and pimiento. Mix all together, adding salt and pepper. On the bottom of a 9×13″ greased casserole, put ½ package of the dressing mix. Cover with the squash mixture. Put remaining dressing mix on top. Drizzle ½ stick melted margarine on top and bake at 350° for 30 minutes or until bubbly.
Yield: 12 servings

Raleigh House Orange Rolls

2   packages dry yeast
1   cup lukewarm water
1   teaspoon salt
⅓   cup sugar

⅓   cup salad oil
2   eggs
4   cups flour, divided

Dissolve the yeast in the water. Add salt, sugar, oil and eggs, beating well. Add 2 cups of flour and continue beating. Add remaining flour and beat until elastic. Cover with a dry cloth and let rise until more than doubled in size — 1-2 hours. Make into rolls; cover and let rise again until more than doubled. Bake at 375° for 15-20 minutes until light brown. Spread each warm roll with orange butter before serving.

Orange Butter:
¼   cup thawed, undiluted frozen
    orange juice
1⅓ sticks butter, softened

1   16-ounce box powdered sugar

Mix and cream all ingredients. Store in a covered container until ready to spread on warm rolls.
Yield: 3½ to 4 dozen

Dinner Party for Twenty

Rockport Shrimp Dip*
Mushroom Bites*
Butterfly Barbeque Legs of Lamb*
Cage Ranch Potatoes
Hot Herbed Tomatoes
Spinach Apple Salad
Ice Box Cloverleaf Rolls*
Lemon and Strawberry Tarts

 To serve 20, 3 legs of lamb, 2 casseroles of potatoes, and 3 dozen rolls will be needed.

Cage Ranch Potato Casserole

1 32-ounce sack frozen potato cubes	2 cups sour cream
1½ sticks butter, divided	2 cups grated Cheddar cheese
½ cup chopped onion	2 cups bread crumbs
1 10¾-ounce can cream of chicken soup	paprika

Thaw potatoes. Melt 1 stick of butter. Put potatoes, onions and butter in a 3 quart casserole and toss. Mix soup, sour cream and cheese; stir into casserole. Top with crumbs mixed with the remaining half stick of melted butter. Sprinkle paprika on top. Bake at 325° about 1 hour.
Yield: 10-12 servings

Variation: Use cream of mushroom soup instead of chicken. Use 2 cups of crushed corn flakes instead of bread crumbs. Add chopped green onions and/or chopped jalapeños.

Hot Herbed Tomatoes

4 pints cherry tomatoes	1½ teaspoons salt
1½ cups soft bread crumbs	⅔ teaspoon dried thyme
¾ cup minced onion	½ teaspoon pepper
¾ cup minced fresh parsley	4 tablespoons olive oil
2 large garlic cloves, minced	

Preheat oven to 400°. Place tomatoes in a single layer in a lightly oiled 9 × 13″ baking dish. Combine remaining ingredients except oil. Sprinkle the mixture over the tomatoes. Drizzle with oil. Bake 6-8 minutes until tomatoes are puffed.
Yield: 20 servings

 This dish can be prepared ahead and refrigerated covered until time to bake.

Spinach Apple Salad

12 bunches fresh spinach
3   cups thinly sliced red onions
3   cups walnuts, coarsely chopped

3   red delicious apples, thinly
    sliced

Wash spinach well and let dry. Add remaining ingredients and toss. **Dressing:**

1   cup lemon juice
1½ cups oil
3   tablespoons sugar

3   small garlic cloves, crushed
3   teaspoons salt

Combine ingredients. Pour over salad and toss.
Yield: 24 servings

Lemon and Strawberry Tarts

Cream Cheese Pastry:
2   cups butter, softened
4   cups flour

4   3-ounce packages cream
    cheese, softened

Combine butter, flour and cream cheese. Chill and roll into small balls. Press to fit into bottom and sides of very small muffin tins. Prick with a fork to keep from puffing. Bake at 375° for 10 minutes.
Yield: Approximately 96-100 shells

Spray muffin tins very lightly with Pam to make removal of pastry easier.

Creamy Lemon Filling:
2   whole eggs
2   egg yolks
¼   cup butter

1   cup sugar
    juice and grated rind of 2 lemons
    Cool Whip

Put whole eggs and yolks into the top of a double boiler. Beat gently until whites and yolks are mixed. Add butter, sugar and lemon juice. Stir with a wooden spoon and cook over boiling water until mixture is the consistency of mayonnaise (20-30 minutes). Fill shells and chill. Garnish with Cool Whip and lemon rind before serving.
Yield: Filling for approximately 24 tarts

Strawberry Filling:
1   10-ounce package frozen
    strawberries
1   8-ounce package whipped
    topping mix
½   cup cold milk

½   teaspoon vanilla
1   15-ounce can sweetened
    condensed milk
½   cup lemon juice
½   teaspoon almond extract

Drain thawed strawberries; reserve juice. Prepare whipped topping with milk and vanilla as directed on package. Mix condensed milk, lemon juice, almond extract and thawed strawberries with 3 tablespoons of the reserved juice. Fold in whipped topping. Spoon into tart shells and freeze at least 4 hours. Set out a few minutes before serving.
Yield: 75-100 tarts

Variation: Use 1 pint of fresh strawberries hulled, sliced and mixed with 2 tablespoons of sugar.

Game Dinner for Ten

Fried Venison Fingers*
Sour Cream Horseradish Sauce
Avocado Halves with Bacon
Birds Paprika*
Spinach and Artichokes*
Wild Rice Casserole
Pistachio Freeze*

Avocado Halves with Bacon

5 avocados, chilled	10 slices bacon, cooked crisp and crumbled

Sauce:

5 tablespoons butter	3 tablespoons sugar
5 tablespoons catsup	3 tablespoons Worcestershire
5 tablespoons cider vinegar	sauce

Put all ingredients for the sauce in the top of a double boiler and heat, but do not boil. Cut the avocados in half lengthwise; remove the seeds but do not peel. Put a slice of crumbled bacon in each avocado half and spoon in 2 tablespoons of hot sauce. Serve as a first course on a crystal plate with a small spoon. The contrast of hot and cold makes this a unique and flavorful dish
Yield: 10 servings

Wild Rice Casserole

1 cup uncooked wild rice	2 teaspoons chopped green
¼ cup butter or margarine	onions
½ cup slivered almonds	1 cup sliced mushrooms
	3 cups chicken broth

Wash and drain wild rice. Melt butter in a large skillet. Add rice, almonds, onions and mushrooms. Cook and stir until almonds are golden — about 20 minutes. Heat oven to 325°. Pour rice mixture into an ungreased 1½ quart casserole. Heat broth to boiling; stir into rice mixture. Cover tightly and bake about 1½ hours or until liquid is absorbed and rice is tender.
Yield: 8-10 servings

 Canned pear halves topped with a spoonful of currant jelly and warmed in the oven are a fine accompaniment to venison. Poached fresh pear halves make this even better, as served with game in Germany in the fall.

 Mix sour cream and horseradish with a few drops of Tabasco to make a delicious sauce for game or beef.

Super Bowl Barbecue Supper for Sixteen

Oven Baked Briskets
Vienna Rolls
Baked Beans Borrachos
Red and White Slaw
Quick Cucumber, Tomato and Onion Salad*
Green Parrot Chocolate Fudge Pecan Pie*

Oven-Baked Briskets

2	4-pound lean beef briskets, well-trimmed	6	tablespoons Worcestershire sauce
1	package dry Lipton onion soup	4	tablespoons liquid smoke
1	teaspoon celery salt	2½	cups Kraft hickory smoked barbecue sauce
¼	teaspoon garlic powder		
2	tablespoons parsley flakes	2	bay leaves

Place briskets on enough heavy-duty foil to wrap well. Combine the dry soup, celery salt, garlic powder and parsley flakes; press into briskets. Combine the liquid ingredients and pour over. Place a bay leaf on each brisket and tightly enclose in foil. Bake at 400° until they sizzle (20-30 minutes). Reduce temperature to 300° and cook for 2½ hours more. Place in the refrigerator in the foil without opening. When cold, open, slice carefully, and reclose. When ready to serve, heat in a 350° oven for 20-30 minutes. This is a fail-safe way; it makes the job easier and prevents the meat from tearing.
Yield: 16 servings

Baked Beans Borrachos

4	15-ounce cans pork and beans	¼	cup brandy
3	4-ounce cans Vienna sausages, sliced	¼	cup sherry
		¼	cup rum
1	8-ounce can crushed pineapple	3	onions, chopped
½	cup grape juice	1	whole garlic clove, crushed
¼	cup molasses		salt and pepper, to taste
1	14-ounce bottle catsup	1	tablespoon Worcestershire sauce
½	cup brown sugar		
½	pound bacon, chopped	2	teaspoons dry mustard
¼	cup bourbon		

Mix all ingredients together in a large greased casserole. Bake at 300° for 6 hours.
Yield: 24 servings

Red and White Slaw

2	medium heads white cabbage, shredded	2	2-ounce jars diced pimientos, drained
2	cups shredded red cabbage	6	green onions, chopped
1	cup diced celery	20	stuffed green olives, chopped
1	cup shredded carrots		
2	small to medium green peppers, chopped		

Mix all ingredients; cover and refrigerate. Toss with dressing just before serving.

Dressing:

1	cup mayonnaise	1	teaspoon Accent
1	cup sour cream	2	level teaspoons celery seed
2	tablespoons lemon juice	½	teaspoon garlic salt
2	teaspoons sugar		salt and pepper, to taste

Mix ingredients. Cover and store in refrigerator.
Yield: 16-18 servings

 A quick and impressive party dessert is coffee ice cream in a toasted coconut crust. Mix 1½ cups angel flaked coconut with 4 tablespoons melted butter and 2 tablespoons sugar. Press into a 9″ pie pan and bake at 350° for 12-15 minutes. Fill the cooled crust with coffee ice cream; top with whipped cream and freeze. Remove from freezer 10 minutes before serving. Drizzle butterscotch sauce over pie and cut into 8 slices.

Luncheon for Ten

Cold Carrot Soup*
Alabama Shrimp Delight
Strawberry Spinach Salad
Margie's Angel Biscuits*
Black Russian Cake*

Alabama Shrimp Delight

1 9-ounce package fresh green
   fettucini
1 bunch green onions, finely
   chopped
3 pounds shrimp, cooked and
   cleaned
1 cup mayonnaise
½ cup sour cream

½ cup yogurt
1 10¾-ounce can cream of
   mushroom soup
2 tablespoons prepared mustard
2 eggs, beaten
1 cup grated sharp cheese
½ cup melted butter

Cook noodles according to package directions and drain well. Toss the hot noodles with the onions and pour into a buttered casserole. Top with the shrimp. Mix mayonnaise, sour cream, yogurt, soup, mustard and eggs and pour over the shrimp. Combine the cheese and butter and pour over the sauce. Bake at 350° for 30 minutes.
Yield: 8-10 servings

Strawberry Spinach Salad

2 bunches fresh spinach, washed
   and torn

1 pint strawberries, halved

Toss spinach and strawberries

Dressing:
½ cup sugar
2 tablespoons sesame seeds
1 tablespoon poppy seeds
1½ tablespoons minced onion

¼ cup Worcestershire sauce
¼ teaspoon paprika
½ cup vegetable oil
¼ cup cider vinegar

Mix well. Pour over salad and serve.
Yield: 10-12 servings

Spring Luncheon for Twelve

Peach Blossoms
Chicken and Crabmeat with Hollandaise
Fresh Asparagus Polanaise
Dilled Tomato Slices
Garden's Ice Box Rolls*
Bourbon Mousse

Peach Blossoms

2½ cups peach schnapps   13½ cups orange juice

Mix and pour over ice.

Yield: 1 gallon

 To make by the drink, fill an all-purpose glass ¾ full with ice, add 1 ounce of peach schnapps and fill glass with orange juice.

Chicken Breasts with Crab Stuffing

12 chicken breasts, skinned and deboned	1 cup herb-seasoned stuffing mix
salt and pepper, to taste	4 tablespoons flour
1 cup chopped onion	1 teaspoon paprika
1 cup chopped celery	2 1.25-ounce packages
⅔ cup butter or margarine, divided	Hollandaise sauce mix
1¼ cups dry white wine, divided	1½ cups milk
2 7½-ounce cans crab meat, drained and flaked	1 cup shredded Swiss cheese

Pound chicken to flatten and sprinkle with salt and pepper. Cook onion and celery in 1 stick butter or margarine until transparent. Remove from heat; add 6 tablespoons wine, crab meat and stuffing. Mix well. Divide mixture among breasts; put some in the center of each breast, roll up and secure with toothpicks. Combine flour and paprika; roll chicken in the mixture to coat. Place prepared breasts in 11 × 7"casseroles. Drizzle 2 tablespoons butter on top of each. Bake at 375° for 1 hour. Blend sauce mix and milk. Cook according to package directions, stirring until thick. Add cheese and remaining wine, stirring until cheese melts and is blended. To serve, pour sauce over chicken or have sauce on the side for guests to serve themselves.
Yield: 12 servings

For Asparagus Polanaise, allow 6 crisp stalks per person. Cook only until tender, approximately 8-10 minutes. Drain well; arrange on a serving platter and decorate with buttered seasoned bread crumbs and a light sprinkling of chopped hard-cooked eggs.

Quick Bourbon Mousse

2   3-ounce packages instant vanilla
     pudding mix
1½ cups milk

1½ cups bourbon
16   ounces Cool Whip
     nutmeg

Put all ingredients in blender, except nutmeg, and mix well. Pour into pots de crème or foil muffin papers. Sprinkle tops with nutmeg and refrigerate.
Yield: 12 servings

Gala Kick-off Coffee for 100

Summer Squash Soup*
Crunchy Chicken Balls
Patsy's Delight*
Pumpkin Bread* Sandwiches with Cream Cheese
Stuffed Party Rolls
Tuna Stuffed Tomatoes*
Sweet and Spicy Almonds*
Fresh Strawberries with Amaretto Cream
Chocoholic Brownies*
Beatriz's Cookies*
Coffee

Crunchy Chicken Balls

2	5-ounce cans chunk chicken	¼	cup chopped water chestnuts
1	cup fine dry bread crumbs	1	tablespoon prepared mustard
¾	cup milk	1	teaspoon poultry seasoning
½	cup mayonnaise	1	teaspoon white pepper
1	egg, slightly beaten		dash of salt
½	cup finely chopped onion	2	cups crushed corn flakes

Preheat oven to 450°. Mix all ingredients in a bowl, except corn flakes. Shape into small balls and roll in corn flake crumbs. Arrange on a greased baking sheet. Bake for 10 minutes or until brown.
Yield: 4 dozen; Do 3 recipes for party of 100

 These can be frozen before or after baking. Thaw before baking.

Stuffed Party Rolls

2	12-ounce cans of Spam	1	medium onion
1	pound Velveeta cheese	100	Pepperidge Farm party rolls

Chill Spam and cheese before grating. Grate all ingredients and mix well. Fill rolls and bake at 350° for 25 minutes.
Yield: 100 rolls

 For Strawberries and Amaretto Cream, serve the berries with stems on; arrange around a bowl of cream for dipping. To serve 100, use 5 16-ounce cartons of sour cream, 10 tablespoons of sugar and Amaretto to taste. Divine!

Christmas Luncheon Party for 150

Finger Sandwiches: Chicken*, Chili Cheese* and Cucumber*
Glazed Ham Balls*
Miniature Spinach Ricotta Quiches*
Assorted Raw Vegetables
Apricot Balls
Frosted Cranberries
Salted Nuts
Cheese Date Dainties*
Golden Brownies*
Scotch Shortbread*
Texas Candy*
Coffee and Wassail

 In making sandwiches for a large group, use day-old bread. Use an electric knife to remove crusts after spreading and to cut into quarters. For moist fillings, butter bread to keep it from becoming soggy. To store overnight, pack in dress boxes lined with plastic wrap. Place dampened paper towels on top before covering and refrigerating.

Apricot Balls

2	pounds dried apricots	2½	cups finely crushed vanilla wafer
2	medium-sized oranges		crumbs, divided
4	cups sugar	1	cup powdered sugar
2	cups shredded coconut		

Grind apricots and whole oranges together. Add sugar and cook in a double boiler over boiling water until sugar is dissolved. Add coconut and ¼ cup crumbs. Remove from heat and set aside until cool. With buttered fingers, roll the apricot mixture into balls about the size of a small walnut. Roll into crumbs and then into powdered sugar. Store in refrigerator in a tightly-covered container until ready to use.
Yield: 150 balls

 These can be frozen, then rerolled in powdered sugar before serving.

Frosted Cranberries

16 ounces fresh cranberries
1 egg white, slightly beaten

16 ounces powdered sugar, sifted

Wash and cull cranberries. Pat dry with paper towels. Put a handful of cranberries at a time into egg white and stir to coat. Remove and shake off excess. Roll in powdered sugar until coated. Place on waxed paper to dry for a couple of hours. Store in an air-tight container.
Yield: 1 pound

Wassail

2 gallons apple cider
2 16-ounce cans frozen orange juice
½ bottle frozen lemon juice (Minute Maid)

3-4 cinnamon sticks
1½ teaspoons ground cloves
1½ teaspoons ground nutmeg
½ cup brown sugar

Mix in a 55-cup percolator. Serve hot.
Yield: 40 cups

Mexican Buffet for 24

Zingy Tortilla Bites
Escabeche Casa del Sol
Margaritas
Pastel Azteca with Salsa Mexicana
Fajitas with Pico de Gallo and Sour Cream*
Warm Flour Tortillas
Green Salad with Avocado Anchovy Dressing*
Flan*

Zingy Tortilla Bites

1	16-ounce jar mild picante sauce	1	2¼-ounce can chopped ripe olives, drained, optional
3	8-ounce packages cream cheese, softened	1	2-ounce jar diced pimientos, drained, optional
1	pint sour cream	20	large flour tortillas
10	green onions, chopped juice of 1 lime		
1-4	jalapeños, seeded and finely chopped		

Mix 1 tablespoon of picante sauce with cream cheese and sour cream. Add the rest of the ingredients, except tortillas. Blend well. Spread filling over tortillas. Roll up tightly, jellyroll fashion. Cover with a damp towel and plastic wrap to prevent drying out. Refrigerate overnight. To serve, cut into ½-¾" slices and use the remaining picante for dipping.
Yield: Approximately 10 dozen

 Substitute 1 4-ounce can drained green chilies for jalapeños if milder taste is desired. These appetizers can be made ahead and frozen.

Margaritas

4	6-ounce cans of frozen limeade	8	limeade cans of tequila
4	limeade cans of Cointreau or Triple Sec		salt

Put the liquids in blender; fill to within an inch of the top with ice and blend. Serve in stemmed glasses with rims dipped in salt.
Yield: 32 5-ounce servings

Escabeche Casa del Sol
(Pickled Vegetables)

24 garlic cloves	6 tablespoons salt
2 medium onions, quartered	2 heads cauliflower, separated
1½ cups olive oil	24 small bay leaves
8 carrots, thinly sliced	6 zucchini, thinly sliced
2 teaspoons whole peppercorns	1½ teaspoons thyme
3 cups white vinegar	1½ teaspoons oregano
2 3½-ounce cans sliced jalapeños	1½ teaspoons marjoram
4 cups water	

In a large Dutch oven sauté the garlic and onions in oil for 3 minutes. Add carrots and peppercorns; sauté for 5 minutes. Add vinegar and simmer covered for 3 minutes. Drain jalapeños, reserving juice. Add jalapeño juice and water to the vegetables. Cover and bring to a boil. Add salt and cauliflower flowerets. Cook covered over moderate heat for 12 minutes. Add jalapeños along with remaining ingredients. Simmer covered for 2 minutes. Cool covered and store in refrigerator.
Yield: 16 cups

 This will keep in refrigerator for 2 weeks.

Pastel Azteca and Salsa Mexicana

1⅓ cups softened butter	4 cups Masa Harina
1 cup sugar	2⅓ cups water
10 eggs, separated and at room temperature	4 tablespoons baking powder

Cream the butter and add the sugar. Beat in the egg yolks, one at a time. Mix the Masa and water and add to the butter mixture. Add baking powder and mix well. Beat the egg whites until stiff and fold into the mixture. Bake at 350° for 50 minutes in an ungreased bundt pan. Serve at room temperature with Salsa Mexicana.

Salsa:

4 tablespoons oil	water to cover
2 medium onions, chopped	4 4-ounce cans Ortega diced
4 garlic cloves, minced	green chilies
5 15-ounce cans of tomato sauce	16 ounces Mozarella cheese, grated
16 chicken breasts	

Heat the oil in a large cooking pot. Sauté the onions and garlic. Stir in the tomato sauce. Cook the chicken breasts in water until tender; cut into bite-size pieces. Strain the broth and add to tomato sauce. Add the undrained peppers. Cover and simmer about 40 minutes. Add the chicken and cheese and cook 10 minutes more. Serve over Pastel Azteca.
Yield: 16-18 servings

 The pastel can be made a day ahead of serving. If a hotter sauce is desired, use jalapeño peppers instead of green chilies. Add black olives if desired. Serve sauce in a chafing dish for a pretty buffet.

Sunday Christening Luncheon for Sixteen

Mimosas
Cheese Marbles
Rolled Chicken Supremes*
Creamed Onions with Peas*
Carrot and Caper Salad*
Pumpkin Rolls

Cheese Marbles

2	3-ounce packages cream cheese	1/2	cup minced pecans
1	4-ounce package blue cheese, crumbled	1	teaspoon minced onion
		1	cup minced parsley
2	2 1/2-ounce cans deviled ham		small pretzel sticks

Mix cheeses until smooth. Stir in deviled ham, pecans and minced onions. Cover and chill in refrigerator. Shape into marble-size balls and roll in parsley. Chill. Use pretzels or toothpicks to spear balls and dip into sauce.

Sauce:

1/2 cup sour cream	dash garlic salt, to taste

Mix and chill until ready to serve
Yield: 40 appetizers

Variation: Use 4 ounces of Cheez Whiz or mild Mexican cheese in place of blue cheese.

Pumpkin Roll

3	eggs	1	teaspoon ginger
1	cup sugar	1	teaspoon nutmeg
⅔	cup pumpkin	1	teaspoon cinnamon
1	teaspoon lemon juice	½	teaspoon salt
¾	cup flour	1	cup chopped pecans
1	teaspoon baking powder		

Beat eggs on high speed of mixer for 5 minutes. Add sugar, pumpkin and lemon juice. Mix dry ingredients and fold into above mixture. Pour into a greased and floured 15×10″ jellyroll pan. Sprinkle nuts over batter. Bake at 375° for 15 minutes. Turn cake out onto a cup towel that has been sprinkled with powered sugar. Roll and cool. Unroll and spread with cheese filling. Re-roll and chill .

Filling:

4	tablespoons margarine, softened	1	cup powdered sugar
1	8-ounce package cream cheese, softened	½	teaspoon vanilla
		½	teaspoon lemon juice

Combine all ingredients and beat until light and fluffy.
Yield: 12 slices

 This can be frozen. Serve on a silver tray and decorate with kumquats and small green leaves, such as holly. A spectacular dessert!

 To make Mimosas, put 5 cubes of ice in each wine glass. Fill with half orange juice and half champagne.

Holiday Christmas Dinner for Twelve

Easy Party Pâté
Mushroom Bites
Crab Dip
Beef Tender*
Tossed Green Salad
Texas Pudding
Biscuit Twists
Festive Bars
Christmas Mints
Cranberry Sherbet*

Easy Party Pâté

¼	cup butter	8	ounces cream cheese, room temperature
½	pound mushrooms, chopped		
½	teaspoon salt	1	hard-boiled egg, chopped
½	teaspoon freshly ground pepper		
½	pound liver sausage, room temperature		

Melt butter over medium heat. Add chopped mushrooms, salt and pepper. Sauté until mushrooms are softened. Combine mushrooms with sausage and cream cheese in food processor. Mix thoroughly. Pack into crock or mold; cover and refrigerate several hours. Garnish with chopped egg and serve on crackers or dark bread.
Yield: 4 cups

Crab Dip

12	ounces cream cheese, softened		garlic salt, to taste
2	tablespoons Worcestershire sauce	6	ounces Heinz chili sauce
1	tablespoon lemon juice	1	6-ounce can Pacific Pearl Snow crab meat, well drained, or 6 ounces fresh crab
2	tablespoons mayonnaise		
1	small onion, grated		parsley or chives, diced

Combine first 6 ingredients and place in shallow glass bowl (not a flat plate). Layer in order: chili sauce, crab meat, parsley or chives. Cover and refrigerate overnight. Serve with crackers.
Yield: 10-12 servings

Mushroom Bites

2	8-ounce cans refrigerated crescent dinner rolls
8	ounces cream cheese, softened
1¼	teaspoons seasoned salt
1	4-ounce can mushroom stems and pieces, drained and chopped
1	eggs well beaten
2	tablespoons poppy seeds

Preheat oven 375°. Separate dough into 8 rectangles, seal the perforations. Combine and mix well cream cheese, salt and mushrooms. Spread each rectangle of dough with the mixture. Starting with the long side, roll up each rectangle as you would a jellyroll; pinch seams to seal. Slice logs into bite-sized 1 " pieces. Brush with egg and top with poppy seeds. Bake, seam side down, in 375° oven for 10-12 minutes.
Yield: 4 dozen

Texas Pudding

4	large eggs
4	cups cooked long-grain rice
2	cups grated Cheddar cheese
2	17-ounce cans cream-style corn
½	cup minced onion
1½	cups finely chopped green pepper
2	teaspoons salt
¼	teaspoon pepper

Beat eggs until foamy. Stir in rice, cheese, corn, onion, green pepper, salt and pepper. Turn into buttered 3 quart casserole. Bake at 350° for about 45 minutes until golden brown around edges and set in center. Let stand 10 minutes before serving.
Yield: 12

 To make biscuit twists, use canned biscuits and roll each one between hands to twist like a snake. Melt 1 stick of butter in an 8×8 " pan in the oven. Lay the twists side by side and sprinkle with sesame seeds or Lawry's seasoned salt or Parmesan cheese. Bake at 475° for 8-10 minutes.

Festive Bars

1	cup flour
1	teaspoon baking powder
½	teaspoon salt
½	cup margarine, melted
1	egg
½	cup evaporated milk
½	cup sugar
1	cup brown sugar, firmly packed
1	cup uncooked oatmeal
1	cup chopped walnuts or pecans
1	cup chopped dates

Combine first 3 ingredients in large bowl. Add next 5 ingredients, beating until well blended. Stir in oatmeal, nuts and dates. Spread mixture in a greased 15×10 " pan. Bake at 350° for 45-50 minutes, checking after 40 minutes. Cool completely. Then glaze in pan.

Glaze:

1	cup sifted powdered sugar
¼	teaspoon salt
2	tablespoons milk
½	teaspoon vanilla
	red and green candied cherries

Combine all ingredients, stirring until smooth. Spread over top. Cut into squares. Decorate each square with ½ red cherry and green cherry pieces to look like holly.
Yield: 63 squares

Christmas Mints

1 3-ounce package cream cheese, room temperature	food coloring, as desired
¼-½ teaspoon peppermint flavoring	granulated sugar, as needed
2½ cups powdered sugar, sifted	holiday rubber candy molds

Beat cream cheese until soft. (Do not use microwave to soften.) Add flavoring. Gradually add sugar, mixing and kneading until consistency of pie dough. Add food coloring. Shape into marble-sized balls, adjusting size to fit into molds and place on waxed paper until all balls are formed. Dip each ball into granulated sugar; press sugared side down into mold; unmold immediately on waxed paper. Let dry several hours. Then turn over to dry other side. Mints will be crisp on outside and creamy inside. Store in airtight container in refrigerator for a week or in the freezer indefinitely.
Yield: 45-50 mints

 For 170-175 mints, use 8 ounces cream cheese, ½-1 teaspoon flavoring and 6¾ cups powdered sugar. Some suggested molds: Christmas tree, Santa Claus, heart, rabbit, roses, leaves.

Mexican Dinner Party for Fifty

Sangria and Mexican Beer
Ceviche* Tostados
Nachos with Beans and Cheese
Green Chili Chicken Enchiladas*
Jalapeño Sauce*
Arroz con Chicharos
Tropical Fruits with Dressing for Fruit Salad*
Cinnamon Strips*
Lemon Milk Sherbet

Sangria

4½ cups fresh lime juice, rinds
reserved
6   cups fresh orange juice, rinds
reserved
6   cups sugar

3   gallons Burgundy wine
orange and lime slices

Combine the fruit juices with sugar until blended. Add the wine and some of the citrus rinds. Let stand for 1 hour. Discard the rinds. Pour over ice in clear glass pitchers and garnish with orange and lime slices.
Yield: 4½ gallons

When preparing ceviche, for those a little squeamish about fish "cooked" only in lime juice, the fish may be gently poached before adding the other ingredients, including the lime juice.

Arroz con Chicharos

6 cups raw rice	2 teaspoons black pepper
4 tablespoons shortening	2 teaspoons salt or to taste
1 large onion, chopped	8 cups tomato juice
6 garlic cloves, chopped	6-8 cups chicken stock
2 teaspoons ground cumin	6 17-ounce cans LeSueur peas, drained

Cook the rice in the melted grease in a heavy Dutch oven until it is no longer transparent. Add the onion and cook until it is limp. Mix the garlic, cumin, pepper and salt into the tomato juice; add to the rice and cook 2-3 minutes. Add 6 cups chicken stock and cook, covered, very slowly for 30 minutes. Check for liquid by using a long fork, not a spoon, to probe to the bottom. (Do not stir.) Add more chicken stock as needed. Add the peas and stir in gently with the fork. Cook 10 minutes and serve.

Yield: 50 servings

 To make Tropical Fruits for 50, combine 5 20-ounce cans pineapple chunks, drained; 5 16-ounce cans mandarin oranges, drained; 16 bananas, sliced; and 16 avocados, sliced.

St. Patrick's Day Dinner Party for Twenty

Spinach Balls
Crab Meat Cobbler with Cheese Biscuit Topping
Sunshine Salad
Creme de Menthe Cake

Spinach Balls

4	10-ounce packages frozen chopped spinach
4	cups Pepperidge Farm herbal stuffing mix
2	onions, chopped
12	eggs, beaten
1½	cups melted butter or margarine

1	teaspoon black pepper
1	cup Parmesan cheese
2	tablespoons minced garlic
1	teaspoon thyme
1	teaspoon red pepper
2	tablespoons Aćcent, optional

Preheat oven to 350°. Cook spinach as directed and drain well. Mix all ingredients together; mold into bite-sized balls and freeze on a cookie sheet. When frozen, store in plastic bags. When ready to serve, heat 20 minutes at 350° and serve.
Yield: 48 small size or 30 large

Variation: For a first course or vegetable put large balls on thick tomato slices before heating.

Crab Meat Cobbler with Cheese Biscuit Topping

1½	cups shortening
1½	cups chopped green pepper
1½	cups chopped onion
1½	cups flour
3	teaspoons dry mustard
1½	teaspoons MSG, optional
3	cups milk

3	cups grated American cheese
3	6½-ounce cans crab meat, drained
4½	cups canned tomatoes, drained and chopped
2	tablespoons Worcestershire sauce
1½	teaspoons salt

Melt shortening in a Dutch oven; add onions and green peppers, cooking until soft — about 10 minutes. Mix flour, mustard and MSG; blend into the vegetables. Add milk and cheese, stirring constantly until cheese is melted and mixture is thick. Add remaining ingredients and blend thoroughly. Pour into 2 greased 9 × 13 " casseroles. Cover and refrigerate overnight. Bake, uncovered, at 350° for 20 minutes. Remove from oven and raise temperature to 450°.

Topping:

3	cups flour
2	tablespoons baking powder
1½	teaspoons salt

¾	cup grated American cheese
6	tablespoons shortening
1½	cups milk

Mix dry ingredients and add cheese. Cut in the shortening. Add milk and lightly mix with a fork. Drop by rounded teaspoonfuls onto the hot crab mixture. Bake for 15-20 minutes.
Yield: 24 servings

 Cobbler may be prepared and frozen. Thaw before baking.

Sunshine Salad

1 head iceberg lettuce	4-6 chopped green onions, tops included
1 head leaf lettuce	
1 head red tip lettuce	2 11-ounce cans mandarin oranges, drained
2½ cups chopped celery	
	½ cup sliced almonds, toasted

Early in the day or the night before, wash and dry all the lettuce. Tear into bite-sized pieces. Wrap loosely in towels and refrigerate. Combine the celery and onions in a large plastic bag.

Dressing:

2 7-ounce packages Good Seasons garlic dressing mix	3 teaspoons sugar
	dash of Tabasco sauce
4 tablespoons water	½ teaspoon dried tarragon
½ cup tarragon vinegar	
⅔ cup salad oil	

Prepare the dressing according to package directions and chill. Add sugar, Tabasco and tarragon. Just before serving, toss all the salad ingredients, except almonds, with the dressing. Sprinkle almonds on top.
Yield: 20 servings

Variation: Grapefruit sections and avocado slices may be added.

Creme de Menthe Cake

1 box white cake mix	chocolate fudge sauce (preferably Hershey's)
7 tablespoons Creme de Menthe	
2 drops green food coloring	1 8-ounce carton Cool Whip shaved chocolate

Prepare cake according to directions, adding 3 tablespoons Creme de Menthe and food coloring to batter. Bake in a 9×13″ pan, sprayed with Pam. Spread cake with fudge sauce while hot, let cool completely. Add remaining Creme de Menthe to Cool Whip and spread over cake. Garnish with shaved chocolate. Refrigerate.
Yield: 24 2″ slices

Lenten Dinner Party for Ten

Indian Cream Cheese Ball
Gulf Shrimp Casserole
Rice
Snow Pea Medley
Garlic Bread Sticks*
Profiteroles

Indian Cream Cheese Ball

1 cup cooked white chicken or 2 large chicken breasts, cooked	2 tablespoons mayonnaise
1½ tablespoons chopped chutney	½ cup blanched slivered almonds
8 ounces cream cheese, softened	½ teaspoon seasoned salt
	¾ tablespoon curry powder
	shredded coconut

Finely chop chicken with the chutney. Combine all ingredients. Chill and shape into a large ball and roll in coconut. Spread on very fresh mushroom slices, jicama root slices or crackers.
Yield: 3 cups

May be shaped into small balls, rolled in coconut and served with toothpicks.

Gulf Shrimp Casserole

9 tablespoons butter	1 teaspoon celery seed
9 tablespoons flour	1 8-ounce can button mushrooms, drained
3 cups milk	
2 cups grated sharp Cheddar cheese	3 tablespoons white vermouth or sauterne
2 pounds shrimp, cleaned and cooked	1 cup Ritz cracker crumbs
	cooked rice

Make a white sauce with butter, flour and milk. Add cheese and stir until smooth. Add other ingredients except crumbs and pour into greased casserole. Then cover with crumbs and bake at 350° for 30 minutes or until bubbly. Serve over rice. Chutney makes a wonderful accompaniment.
Yield: 10-12 servings

Mix fresh snow peas, cooked al dente, with drained LeSeuer peas. Season with melted butter, salt and pepper.

For a quick and impressive dessert, make Profiteroles using a 15-ounce package Stella D'oro anginettis, vanilla ice cream and Hershey's chocolate fudge sauce. Split the anginettis and put one tablespoon vanilla ice cream on each bottom slice. Replace the pastry crown. Prepare 2 per person. Freeze. When ready to serve, place on crystal plate and spoon on heated fudge sauce. Sprinkle with chopped pecans. Variation: Use pumpkin ice cream and caramel sauce.

Equivalents

Flour — 1 pound
　　All purpose, sifted　　　　　4 cups
　　Cake　　　　　　　　　　　4½ – 5 cups

Sugar —
　　Granulated, 1 pound　　　　2¼ – 2½ cups
　　Brown, firmly packed, 1　　2¼ cups
　　pound
　　Confectioners, sifted, 1 pound　4½ – 5 cups

Cheese —
　　American, Swiss or Monterey　2 cups
　　Jack, ½ pound, grated
　　Cottage, ½ pound　　　　　1 cup
　　Cream, 3 ounces　　　　　6 tablespoons

Eggs —
　　Yolks, 12 – 14　　　　　　1 cup
　　Whites, 8 – 10　　　　　　1 cup

Crackers
　　Saltines, 15 crackers　　　1 cup
　　　　　34 (stack), crushed　2¼ cups

Ritz — 22 crushed　　　　　　1 cup

Bread —　　　　　　　　　　22 slices in a loaf

Rolls —　　　　　　　　　　7 dozen for 50

Dip —　　　　　　　　　　　4 – 6 cups for 50

Ice —　　　　　　　　　　　2 – 4 large bags for
　　　　　　　　　　　　　　50

For 50 People You Will Need:

Beverages —
coffee — 1½ pounds for 75 cups
punch or lemonade — 2½ gallons
tea, iced, 12-ounce glass — 6 1-ounce family size tea bags and 3 gallons water
tea, hot — ½ pound tea for 75 cups
half & half, cream for coffee — 1½ pints
lemons for tea — 6, cut in 8 wedges or 8 slices
sugar for tea, coffee — ¾ pound

Meats: —
Beef, lamb, roasted sliced — 16 – 18 pounds
Ham, bone in, sliced — 22 pounds
Ham, boneless, sliced — 15 pounds
Ham, ground (for loaf, etc.) — 12 pounds
Turkey, sliced — 2 20-pound turkeys
Turkey, for casserole or spaghetti — 1 12-pound turkey

* Chicken, whole, cooked and cubed for casseroles — 6 4-pound chickens
Chicken for salad — 4 quarts, cubed (see above) with 4 quarts celery 2 quarts mayonnaise
Chicken, creamed — 6 quarts chicken cubed 3½ quarts white sauce

Salads —
Fruit salad — 7 quarts prepared fruit, drained
Gelatin — 10 envelopes gelatin, 3 quarts liquid, 2½ quarts solid ingredients
Lettuce — 4 heads for leaf under salad 7 heads for a tossed salad
Salad dressing — 1 quart
Mayonnaise for "dollops" — 1 quart: 1½ tablespoons each serving
Cabbage (for slaw) — 5 pounds

Desserts —
Ice Cream — 2 gallons
Salted nuts — 3 – 4 pounds
Whipping cream for garnish — 1 quart: 1½ tablespoons each
Cakes — 3 or 4 9-inch layer or 10-inch angel food (14 – 16 slices each)

Soups — 4 gallons

Dairy products —
Butter: for table — 1 pound: 72 pats per pound
for sandwiches — 1 pound for 100 slices bread
for vegetable seasoning — ½ pound; ½ teaspoon each serving
Cheese for sandwiches or with cold cuts — 5 pounds

*It is more economical to substitute turkey for cooked cubed chicken. Two 4-pound hens will make spaghetti for 16; one 8-pound turkey will make spaghetti for 30.

Rice, raw   4 pounds = 8 cups = ½ cup servings
                                                each

Vegetables, cooked   6 – 7 quarts, ½ cup per serving

Can Sizes

1 #303 can = 2 cups
1 #2 can   = 2½ cups
1 #2½ can   = 3½ cups
1 #3 can   = 5½ cups
1 #10 can   = 12 cups

1 #10 can   = 7 #303 cans
                 5 #2 cans
                 4 #2½ cans
                 2 #3 cans

Index